www.ingramcontent.com/pod-product-compliance
Lightning Source LLC
Chambersburg PA
CBHW081217230426
43666CB00015B/2767

TEACHER'S EDITION

Scott E. Blumenthal

Behrman House Publishers

Dedicated to my mentors
and colleagues at Behrman House:
David E. Behrman,
Gila Gevirtz, Terry Kaye,
and Robert Tinkham

Book and Cover Design: Itzhack Shelomi

Copyright © 2003 Behrman House, Inc.
Millburn, New Jersey
www.behrmanhouse.com
ISBN 978-0-87441-161-4

Manufactured in the United States of America

Table of Contents

PREFACE 4

INTENT AND PURPOSE OF SHALOM IVRIT 1 4

HOW TO USE THE TEXTBOOK 4
    Using This Teacher's Edition to Teach the Textbook
    Structure of the Teacher's Edition
    Strategies for Teaching Chapter Stories
    Pacing
    Homework
    Family Education

SCOPE AND SEQUENCE CHART 7

ENRICHMENT AIDS AND ACTIVITIES 14
    Using the Chalkboard
    Using the Prayer Companion
    Using the Word Cards
    Using the Picture Cards
    Classroom Games

SHALOM IVRIT 1 WORD CARDS: MASTER LIST 19

TIME MANAGEMENT 21

SAMPLE CLASS SESSIONS 22

BLACK-LINE MASTERS 24
    Lesson Plan Form
    Sample Letter to Parents
    Picture Cards

TEACHING TECHNIQUES 35

ENGLISH TRANSLATIONS OF CHAPTER STORIES, POEMS, AND SONGS ... 164

Preface

You are about to introduce your students to the exciting world of modern Hebrew. In doing so, you will help them to experience the thrill of adventure that comes with learning a new language, while connecting them to Israel and to the language of the Jewish people.

Shalom Ivrit 1 will teach your students to read and understand modern Hebrew. Through stories, dialogues, and poems, *Shalom Ivrit* will develop a level of reading fluency and comprehension that will surprise and delight your students. The fun, interactive comprehension activities—including puzzles, sentence-completion exercises, true and false, and word–picture matches—will reinforce instruction and assess progress while engaging and reassuring the young learner.

Intent and Purpose of Shalom Ivrit 1

Shalom Ivrit 1 is the first in a three-volume series that will teach fluent reading and comprehension of modern Hebrew, including a gentle introduction of Hebrew vocabulary and grammar. *Shalom Ivrit* will:

- Help students acquire Hebrew language skills through use of the language, rather than through learning rules in isolation or by rote.
- Build skills sequentially and incrementally, while at the same time reinforce and assess students' learning.
- Introduce carefully selected and controlled vocabulary—often represented pictorially—in short, digestible lists: the *milon* (dictionary), containing words that recur throughout the series; and the *tarmilon* (literally "backpack"), which contains words that are unique to the chapters in which they appear.
- Present Hebrew grammar rules simply and clearly, after students have encountered them in the context of the chapter story.

Shalom Ivrit 1 teaches Hebrew language skills in the context of a Jewish holiday celebration. By teaching everyday, core vocabulary as well as both new and familiar cultural words, *Shalom Ivrit 1* will contribute to the student's sense of belonging and participation in Jewish tradition. And the familiar cultural words will ease them into usage of modern Hebrew vocabulary.

Shalom Ivrit is designed to make the acquisition of Hebrew language skills a joy for your students—and to inspire and encourage them to learn more.

How To Use the Textbook
Using This Teacher's Edition to Teach the Textbook

This Teacher's Edition contains the entire text of *Shalom Ivrit 1*, reproduced in reduced size. The pages are annotated with suggested activities, teaching methods, and other information to assist you—every step of the way. Every element in the textbook is covered, including the introduction of new vocabulary, the reading of each chapter story, and the review and reinforcement of all material.

Keep in mind that students learn in different ways, and a student's primary learning mode may be aural, visual, or tactile. Similarly, teachers teach in different ways. Don't feel obligated to use a method that feels uncomfortable for your personal teaching style. By the same token, remember that since students learn in different ways, you should vary your teaching methods accordingly. Feel free to repeat an activity or method that works especially well for you and your students.

> The information and suggestions in this Teacher's Edition are intended to assist you in developing your own teaching plan. You do not need to follow every suggestion on every page. Rather, allow the guide to provide you with many different options from which to choose. Only you, the teacher, knows what works best for your class and with your teaching style.

Structure of the Teacher's Edition

This Teacher's Edition provides teaching techniques and suggestions that correspond to features in the textbook. Each section of the Teacher's Edition indicates the corresponding page number in the student text.

In addition, each chapter in the Teacher's Edition contains the following features:

- **Lesson Objectives** Specific learning goals for each chapter, including an overview of the chapter's new language concepts and a chart of new vocabulary words and phrases.
- **New Milon Words and Phrases** A comprehensive list of the chapter's new core vocabulary.
- **What We'll Need** A checklist of materials that will come in handy as you teach the lesson.
- **Where We Are** A brief synopsis of where we are in *Shalom Ivrit*'s "story," to help familiarize students with

the book's theme and recurring characters.
- **Let's Review** An interactive exercise to review grammar and vocabulary from the previous lesson.
- **Introducing the Lesson** A warm-up exercise to gently introduce vocabulary that is central to the new lesson.
- **Mastering the Milon** Ideas and techniques to introduce each new word (or phrase) individually and to ensure that students have absorbed its meaning.
- **Looking Ahead** A brief introduction of material to be learned in the following chapter.

Each chapter in this Teacher's Edition also contains many of the following enrichment ideas, supplementary information, and activities:

Ready for Reading Warm-up questions and exercises to prepare your students for reading the chapter's main stories.

Read Aloud! Ideas and techniques to help your class fully absorb—and enjoy—the chapter's main stories.

The Extra Mile Questions and fill-ins for reviewing each chapter's stories, dialogues, and poems.

Put It Together Exercises to help your students synthesize new vocabulary by combining words and phrases.

Captain Grammar Helpful hints to clarify and explain rules of Hebrew grammar and syntax.

Using the Photograph Ideas for using the book's photos and captions as teaching tools.

Our Tradition Tidbits of Jewish ritual and tradition to highlight the sacred nature of the Hebrew language.

Bring It to Life Ideas for teaching through art, song, movement, *and food!*

Conversation Corner Short dialogue games and activities to encourage students to speak Hebrew with one another.

Game Box Review exercises and activities to enhance the lesson's learning experience.

Strategies for Teaching Chapter Stories

Every chapter in *Shalom Ivrit 1* contains at least one Hebrew story (used here to mean narratives, dialogues, songs, and poems) that gently immerses your students into reading and speaking רַק עִבְרִית—Hebrew only. This Teacher's Edition contains techniques and strategies for teaching all chapter stories and the material that follows them.

Here are some general techniques for reading and reviewing chapter stories:

- Ask questions that will help the class prepare to read together. For example, before reading "הַסֵּדֶר," ask your students to share some of their families' special Passover traditions. Ask which of the objects in the illustration look familiar, and list them on the board.
- First read the entire story aloud to your class. Have students follow along with their fingers or by pointing to each word as you read it. Read slowly and clearly, with particular attention to new words and phrases. If the story has rhyme or a regular rhythm, be sure to emphasize it. You may wish to have students repeat each line or stanza after you say it. Encourage students to raise their hands and ask questions when you are finished.
- Have the class read the chapter story twice: a "slow read," during which students familiarize themselves with new words and grammatical constructions, and a "fast read," during which they challenge themselves to read smoothly and clearly.
- Assign reading parts to individual students (this works best with the dialogues). Have students read at their desks or come to the front of the class and "perform" the story. If time allows, have students rehearse their parts, then perform the story for a younger class!

Pacing

Students differ in ability. Teachers differ in style. Schools differ in the number of class sessions scheduled each week. Ultimately, you must decide how to pace your class through the text.

The chapters in *Shalom Ivrit 1* vary in length. Some may take only one or two class sessions to cover, while others may take three or four. A short, but more difficult, lesson may take more time to teach than a longer, simpler lesson.

Homework

Whether or not to give homework is a question that should be addressed by your school principal. Homework can provide students with additional contact, repetition, and reinforcement of material that has already been learned in class. But homework should not be used as a tool to teach new information.

If you do give homework, *Shalom Ivrit 1* makes assigning it easy. Built into each lesson are a variety of exercises that reinforce reading comprehension. Any one of these exercises—especially the "Checkpoint" features, which appear after every three chapters—can be used for homework.

Be sure to review homework assignments during the following class session. Doing this reassures the students that their efforts were noted and were a worthwhile expenditure of time.

Family Education

A partnership between home and school will help your students reach their greatest potential, and every effort should be made to facilitate this partnership. One way to do this is to include parents in the learning of some basic modern Hebrew vocabulary.

- Send home a letter after the first day of class to tell them about their child's Hebrew program and to teach a few simple words. A sample black-line master is provided on page 25.
- Send home short letters periodically throughout the year to help bring some Hebrew vocabulary into your students' homes. Black-line masters are included after Chapters 3, 6, 9, and 12.

Scope and Sequence Chart for: שָׁלוֹם עִבְרִית 1

Chapter	Story	Page	Nouns	Verbs	Other	תַּרְמִילוֹן
1	שָׁלוֹם	4	שָׁלוֹם יֶלֶד יַלְדָה עַכְבָּר		אֲנִי	
	מִי בַּבַּיִת?	5	בַּיִת אַבָּא אִמָּא	גָר/גָרָה	מִי בְּ___ הִנֵּה כֵּן	
2	אֵיפֹה הַדְבַשׁ?	10	מִשְׁפָּחָה נֵר/נֵרוֹת חַלָּה יַיִן תַּפּוּחַ		אֵיפֹה הַ___, הָ___ יֵשׁ לֹא טוֹב/טוֹבָה וְ___	יְבַשׁ רֹאשׁ הַשָּׁנָה שָׁנָה טוֹבָה
	קוֹל שׁוֹפָר	14			לְ___	קוֹל שׁוֹפָר
	הָעַכְבָּר בַּשׁוֹפָר	16				
3	בַּסּוּכָּה	18	סַבָּא סַבְתָּא חַג		אַתָּה אַתְּ אֶת גַּם	סוּכָּה לוּלָב אֶתְרוֹג חַג שָׂמֵחַ
	עַכְבָּר בַּסּוּכָּה	20	גֶּשֶׁם יְלָדִים קוּפְסָה		לְ___, לַ___ קַר	
	תּוֹרָה—מַתָּנָה טוֹבָה	24	תּוֹרָה מַתָּנָה			שִׂמְחַת תּוֹרָה
	גֶּשֶׁם	25	מְעִיל כּוֹבַע מִטְרִיָּה	הוֹלֵךְ/הוֹלֶכֶת		
		26	Checkpoints			

Scope and Sequence Chart for: שָׁלוֹם עִבְרִית 1

Chapter	Story	Page	Nouns	Verbs	Other	תַּרְמִילוֹן
4	מִשְׁפָּחָה	28	אָח אָחוֹת		יֵשׁ לִי גָּדוֹל/גְּדוֹלָה קָטָן/קְטַנָּה מַה	
	לֵילִי לֹא לֹא	32	שׁוּלְחָן לֶחֶם עוּגָה	רוֹצֶה/רוֹצָה בּוֹכֶה/בּוֹכָה	כּוּלָם עַל-יַד אוּלַי שָׂמֵחַ/שְׂמֵחָה אוֹ	אוֹכְלִים שְׂמֵחִים
	אֲנִי קְטַנְטַנָּה	35	נְמָלָה			קְטַנְטַנָּה
5	בַּכִּתָּה	36	כִּתָּה שֶׁקֶט מוֹרֶה/מוֹרָה לוּחַ	בָּא/בָּאָה כּוֹתֵב/כּוֹתֶבֶת	חָדָשׁ/חֲדָשָׁה מְאֹד עַל כִּי	טוֹבִים
	דּוֹרוֹן בַּכִּתָּה	38	כִּסֵּא מַחְבֶּרֶת עִפָּרוֹן סֵפֶר מִשְׁקָפַיִם אָרוֹן		יֵשׁ לְךָ/יֵשׁ לָךְ אֲבָל אֵין לִי	
	נְמָלָה בַּכִּתָּה	42		שָׁר/שָׁרָה	אֵין	סְפָרִים מַחְבָּרוֹת תַּפּוּחִים עוּגוֹת חַלּוֹת אֲרוֹנוֹת

Shalom Ivrit 1 • Teacher's Edition

Scope and Sequence Chart for: שָׁלוֹם עִבְרִית 1

Chapter	Story	Page	Nouns	Verbs	Other	תַּרְמִילוֹן
6	שַׁבָּת שָׁלוֹם	44	פֶּרַח/פְּרָחִים שַׁבָּת		יָפֶה/יָפָה	שַׁבָּת שָׁלוֹם
	מִי בַּבַּיִת בְּשַׁבָּת?	46	בְּרָכָה	אוֹהֵב/אוֹהֶבֶת אוֹכֵל/אוֹכֶלֶת		
	יוֹם שַׁבָּת, יוֹם מְנוּחָה	50	יוֹם מְנוּחָה עֲבוֹדָה	עוֹבֵד/עוֹבֶדֶת	עָיֵף/עֲיֵפָה	כָּל יוֹם מִסְתּוֹבֵב/ מִסְתּוֹבֶבֶת
		52	Checkpoints			
7	חֲנוּכָּה	56	אוֹר הַיוֹם נֵר/נֵרוֹת	מַדְלִיק/ מַדְלִיקָה	רִאשׁוֹן שֶׁל	חֲנוּכָּה לְהַדְלִיק חֲנוּכִּיָּה מַדְלִיקִים שָׁרִים בְּרָכוֹת
	חַג הָאוֹר	60			חַם יֵשׁ לָנוּ	שַׁמָּשׁ לְבִיבָה/ לְבִיבוֹת נֵס גָּדוֹל הָיָה שָׁם
	הָעַכְבָּר בַּסְּבִיבוֹן	62	רֹאשׁ	עוֹשֶׂה/עוֹשָׂה נוֹתֵן/נוֹתֶנֶת אוֹמֵר/אוֹמֶרֶת		סְבִיבוֹן מַתָּנוֹת אוֹמְרִים

Scope and Sequence

Scope and Sequence Chart for: שָׁלוֹם עִבְרִית 1

Chapter	Story	Page	Nouns	Verbs	Other	תַּרְמִילוֹן
8	דִינָה שְׂמֵחָה	64	שָׁבוּעַ יוֹם רִאשׁוֹן יוֹם שֵׁנִי יוֹם שְׁלִישִׁי יוֹם רְבִיעִי יוֹם חֲמִישִׁי יוֹם שִׁישִׁי יוֹם שַׁבָּת		כָּל	
	מָה בָּרָא אֱלֹהִים?	66	אֱלֹהִים	בָּרָא		עֵצִים כּוֹכָבִים דָּגִים צִפֳּרִים חַיּוֹת אֲנָשִׁים חֹשֶׁךְ מַיִם שָׁמַיִם יָרֵחַ שֶׁמֶשׁ
9	חַג לָעֵצִים	72	עֵץ/עֵצִים בּוֹקֶר יוֹם הֻלֶּדֶת פֵּרוֹת תּוֹדָה			ט״וּ בִּשְׁבָט שְׁקֵדִיָּה
	יוֹם הֻלֶּדֶת לָעַכְבָּר	74	לַיְלָה חֲגִיגָה שִׂמְחָה	עוֹמֵד/עוֹמֶדֶת		צִפּוֹר/צִפֳּרִים הַר פַּרְפַּר חָבֵר
	לִילִי רוֹצָה מַתָּנָה	78	עֵינַיִם		עִם לְךָ/לָךְ	
		80	Checkpoints			

Scope and Sequence Chart for: שָׁלוֹם עִבְרִית 1

Chapter	Story	Page	Nouns	Verbs	Other	תַּרְמִילוֹן
10	עוֹלָם יָפֶה	82	עוֹלָם צֶבַע דַף	מְצַיֵּר/מְצַיֶּרֶת	הַרְבֵּה יָרוֹק צָהוֹב כָּחוֹל שָׁחוֹר אָדוֹם לָבָן	מְצַיְּרִים בְּצֶבַע צְבָעִים
	לֵיצָן	86	פֶּה אוֹזְנַיִם אַף			
	רָן הַלֵּיצָן	87	לֵיצָן גַן		זֶה	
11	הַיוֹם פּוּרִים	88	מֶלֶךְ יְהוּדִי מַלְכָּה סוּס רַעַשׁ	קוֹרְאִים לִהְיוֹת מְדַבֵּר/ מְדַבֶּרֶת	הוּא/הִיא טִפֵּשׁ חָכָם רַע	פּוּרִים מְגִילָה מַסֵּכָה/ מַסֵּכוֹת רַעֲשָׁן עוֹשִׂים אָזְנֵי הָמָן
	הַיוֹם שְׂמֵחִים	92	יְלָדוֹת		אַחֲרֵי	כֶּתֶר אִישׁ
	אִם...	95			אִם יֵשׁ לְ___	

Scope and Sequence

Scope and Sequence Chart for: שָׁלוֹם עִבְרִית 1

Chapter	Story	Page	Nouns	Verbs	Other	תַּרְמִילוֹן
12	הַסֵּדֶר	96		קוֹרֵא/קוֹרֵאת לוֹקֵחַ/לוֹקַחַת	מִ___	סֵדֶר פֶּסַח מַצָּה/מַצּוֹת קְעָרָה מַה נִּשְׁתַּנָּה הַגָּדָה פַּרְעֹה יְהוּדִים מִצְרַיִם עֲבָדִים יוֹצְאִים בְּנֵי חוֹרִין
	חַג הַפֶּסַח, חַג הָאָבִיב	100				דָּג אָבִיב חֲרוֹסֶת מָרוֹר חַד־גַּדְיָא
	אֵין לֶחֶם	102	עוּגִיָּה בֵּיצָה	לֶאֱכוֹל חוֹשֵׁב/חוֹשֶׁבֶת	רָעֵב/רְעֵבָה	
		104	Checkpoints			

Scope and Sequence Chart for: שָׁלוֹם עִבְרִית 1

Chapter	Story	Page	Nouns	Verbs	Other	תַּרְמִילוֹן
13	דֶּגֶל כָּחוֹל וְלָבָן	108	דֶּגֶל		לָמָּה לִי	יִשְׂרָאֵל יוֹם־הָעַצְמָאוּת
	יוֹם הוּלֶדֶת לְיִשְׂרָאֵל	110	עַם אֶרֶץ			תּוֹדָה לָאֵל עַם יִשְׂרָאֵל חַי אֶרֶץ יִשְׂרָאֵל אֶרֶץ אֲבוֹתַי
	יֵשׁ לָנוּ דֶּגֶל	112				
14	כָּל שָׁנָה	114	שָׁנָה			מְבָרְכִים הוֹלְכִים דְּגָלִים שָׁבוּעוֹת מַתַּן תּוֹרָה
	עַכְבָּר שָׂמֵחַ	118				חַלָּה עֲגוּלָה צִמּוּקִים מָתוֹק מַר גְּבִינָה

Enrichment Aids and Activities

Using the Chalkboard

Use the chalkboard to introduce new words and phrases, demonstrate similarities between words, answer questions, play games, and present assignments.

Remember to vary the way in which you use the chalkboard. This can be as simple as changing the chalk color or varying the size of the words you write.

Draw a picture on the chalkboard to help illustrate the lesson. (The less polished an artist you are, the more the class will love your drawings.) For example, draw a silly face on the board to teach the words פֶּה, עֵינַיִם, and אַף.

Incorporate your students' need for physical movement. Plan quick-paced exercises that involve coming to the board. For example, have the students illustrate a word that you have written on the chalkboard. There is really nothing more special about writing on a chalkboard than on paper—unless you are a child. Coming to the front of the room and writing on the chalkboard is exciting to many students. If they enjoy using the chalkboard, let them do it.

Using the Prayer Companion

In order to help you incorporate prayer learning into your class, the *Shalom Ivrit Prayer Companion 1* is available for use with *Shalom Ivrit 1*. The *Prayer Companion* presents blessings for the home and synagogue, including Shabbat and holiday blessings and selected prayers from the Friday evening and Shabbat morning services. Its structure and organization is parallel to those of *Shalom Ivrit*.

Techniques for integrating the *Prayer Companion* into your *Shalom Ivrit* program include:

1. Teach a *Prayer Companion* chapter after each *Shalom Ivrit* chapter. Each chapter of the *Prayer Companion* is tied thematically to the *Shalom Ivrit* text. For example, after teaching that אִמָּא and אַבָּא mean "mother" and "father" in *Shalom Ivrit*, the *Prayer Companion* will teach that men and boys say מוֹדֶה אֲנִי and women and girls say מוֹדָה אֲנִי.
2. Designate a portion of your day for prayer study. Use the *Prayer Companion* for 10–15 minutes of each session as a complement to your Hebrew language study.
3. Link *Prayer Companion* chapters to your class holiday discussions. For Sukkot, you can review the blessing for dwelling in the sukkah, then read about the various names of the holiday. For Purim, review the blessings recited before the *megillah* reading and read about Purim rituals and mitzvot.

Using the Word Cards

There is also a set of *Shalom Ivrit* Word Cards. These cards, printed on durable, heavy cardboard, include all *milon* words introduced in the book. (Each Word Card is numbered for easy reference when working on activities in this Teacher's Edition.) The English meaning is on the back of each Word Card.

Word Cards may be used by individuals or small groups of students, or by the class as a whole. Possible games and teaching strategies using Word Cards are endless, and each teacher can develop many ways of using them. The following suggestions may be implemented as presented here or adapted as necessary.

Remember to use the Word Cards regularly and with a variety of techniques.

General Word Card Techniques and Games

1. Display a number of Word Cards on the chalkboard ledge. Provide a clue about one of the words and ask the students to read the correct word. For example, מָה עַל הַשּׁוּלְחָן? (עוּגָה)
2. Distribute Word Cards to the class. Call out, one at a time, English meanings of the Hebrew words or phrases found on the cards. Ask the student with the corresponding card to stand up, display the card, and read the word or phrase.
3. Display on the chalkboard ledge Word Cards that create a sentence of 4–6 words. Have students, one at a time, come to the board and replace one of the Word Cards with another Word Card that would change the meaning of the sentence, but still make sense!
4. Post at least six words in a column on the board. Ask individuals or teams to take turns "climbing up the ladder" by reading and translating the words in the column in ascending order. Score one point for each word translated correctly. Then play again by having students read the words in descending order to climb down the ladder.
5. Have students display new Word Cards to the class and teach their meanings through "student pantomime," in which they are allowed to use the Hebrew word and no other verbal clues!

Shalom Ivrit 1 • Teacher's Edition

Using the Picture Cards

You may wish to use illustrations in addition to Word Cards to teach and review new vocabulary. This Teacher's Edition includes a set of eight black-line masters, each containing four Picture Cards (see pages 26–33). Like the Word Cards, the Picture Cards are numbered for easy reference when working on activities included in this Teacher's Edition.

These Picture Cards include objects that may not be readily accessible in your classroom. For example, you may be able to teach that עִפָּרוֹן means "pencil" or that אָרוֹן means "closet" by referring to the actual objects in your classroom or school. But it will be more difficult to find an example of "mouse" or "king."

Like the Word Cards, the Picture Cards may be used in a wide variety of ways, including those suggested in "General Word Card Techniques and Games" above. You may wish to color the set of Picture Cards to make them more lively, or duplicate a set for each student to use for classroom games. Additional Picture Card ideas and techniques include:

1. Display a series of Picture Cards, one at a time, to the class. Have students provide the correct Hebrew words. You may wish to make it a game, timing individual students to see who can first correctly identify ten randomly chosen Picture Cards in the shortest time.
2. Create a sentence on the chalkboard ledge that uses both Word Cards and Picture Cards. Have individual students read the sentence, using the correct Hebrew words for the Picture Cards.
3. Combine pairs of Picture Cards and display them. Have students create silly sentences to describe the combination. For example, if you show Picture Cards for hat and cake, a student might say: יֵשׁ עוּגָה בַּכּוֹבַע ("There is cake in the hat").

Classroom Games

Games can add variety and energy to your classroom. They reinforce learning and capture students' attention through a fun, lively medium. As you plan to use the games below, or others you may develop or choose to use, keep the following considerations in mind:

1. *Use games that move quickly*. Some games below require physical movement; some are timed; some challenge students to think and respond on the spot.
2. *Stop when students' interest begins to lag*. If the game does not capture your students' attention, it's best to move on to another activity or version of the game.
3. *See that all students are actively involved*. The games below include participation by all members of the group. If you find that some of the students are bored or feel excluded, you may wish to assign those students specific roles, such as scorekeeper or team captain. Or make a rule that each student may only answer two or three times, in order to allow all students the opportunity to answer.
4. *Choose games that contribute to improving specific skills*. If your goal is to improve reading fluency, play "מָצָאתִי—I Found It!" or "Jeopardy!" If you're ready to reinforce reading comprehension, play "Hebrew Match-Up" or "Concentration." This Teacher's Edition will provide specific suggestions for games (and varieties of games) in each chapter.
5. *Maintain control of the class*. Games are effective because they provide a sense of excitement and variety. Make sure that students understand that while they are having fun, excessive noise and disruptive behavior will not be tolerated.

The Magic Stone

Have the class sit or stand in a circle. Provide a student with a tennis ball or bean bag—the "magic stone." The student holding the magic stone is the Wizard. The student to the Wizard's right is the Apprentice. The Wizard "tests" the Apprentice in one of the following ways:

1. Shows the Hebrew side of a Word Card and asks for its English translation.
2. Shows the English side of a Word Card and asks for its Hebrew translation.
3. Shows a Picture Card and asks for the Hebrew name of the object pictured.
4. Using the textbook, asks questions based on chapter story or exercise. Depending on your students' level, you may choose to have the Wizard ask questions in Hebrew or English. Answers should always be provided in Hebrew.

If the Apprentice answers correctly, he or she receives the magic stone and becomes the Wizard. If the Apprentice answers incorrectly, that student must step out of the circle, and the Wizard asks the next Apprentice a different question. The last student left holding the magic stone is the winner.

מָצָאתִי—I Found It!

Have students locate a word or phrase on a given page, based on clues that you provide.

Sample clues may include:
- Find the word for a male teacher.
- Find the two words that mean, "Achbar is in the closet."
- Find the name of our patriarch Abraham's wife.

Have students call מָצָאתִי! (I found it!) when they locate the word or phrase. The first student who calls מָצָאתִי! should read the word or phrase correctly. If that student reads correctly, he or she receives a point. If that student does not, the other students have an opportunity to call מָצָאתִי! and read the word or phrase.

An alternate form of the game requires the students to read the word *before* and the word *after* the word or phrase in question.

Hebrew Baseball

Using four chairs (one for each base), create a mock baseball diamond in your classroom. Divide the class into two teams and have them sit on opposite sides of the room. Choose a team to be at bat. That team will send one student at a time to home plate, who will then choose the difficulty level of the question that will be asked of him or her: a single, double, triple, or home run. The higher the chosen hit, the more difficult the question you will ask. You may wish to prepare questions for each level beforehand.

Sample questions are:
- For a single: What is the English translation of the word "holiday"?
- For a double: In Hebrew, name three words found in the Haggadah.
- For a triple: Translate אִמָּא אוֹכֶלֶת עוּגָה ("mother eats cake") into English.
- For a home run: Translate "The children eat eggs in the morning" (הַיְלָדִים אוֹכְלִים בֵּיצִים בַּבּוֹקֶר) into Hebrew.

If the answer is correct, the student advances the number of bases tried for (and anyone on base will advance the same number of bases). If the student is incorrect, he or she is out.

After three outs the next team comes to bat. Play as many innings as you'd like, but make sure the second team gets its final turn at bat.

Beat the Clock

Individual Competition

Using a stopwatch or a watch with a second hand, time individual students as they read an assigned set of lines (dialogue stories will work best). Students should try to improve their previous records. If a student reads a word incorrectly, two seconds are added to the total time. Allow each student a maximum time of 60 seconds before proceeding to the next student. You may wish to challenge your students to reach a target time, perhaps 25 seconds.

Teams

Divide the class into two teams—א and ב. Ask each member of א to read a line, in turn, until the passage is completed, while timing the team with a stopwatch. Then ask ב to try to achieve a better time while reading the same selection in the same way. Then reverse the order, using a different set of lines, with ב going first.

If a reader makes a mistake, ask that student to read the word correctly before proceeding, or "pass along" the word to the next student, who finishes the first student's word(s) and then continues with his or her own.

Class

Announce a "target time"—a period of time for the class to beat while reading a particular set of lines. Ask each student to read one word in turn. If the class beats the target time, ask them to repeat the lines, to beat the time again!

Concentration

Create one set of 5" x 7" index cards with Hebrew words, and one set of cards with their English translations (or illustrations). All cards should be blank on one side. Combine both sets and shuffle together.

Place all cards, word-side up, on the floor or a large table. Then turn the cards over, so that the blank side faces up. Ask students individually (or in teams) to try to match the Hebrew and English word pairs by turning over any two cards.

If they match, award the player or team a point and remove the matched pair of cards. If they do not match, place the cards back in their original position and ask another student or team to go. Continue the game until all cards have been removed. The player or team with the most points wins.

Tic-Tac-Toe on the Go

Arrange nine chairs in three rows of three chairs each. Prepare ten strips of paper—five white and five blue—to use as "markers" for each tic-tac-toe spot. Divide the class into two teams—לָבָן (white) and כָּחוֹל (blue). Give the strips of paper to the students.

Show a student from the לָבָן team the Hebrew side of a Word Card, or ask a question based on the chapter story or exercise. If the student answers the question correctly, he or she may choose to sit—with the team's "marker"—in any of the nine chairs. Then ask a student from the כָּחוֹל team a question. If that student answers correctly, he or she may choose to sit in any of the remaining chairs. The team that gets three in a row, in any direction, wins.

Around the World

Have students sit in a semicircle. Assign a "world traveler" to stand behind the student at either end of the semicircle. Ask for the English translation of a Word Card, or ask a question based on the chapter story. Only the "world traveler" and the student seated in front of him or her may answer. The first of the two students to answer correctly stands behind the next student in the semicircle; the student who did not answer is "out." If neither student answers correctly, provide the correct answer and read another.

The goal is for the "world traveler" to travel completely around the "world" (the class) by correctly answering all the questions. If both students answer correctly at the same time, provide another question.

מַה הַמִילָה—What's the Word?

Have a student choose a word from the chapter. The other students must guess what the word is, based on questions they ask. They can ask any question—in English—that will help them guess the word.

Suggested questions are:
- Is the word masculine or feminine?
- Is the word a person, place, or thing?
- How many letters are there in the word?

The class may ask as many questions as they like, but each student may guess only once. The student who guesses correctly receives a point and chooses the next word. The student with the most points at the end of ten rounds is the winner.

Hebrew Match-Up

Write questions in Hebrew based on the *milon* or chapter story on colored paper—one for each student in the class—and put them in a box. Write answers, also in Hebrew, to the questions on white paper and put them in a second box. Divide the class into א and ב. Ask each student on א to take a question from the question box, and each student on ב to take an answer from the answer box. Ask a player from א to read his or her question. The player from ב who believes his or her card has the correct answer should read the card.

If that student is correct, ב receives a point. Continue this way, asking another א member to read a question, and ב to try to find the correct answer.

After all the questions and answers have been correctly matched, collect and return them to their respective boxes and reverse the assignments so that members of ב have the questions, and א answers. The team with the most points at the end of three rounds wins.

Jeopardy!

Draw the following chart on the board:

Read It!	Know It!	Say It!
1	1	1
2	2	2
3	3	3
4	4	4
5	5	5

Prepare 15 Word Cards and questions, one for each number on the chart.
- For the "Read It!" category, prepare to show the Hebrew side of five Word Cards, at varying levels of difficulty. Students will be asked to accurately read the Hebrew.
- For the "Know It!" category, prepare to show the English side of five different Word Cards, also at varying levels of difficulty. Students will be asked to translate the word into Hebrew.
- For the "Say It!" category, prepare five questions (in English or Hebrew, depending on your students' skill levels), based on the *milon* words or chapter story you are reviewing.

Divide the class into two teams—א and ב. Select a student from א to pick a category and a number below it, determining the level of difficulty (1 is easy; 5 is hard). Then, allow anyone in the class to answer. Call on the student who raises his or her hand first. Cross off the number from the chart, and do not use it again.

If the student answers correctly, the question's point value is awarded to his or her team. If the student answers incorrectly, the question's point value is deducted from his or her team, and the other team may answer. The team with the most points after all 15 questions have been asked is the winner.

Variations on the game may include:
- *Double Up!* Once all 15 questions have been asked, complete the chart with doubled point values (2, 4, 6, etc.), and continue playing.
- *Risk It!* Once all 15 questions have been asked, have each team decide how many points it wishes to "risk" (an amount between 0 and the number of points they have). Then ask a question that includes all three category skills. For example: "Read aloud the sixth and seventh lines on page 96, then translate them." Each team has an opportunity to do so. If the team is correct, their amount "risked" is added to their score. If the team is incorrect, their amount is deducted. The team with the most points after "Risk It!" is the winner.

Scrambled!

Give each student a blank sheet of paper and a pencil. Challenge the students to create as many complete sentences as they can in five minutes, using a given set of words from a chapter story or activity.

After the time has expired, have each student read one sentence aloud. Determine whether the sentence is correct, based on gender and number. (אֲנִי נֵרוֹת and אָחוֹת חָדָשׁ, for example, are not, and therefore don't count.) Have all students with the same sentence cross theirs out.

Students receive points for unique sentences, based on the number of words in the sentence:

2 words .... 1 point
3 words .... 2 points
4 words .... 3 points

The student with the most points at the end of the game is the winner.

Shalom Ivrit 1 Word Cards: Master List

The following is a list of Word Cards included in Shalom Ivrit 1:

brother	אָח	40	hello	שָׁלוֹם	1
sister	אָחוֹת	41	I	אֲנִי	2
big (m/f)	גָּדוֹל/גְּדוֹלָה	42	boy	יֶלֶד	3
small (m/f)	קָטָן/קְטַנָּה	43	girl	יַלְדָּה	4
what	מָה	44	mouse	עַכְבָּר	5
everyone	כֻּלָּם	45	who	מִי	6
next to	עַל־יַד	46	in the	בַּ__	7
table	שֻׁלְחָן	47	house	בַּיִת	8
wants (m/f)	רוֹצֶה/רוֹצָה	48	here is, here are	הִנֵּה	9
bread	לֶחֶם	49	mother	אִמָּא	10
maybe	אוּלַי	50	father	אַבָּא	11
cake	עוּגָה	51	yes	כֵּן	12
happy (m/f)	שָׂמֵחַ/שְׂמֵחָה	52	lives (m/f)	גָּר/גָּרָה	13
cries (m/f)	בּוֹכֶה/בּוֹכָה	53	where	אֵיפֹה	14
or	אוֹ	54	the	הַ__	15
ant	נְמָלָה	55	family	מִשְׁפָּחָה	16
very small (f)	קְטַנְטַנָּה	56	there is, there are	יֵשׁ	17
class, classroom	כִּתָּה	57	no	לֹא	18
comes (m/f)	בָּא/בָּאָה	58	and	וְ__	19
quiet	שֶׁקֶט	59	good (m/f)	טוֹב/טוֹבָה	20
teacher (m/f)	מוֹרֶה/מוֹרָה	60	to, for	לְ__	21
new (m/f)	חָדָשׁ/חֲדָשָׁה	61	you (m)	אַתָּה	22
very	מְאֹד	62	you (f)	אַתְּ	23
writes (m/f)	כּוֹתֵב/כּוֹתֶבֶת	63	grandfather	סַבָּא	24
on	עַל	64	grandmother	סַבְתָּא	25
chalkboard	לוּחַ	65	also	גַּם	26
because	כִּי	66	holiday	חַג	27
chair	כִּסֵּא	67	rain	גֶּשֶׁם	28
you have (m/f)	יֵשׁ לְךָ/יֵשׁ לָךְ	68	cold	קַר	29
notebook	מַחְבֶּרֶת	69	children, boys	יְלָדִים	30
but	אֲבָל	70	to the, for the	לַ__ , לָ__	31
I do not have	אֵין לִי	71	box	קוּפְסָה	32
pencil	עִפָּרוֹן	72	Torah	תּוֹרָה	33
book	סֵפֶר	73	gift	מַתָּנָה	34
eyeglasses	מִשְׁקָפַיִם	74	goes, walks (m/f)	הוֹלֵךְ/הוֹלֶכֶת	35
closet	אָרוֹן	75	coat	מְעִיל	36
there is/are not	אֵין	76	hat	כּוֹבַע	37
sings (m/f)	שָׁר/שָׁרָה	77	umbrella	מִטְרִיָּה	38
a peaceful Shabbat	שַׁבָּת שָׁלוֹם	78	I have	יֵשׁ לִי	39

English	Hebrew	#		English	Hebrew	#
stands (m/f)	עוֹמֵד/עוֹמֶדֶת	121		flower(s)	פֶּרַח, פְּרָחִים	79
eyes	עֵינַיִם	122		nice, pretty (m/f)	יָפֶה/יָפָה	80
with	עִם	123		Shabbat	שַׁבָּת	81
to you (m/f)	לְךָ/לָךְ	124		likes, loves (m/f)	אוֹהֵב/אוֹהֶבֶת	82
world	עוֹלָם	125		blessing	בְּרָכָה	83
draws (m/f)	מְצַיֵּר/מְצַיֶּרֶת	126		eats (m/f)	אוֹכֵל/אוֹכֶלֶת	84
crayon, color	צֶבַע	127		day	יוֹם	85
sheet (of paper)	דַּף	128		rest	מְנוּחָה	86
many	הַרְבֵּה	129		tired (m/f)	עָיֵף/עֲיֵפָה	87
clown	לֵיצָן	130		work	עֲבוֹדָה	88
garden	גַּן	131		works (m/f)	עוֹבֵד/עוֹבֶדֶת	89
this, this is (m)	זֶה	132		light	אוֹר	90
read (pl)	קוֹרְאִים	133		today	הַיּוֹם	91
to be	לִהְיוֹת	134		first	רִאשׁוֹן	92
king	מֶלֶךְ	135		of, belonging to	שֶׁל	93
he/she	הוּא/הִיא	136		lights (m/f)	מַדְלִיק/מַדְלִיקָה	94
foolish (m)	טִפֵּשׁ	137		candle(s)	נֵר/נֵרוֹת	95
wise (m)	חָכָם	138		warm	חַם	96
Jew, Jewish	יְהוּדִי	139		we have	יֵשׁ לָנוּ	97
queen	מַלְכָּה	140		makes, does (m/f)	עוֹשֶׂה/עוֹשָׂה	98
horse	סוּס	141		gives (m/f)	נוֹתֵן/נוֹתֶנֶת	99
speaks (m/f)	מְדַבֵּר/מְדַבֶּרֶת	142		says (m/f)	אוֹמֵר/אוֹמֶרֶת	100
noise	רַעַשׁ	143		head	רֹאשׁ	101
bad (m)	רַע	144		all, every	כָּל	102
girls	יְלָדוֹת	145		week	שָׁבוּעַ	103
after	אַחֲרֵי	146		Sunday	יוֹם רִאשׁוֹן	104
if	אִם	147		Monday	יוֹם שֵׁנִי	105
has	יֵשׁ לְ___	148		Tuesday	יוֹם שְׁלִישִׁי	106
reads (m/f)	קוֹרֵא/קוֹרֵאת	149		Wednesday	יוֹם רְבִיעִי	107
takes (m/f)	לוֹקֵחַ/לוֹקַחַת	150		Thursday	יוֹם חֲמִישִׁי	108
from	מִ___	151		Friday	יוֹם שִׁשִּׁי	109
hungry (m)	רָעֵב	152		Shabbat, Saturday	יוֹם שַׁבָּת	110
to eat	לֶאֱכֹל	153		created (m)	בָּרָא	111
cookie	עוּגִיָּה	154		God	אֱלֹהִים	112
thinks (m/f)	חוֹשֵׁב/חוֹשֶׁבֶת	155		tree(s)	עֵץ/עֵצִים	113
egg	בֵּיצָה	156		morning	בֹּקֶר	114
flag	דֶּגֶל	157		birthday	יוֹם הוּלֶדֶת	115
why	לָמָּה	158		fruit (pl)	פֵּרוֹת	116
to me	לִי	159		thank you	תּוֹדָה	117
nation, people	עַם	160		night	לַיְלָה	118
land	אֶרֶץ	161		party	חֲגִיגָה	119
year	שָׁנָה	162		joy, happiness	שִׂמְחָה	120

Shalom Ivrit 1 • Teacher's Edition

Time Management

One of the most difficult things to do when planning a curriculum is to decide exactly how to use the class time. The following charts are designed to help you decide how to allocate the time available. Each class session should be divided into at least four distinct components:

1. An opening activity, to review previous material or to set up the class session
2. Introduction of new material
3. Reinforcement of new material
4. A closing activity to summarize and reinforce the class session's content

The amount of time spent on each component should depend on the overall amount of time available for Hebrew instruction and on what you wish to accomplish. Completing a Lesson Plan Form (sample black-line master included on page 24) in advance of every class session will help you to manage your time so that your goals can be met.

If You Meet Once a Week for Hebrew Instruction...

If your school meets 1–1½ hours per week for thirty weeks, you should allow approximately two classroom sessions per chapter. Keep in mind that some chapters will introduce 15–20 new words and phrases, while others will introduce only a few. Therefore, some chapters will require more than two classroom sessions, while other weeks you may be able to cover a chapter in one class session.

If You Meet Twice a Week for Hebrew Instruction...

If your school meets 2–3 hours per week for thirty weeks, you should allow two to four classroom sessions per chapter. You will need to take into consideration the number of *milon* words introduced in each chapter and pace your class accordingly.

Sample Class Sessions (60 Minutes)

Chapter 6 of *Shalom Ivrit 1* contains 12 new words. Although it will depend on the length of the sessions, you will probably need two class sessions to teach this chapter. Here are sample outlines for these two sessions. Remember that detailed teaching instructions for each chapter are included in this Teacher's Edition.

Lesson 6, "Shabbat Shalom," Textbook pages 44–45, Teacher's Edition pages 79–81.

Activity	Purpose	Examples	Time
Opening Activities • "Where We Are" • "Let's Review" • "Introducing the Lesson"	Reinforce previous learning; create interest in new material	• Read "Where We Are" aloud. • Review Chapter 5 vocabulary with a "tour" of objects found in the classroom. Include יֵשׁ לְךָ/יֵשׁ לָךְ. • Introduce מְנוּחָה and עֲבוֹדָה using Word Cards 86 and 88, and through pantomime.	10 min.
Introduction of New Material • "Mastering the Milon" (p. 44) • Chapter Story: "שַׁבָּת שָׁלוֹם" (p. 44)	Present core curriculum materials	• Teach the four words and phrases from the *milon* on page 44, using the techniques in this Teacher's Edition; then ask students to create noun/adjective pairs in "Put It Together." • Have students read "שַׁבָּת שָׁלוֹם" aloud. Ask "The Extra Mile" questions after each stanza.	25 min.
Reinforcement • "Yes or No?" (p. 45) • "Word Match" (p. 45)	Refine reading fluency and comprehension; reinforce new material	• Have students complete "Yes or No" by restating each sentence as a question. • Have students complete "Word Match," then read answers aloud.	15 min.
Closing Activity Play "Scrambled!"	Reinforce material	Have students create as many sentences as they can, using the vocabulary in "Word Match."	10 min.

Lesson 6, "Shabbat Shalom," Textbook pages 46–50, Teacher's Edition pages 82–87.

Activity	Purpose	Examples	Time
Introduction of New Material • "Mastering the Milon" (p. 46) • Chapter Story: "מִי בַּבַּיִת בְּשַׁבָּת?" (p. 46)	Present core curriculum materials	• Teach the three words from the *milon* on page 46, using the techniques in this Teacher's Edition; follow up by having students list foods they like to eat in "Put It Together." • Have students read "מִי בַּבַּיִת בְּשַׁבָּת?" aloud, using fun "squeaky mouse" voices. Ask "The Extra Mile" questions for review.	15 min.
Reinforcement • "He or She?" (אוֹכֵל/אוֹכֶלֶת) (p. 47) • "Where Is It?" (p. 48) • "He or She?" (אוֹהֵב/אוֹהֶבֶת) (p. 49)	Refine reading fluency and comprehension; reinforce new material	• Have students complete "He or She?" then review dialogues with "Conversation Corner." • Have students complete "Where Is It?" and the next "He or She?" then play the memorization game "Check, Please!"	15 min.
Introduction of New Material • "Mastering the Milon" (p. 50) • Chapter Story: "יוֹם שַׁבָּת, יוֹם מְנוּחָה" (p. 50)	Present core curriculum materials	• Teach the five words from the *milon* on page 50, using the techniques in this Teacher's Edition; have students pantomime words in "Put It Together." • Have students pretend to be reporters as they read the story aloud.	20 min.
Reinforcement • Photo caption (p. 51) • "He, She, or They?" (p. 51)	Refine reading fluency and comprehension; reinforce new material	Have students practice plurals with "He, She, or They?"	10 min.
Closing Activity Play "Listen Up!"	Provide reinforcement	See how long your students can keep up in this Hebrew version of Simon Says.	If time allows

Lesson Plan Form

Teacher's Name _____ Grade _____ Lesson Date(s) _____

Text pages in *Shalom Ivrit 1* to cover _____

Goals:
Review
Introduce
Practice

Instructional Materials Needed

Planned Activities	Time Estimate

Homework Assigned

Notes

Dear Parent,

This year our class will acquire an exciting new skill—reading and understanding modern Hebrew.

Today your child received a new textbook called *Shalom Ivrit*—the first book in a three-year series. With *Shalom Ivrit*, your child will not only continue to develop and sharpen his or her Hebrew reading skills, but will also *understand* the meaning of the words. And, of course, we will focus on modern language skills—words and phrases that are used in Israel today. We hope that your child will experience the joy of discovery that comes with learning a new language, and will also build a strong connection to Israel and to the language of the Jewish people.

There are a number of ways you can participate in your child's Hebrew learning, even if you don't know Hebrew yourself. Try to express your interest, praise your child's achievements, and motivate your child to learn. And perhaps each week, ask him or her to share a few new words from that week's *Shalom Ivrit* lesson.

Here are some words your child will learn during the first few weeks that you may wish to incorporate into your daily conversations:

hello	*shalom*	שָׁלוֹם
mother	*ima*	אִמָא
father	*aba*	אַבָּא
house	*bayit*	בַּיִת
yes	*kein*	כֵּן
no	*lo*	לֹא

Learning to understand Hebrew can be a very exciting experience. We hope you will encourage your child and share the excitement!

B'Shalom,

2

1

4

3

6

5

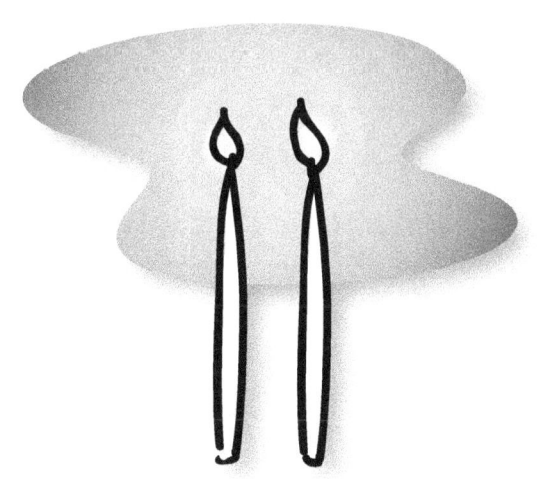

8

7

10

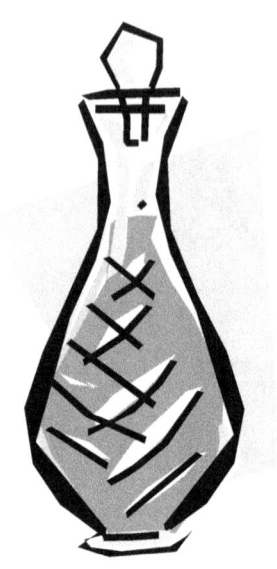

9

12

11

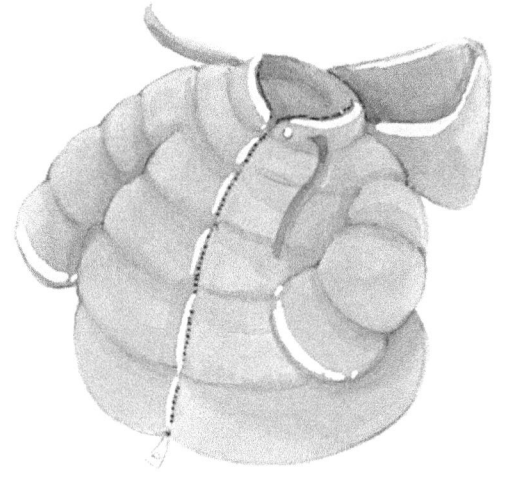

14

13

16

15

17

18

19

20

22

21

24

23

26

25

28

27

29

30

31

32

Lesson Objectives

Students will:
- Begin to build their base of Hebrew vocabulary, starting with words for members of the family and the pronouns אֲנִי and מִי.
- Build their first short sentences.

New Milon Words and Phrases

Core Vocabulary

hello	שָׁלוֹם
I	אֲנִי
boy	יֶלֶד
girl	יַלְדָה
who	מִי
in the	בַּ___
house	בַּיִת
here is, here are	הִנֵה
mother	אִמָא
father	אַבָּא
yes	כֵּן
lives (m/f)	גָר/גָרָה

Other Useful Vocabulary

mouse	עַכְבָּר

What We'll Need

- ❑ Text pages 4–9
- ❑ Word Cards 1–13
- ❑ Picture Cards 1–6
- ❑ Helpful props: a tennis ball, markers, and construction paper

Where We Are

In this first chapter, we'll meet Dinah, Doron, and their family—as well as the mischievous mouse Bar. Dinah, Doron, and their friends will appear throughout *Shalom Ivrit*, as we learn vocabulary relating to Jewish holidays and everyday life.

Introducing the Lesson

Draw a house on the chalkboard. Display Picture Cards 1–4 on the chalkboard ledge. Point to the cards, one at a time, and say:

- הִנֵה אִמָא.
- הִנֵה אַבָּא.
- הִנֵה יֶלֶד.
- הִנֵה יַלְדָה.

Place the אַבָּא Picture Card in the "house," say:

אַבָּא גָר בַּבַּיִת.

Repeat with the other three Picture Cards.

Lift the אַבָּא Picture Card. Place it in the "house" as you ask the class: אַבָּא גָר בַּבַּיִת?

Nod your head as you prompt them to reply: כֵּן.

Repeat with the other three Picture Cards. Encourage students to reply כֵּן each time.

Mastering the Milon (p. 4)

• שָׁלוֹם • Explain that in this chapter, שָׁלוֹם is used as "hello." Ask your students: What else can שָׁלוֹם mean? (*Most students will know that* שָׁלוֹם *also means "goodbye" and "peace."*)

• אֲנִי • Point to yourself and say אֲנִי. Have each student, in turn, do the same.

Bring It to Life Teach the words for "teacher"— מוֹרָה (f) and מוֹרֶה (m).
Say: אֲנִי מוֹרֶה/מוֹרָה.
Have each student introduce him or herself:

שָׁלוֹם מוֹרָה. אֲנִי דָוִד.

• יֶלֶד and יַלְדָּה • Call a boy to the front of the class.
Say: [boy's name] יֶלֶד.
Call a girl to the front of the class.
Say: [girl's name] יַלְדָּה.
Ask: What do you think יֶלֶד and יַלְדָּה mean? Continue this way until students understand that יֶלֶד means "boy," and יַלְדָּה "girl."

Put It Together Break the class into pairs. Have students introduce themselves to one another using the following formula:

שָׁלוֹם, יֶלֶד/יַלְדָּה. אֲנִי יֶלֶד/יַלְדָּה.

• עַכְבָּר • Display Picture Card 6. Using a "squeaky-mouse" voice, say: שָׁלוֹם, אֲנִי עַכְבָּר.
Ask: What do you think עַכְבָּר means? You may wish to have students take turns to see who can say, "אֲנִי עַכְבָּר" in the best "squeaky-mouse" voice!

Chapter Story: שָׁלוֹם (p. 4)

Ready for Reading Read the entire story aloud to the class. Read clearly and slowly in order to allow students to become familiar with the correct reading. Ask: What is the name of the story? (שָׁלוֹם) What do you think this story is about? (*Students will likely answer that the story is about people greeting one another.*) Explain that דּוֹרוֹן, דִּינָה, and בָּר are the names of characters in the story.

Read the first two lines again. Have students repeat each line. Ask: Which words do you know? (*Students should be able to identify all words.*) Read the second and third set of lines. Have students repeat the reading after each line.

Read Aloud! Assign three students to read the parts of דּוֹרוֹן, דִּינָה, and בָּר. Instruct the rest of the class to read the three lines that begin with שָׁלוֹם. Have the assigned students read all six lines.

Ask volunteers to identify the lines that mean:

- Hello, Doron. (*Line 2:* שָׁלוֹם דּוֹרוֹן.)
- Hello, Dinah. (*Line 4:* שָׁלוֹם דִּינָה.)
- I am Bar; I am a mouse. (*Line 5:* אֲנִי בָּר, אֲנִי עַכְבָּר.)

Mastering the Milon (p. 5)

- **בַּיִת** • Draw, or have students draw, a house on the chalkboard. Or display Picture Card 5. Ask: What does בַּיִת mean?

- **בַּ___** • Display Word Card 7 and explain that this prefix combines ___בְּ, meaning "in," and ___הַ, meaning "the." It will always appear together with another word—that's why we see the blank line!

- **כֵּן** • Explain to your students that they should use כֵּן instead of "yes" when answering in the affirmative. Practice by asking students a series of arbitrary (even silly!) questions to which the answer is כֵּן. For example, ask: Does Hanukkah have eight nights this year? (!כֵּן)

**Put It Together** Draw, or have a student draw, a stick figure of a girl inside the drawing of a house. Teach a new word: לֹא, meaning "no."
Ask: יַלְדָּה בַּבַּיִת? (Class should respond: כֵּן.)
Ask: יֶלֶד בַּבַּיִת? (Class should respond: לֹא.)
Then:
- Add a stick figure of a boy and repeat the questions.
- Erase one of the figures and repeat the questions.
- Add a stick figure of a mouse and ask:
עַכְבָּר בַּבַּיִת?

- **מִי** • Teach that מִי is their first "question word." Draw a stick figure of a boy and ask: מִי בַּבַּיִת?
Answer: יֶלֶד בַּבַּיִת.
Continue this way until students understand that מִי means "who."

**Put It Together** Refer to the drawing of the house on the board. Include only a boy inside. Ask:
מִי בַּבַּיִת? (יֶלֶד בַּבַּיִת.)
Replace the boy with a girl. (יַלְדָּה בַּבַּיִת.)
Then, a mouse. (עַכְבָּר בַּבַּיִת.)

Captain Grammar Explain that in many ways, Hebrew is more compact than English; we can convey a message using fewer words. For example, in Hebrew we say "in the" using the letter-vowel combination בַּ. What's more, we connect it to the word that follows, as in בַּבַּיִת.

- **הִנֵּה** • Point to students in the classroom and say, הִנֵּה יַלְדָּה or הִנֵּה יֶלֶד. Explain that הִנֵּה means both "here is" and "here are."

- **אִמָּא** and **אַבָּא** • Display Picture Card 1, say: אִמָּא.
Picture Card 2: אַבָּא.
Point to the אִמָּא card and ask the class: מִי? (אִמָּא)
To the אַבָּא card: מִי? (אַבָּא)

**Put It Together** On the board, draw a picture of a mother and a father inside a house. Point to each, say: הִנֵּה אִמָּא and הִנֵּה אַבָּא. Ask:
- אִמָּא בַּבַּיִת? (כֵּן.)
- אַבָּא בַּבַּיִת? (כֵּן.)
- עַכְבָּר בַּבַּיִת? (לֹא.)
Leave the drawing on the board for גָּר/גָּרָה.

- **גָּר/גָּרָה** • Explain to your students that גָּר/גָּרָה is their first Hebrew verb, meaning "lives." Explain that Hebrew verbs, like many Hebrew words, have different forms for masculine and feminine. The masculine form of this verb is גָּר, the feminine form is גָּרָה.

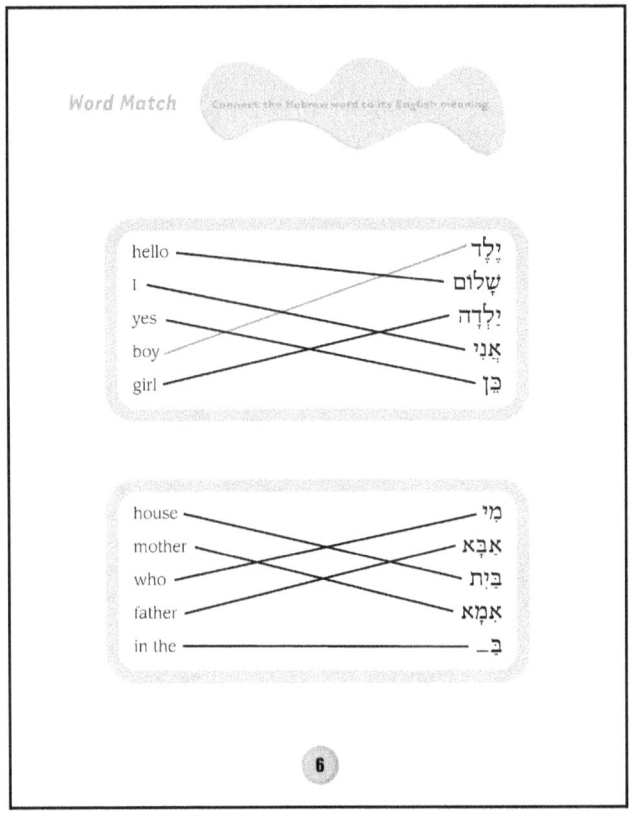

Point to the drawing of the father on the board and say:

אַבָּא גָר בַּבַּיִת.

Point to the mother, say:

אִמָא גָרָה בַּבַּיִת.

Chapter Story: מִי בַּבַּיִת (p. 5)

Read Aloud! Read the entire story on page 5 aloud. Assign five students to read the short poems on page 5 (three for the top of the page, two for the bottom). Have each student read his or her poem aloud.

The Extra Mile Once your students have read the entire story, ask the following questions. Have them answer using complete Hebrew sentences.

- אִמָא בַּבַּיִת? (כֵּן, אִמָא בַּבַּיִת.)
- אַבָּא בַּבַּיִת? (כֵּן, אַבָּא בַּבַּיִת.)
- בַּר בַּבַּיִת? (כֵּן, בַּר בַּבַּיִת.)
- בַּר גָר בַּבַּיִת? (כֵּן, בַּר גָר בַּבַּיִת.)

Word Match (p. 6)

Have students complete the two Word Match exercises on page 6 by connecting each Hebrew word to its English meaning. Check answers by having students read each Hebrew/English pair aloud.

Game Box Shuffle the ten Word Cards that correspond to the words used on page 6 (cards 1–12, minus 5 and 9). Divide the class into two teams: א and ב.

Here are two versions of the "Don't Peek!" game:

A Time to Think

Place a card, English side up, on each student's desk. (If you have fewer than ten students, use fewer words for each round; if you have more, assure your students that everyone will have at least one turn.)

Have a student from א translate the Word Card into Hebrew, then flip it over to check whether the answer is correct. Then a student from ב translates his or her word, checks the answer, and so on. Each correct response earns the student's team 1 point.

▼

Once all the cards have been used, collect, reshuffle, and distribute them again. The team with the most points at the end of three rounds is the winner.

Think Fast!

Place Word Cards on students' desks just before their turn. Begin a stopwatch. If a student guesses the Hebrew translation in 1–3 seconds, that team earns 2 points. If 4–10 seconds, then 1 point. If more than 10 seconds, the team loses 1 point.

◀

 **Game Box** Divide the class into א and ב. Have each team form a line and face the other team. Members of א should hold their books open to page 6; ב should not have books.

Have the first student on א "serve" by choosing a Hebrew word from page 6 and reading it aloud. The first student on ב must "return" by responding with the correct English translation. The second student on א then serves by reading the same Hebrew word and adding another. The second student on ב must return with the correct English translations for both words. The next student on א then repeats the same two Hebrew words and adds a third, and so on. Students may choose to use a word more than once. ב receives a point for every new word it can return in the series. If every student on א has served, continue with the first student in the line.

Continue until a member of ב is unable to return a serve—either by forgetting the sequence or mistranslating a word. Then the serve switches to ב. The team with the most points after both teams have served is the winner.

An alternate version of the game includes students serving in English and returning in Hebrew.

Family Portraits (p. 7)

Have students complete the exercise on page 7 by placing the correct number beneath each box and drawing pictures of themselves in the box specified.

Review answers by having students point to the illustrations and give the correct number and Hebrew word.

 Captain Grammar Explain to your students that Hebrew does not have words for "is," "are," or "am." Instead, we simply say: אֲנִי יַלְדָּה—"I [am a] girl."

 Bring It to Life Using markers and construction paper, have your students draw pictures of their own families inside rooms of their home. Have them label each person (or pet!) with the correct Hebrew word.

Use this project as an opportunity to teach a few more words. Write the following Hebrew words on the board:

סָבָא — grandfather
סַבְתָּא — grandmother
כֶּלֶב — dog
חָתוּל — cat

 **Conversation Corner** Display the family portraits on the chalkboard or around the room. Have students present their "works of art" to the class. They may say, אֲנִי בַּבַּיִת, הִנֵּה שָׂרָה, הִנֵּה אַבָּא, etc. OR שָׂרָה בַּבַּיִת, אִמָּא בַּבַּיִת, etc.

Encourage students to raise their hands and ask the "artist" about his or her picture. Have them introduce themselves by saying:

שָׁלוֹם, דָּוִד. אֲנִי רָחֵל.
The "artist" should respond, שָׁלוֹם, רָחֵל. אֲנִי דָּוִד.
They may ask questions about the picture:
מִי הַיֶּלֶד?—Who is the boy?;
כֶּלֶב בַּבַּיִת?—Is a dog in the house?; etc.

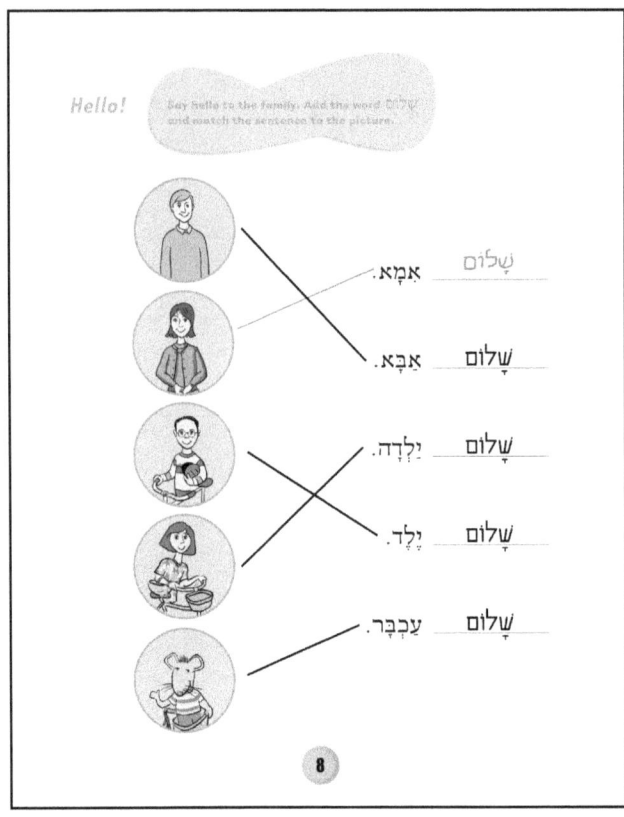

Hello! (p. 8)

Have your students complete the activity by adding the word שָׁלוֹם in each blank line, then drawing a line from each sentence to its corresponding picture.

Who Is Home? (p. 9)

Have students complete the exercise on page 9 by writing the number of each picture next to the matching word, then completing the sentence. You may wish to allow students to work in pairs or groups as they complete the exercise. Check student answers by walking around the class to see that students have written the correct number on each line and have completed each sentence with the word בַּבַּיִת.

Game Box Play a version of "The Magic Stone," as described on page 16. Give the tennis ball to the student whose birthday is coming next to begin the game.

In this version of the game, the Wizard (the student with the ball) reads any Hebrew sentence found in Chapter 1. The Apprentice (the student to his or her right) then has 5 seconds to say the sentence in English. If that student is correct, he or she receives the ball and offers the next "challenge." If that student is incorrect, he or she steps out of the circle and the student with the ball offers another "challenge."

Continue until only one student remains in the circle. That remaining student is the winner.

Looking Ahead Explain to your students that they will now learn Hebrew words having to do with Jewish holidays, beginning with the Head of the Year—Rosh Hashanah.

Ask your students to brainstorm Hebrew Rosh Hashanah words. (*Answers may include: Rosh Hashanah—Head of the Year; shanah tovah—a good year; shofar.*)

Shalom Ivrit 1 • Teacher's Edition

Lesson Objectives

Students will:
- Understand that ‏‎ַה‎‏, ‏‎וְ‎‏, and ‏‎לְ‎‏ are prefixes, joining the word that follows.
- Begin to differentiate between masculine and feminine forms of verbs.

New Milon Words and Phrases

where	אֵיפֹה
the	הַ___
family	מִשְׁפָּחָה
there is, there are	יֵשׁ
no	לֹא
and	וְ___
good (m/f)	טוֹב/טוֹבָה
to, for	לְ___

What We'll Need

❏ Text pages 10–17
❏ Word Cards 14–21
❏ Helpful props: a round ḥallah, grape juice (to symbolize wine), two candles with candlesticks, and an apple, to set a "real" Rosh Hashanah table; markers and construction paper. If you prefer, you can substitute Picture Cards 7–10 for these props.

Where We Are

In Chapter 2, we join Dinah, Doron, and their family as they celebrate Rosh Hashanah. We'll learn words for familiar Rosh Hashanah objects, including one in which little Bar has built a home!

Let's Review

Draw a house on the chalkboard (as in Chapter 1), with יַלְדָה, יֶלֶד, אַבָּא, אִמָא inside. Say: הִנֵה בַּיִת.
Ask your students:

- יֶלֶד בַּבַּיִת? (כֵּן, יֶלֶד בַּבַּיִת.)
- יַלְדָה בַּבַּיִת? (כֵּן, יַלְדָה בַּבַּיִת.)
- אַבָּא גָר בַּבַּיִת? (כֵּן, אַבָּא גָר בַּבַּיִת.)
- אִמָא גָרָה בַּבַּיִת? (כֵּן, אִמָא גָרָה בַּבַּיִת.)

Keep the drawing on the chalkboard as you begin Chapter 2.

Introducing the Lesson

Point to the chalkboard drawing of the family inside the house. Ask: אֵיפֹה הַיֶלֶד?
Say: הַיֶלֶד בַּבַּיִת.
Ask the class: אֵיפֹה הַיַלְדָה? (הַיַלְדָה בַּבַּיִת.)

Point to the entire house, ask: אֵיפֹה הַמִשְׁפָּחָה?
Say: (הַמִשְׁפָּחָה בַּבַּיִת.)

Draw a mouse inside the house, ask: הָעַכְבָּר בַּבַּיִת? (כֵּן, הָעַכְבָּר בַּבַּיִת.)
Erase the mouse, repeat the question, and answer: לֹא, הָעַכְבָּר לֹא בַּבַּיִת.

41   Chapter 2

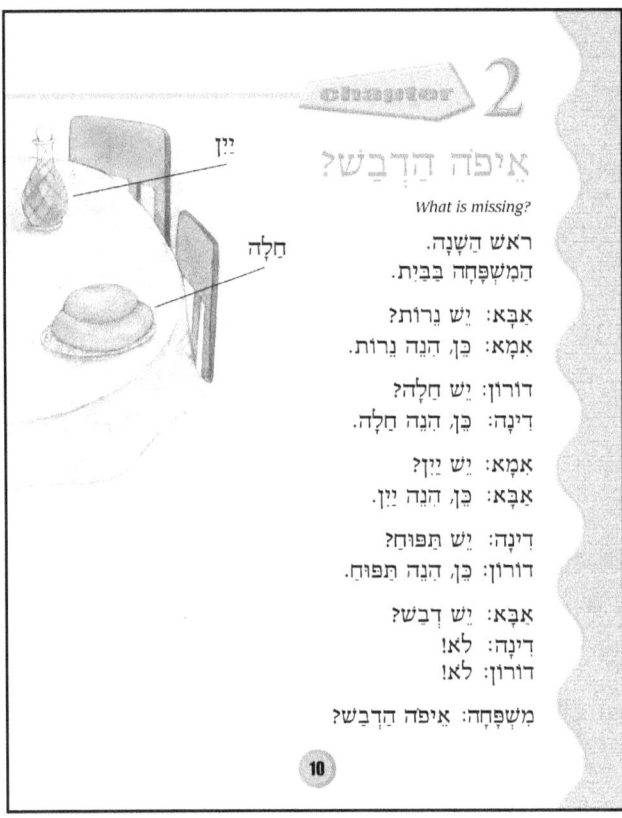

Mastering the Milon (p. 11)

Place the ḥallah, grape juice, candles with candlesticks, and apple (or Picture Cards 7–10) on a table, as pictured on pages 10–11.

• **אֵיפֹה** • Ask: ‎?אֵיפֹה [name of a student in your class]? Pretend you are searching the room. Do not look at the student as you ask the question. Then look at the student and say: ‎הִנֵה [student]! Ask: What do you think ‎אֵיפֹה means?

• **הַ___** • Stressing the ‎הַ, ask: ‎אֵיפֹה הַחַלָה?
Then: ‎אֵיפֹה הַחַלָה וְהַתַפוּחַ?
Ask: What do you think ‎הַ___ means? Explain that like ‎וְ___, ‎הַ___ joins the word that follows it.

Continue by teaching the words that surround the table on pages 10–11 (these are *tarmilon* words—words that are unique to the chapters in which they appear). Have students come up to the table as you teach each new word.

• **חַלָה** • Ask: ‎אֵיפֹה הַחַלָה? Have the student point to the ḥallah and say: ‎הִנֵה הַחַלָה.

• **יַיִן** • Ask: ‎אֵיפֹה הַיַיִן?
Pretend to take a sip of wine. Have the student point to the wine (juice) and say: ‎הִנֵה הַיַיִן.

• **נֵרוֹת** • Ask: ‎אֵיפֹה הַנֵרוֹת?
Make the gesture of bringing in the Shabbat candles. Have a student point to the candles and say: ‎הִנֵה הַנֵרוֹת.

• **תַפוּחַ** • Rub your stomach as if you are hungry.
Ask: ‎אֵיפֹה תַפוּחַ?
Have a student point to the apple and say: ‎הִנֵה תַפוּחַ.

**Put It Together** Call up students, one at a time, to the table. Have them point to objects as you ask about them:
• ‎אֵיפֹה נֵרוֹת? (הִנֵה נֵרוֹת.)
• ‎אֵיפֹה חַלָה? (הִנֵה חַלָה.)
• ‎אֵיפֹה יַיִן? (הִנֵה יַיִן.)

You may wish to ask these questions more and more quickly as the class masters the vocabulary.

• **וְ___** • Point to each object as you say:
‎הִנֵה חַלָה וְנֵרוֹת וְתַפוּחַ וְיַיִן.

Ask: What do you think ‎וְ___ means? (*Students will likely understand that ‎וְ___ means "and."*) Explain that the prefix ‎וְ___ joins the word that follows it.

**Put It Together** Call individual students to the table. Have them point to the objects as you list them:
• ‎תַפוּחַ וְיַיִן
• ‎חַלָה וְנֵרוֹת
• ‎נֵרוֹת וְחַלָה וְיַיִן

Have students provide answers in full sentences while pointing to the objects you name:
• ‎אֵיפֹה תַפוּחַ וְנֵרוֹת? (הִנֵה תַפוּחַ וְנֵרוֹת.)
• ‎אֵיפֹה חַלָה וְיַיִן וְתַפוּחַ? (הִנֵה חַלָה וְיַיִן וְתַפוּחַ.)
• ‎אֵיפֹה יַיִן וְחַלָה וְנֵרוֹת? (הִנֵה יַיִן וְחַלָה וְנֵרוֹת.)

Set the table with only one object, then a combination of two, then three. Have students describe what they see. Possible descriptions include:
• ‎הִנֵה תַפוּחַ.
• ‎הִנֵה נֵרוֹת וְיַיִן.
• ‎הִנֵה חַלָה וְנֵרוֹת וְתַפוּחַ.

• **לֹא** • Point to the ḥallah and ask: ‎חַלָה? (כֵּן.)
To the candles: ‎תַפוּחַ? (לֹא.)
To the wine: ‎חַלָה? (לֹא.)

Shalom Ivrit 1 • Teacher's Edition

 • יֵשׁ • Point to objects on the table and say:

יֵשׁ חַלָּה; יֵשׁ יַיִן; יֵשׁ נֵרוֹת.

Explain that יֵשׁ, meaning "there is" and "there are" may be easily confused with הִנֵּה, meaning "here is" and "here are." Explain that we use יֵשׁ when speaking generally, and הִנֵּה when speaking in more specific terms. For example:

יֵשׁ יְלָדִים בַּבַּיִת. (There are children in the house);
הִנֵּה יֶלֶד. (Here is a boy).

Put It Together Set the table with all the objects. Call individual students up, and ask them to answer using יֵשׁ, then כֵּן or לֹא.

• יֵשׁ חַלָּה? (כֵּן, יֵשׁ חַלָּה.)
• יֵשׁ תַּפּוּחַ? (כֵּן, יֵשׁ תַּפּוּחַ.)
• יֵשׁ יַיִן וְנֵרוֹת? (כֵּן, יַיִן וְנֵרוֹת.)

Set the table with an apple and candles only. Ask students to answer using only כֵּן or לֹא:

• יֵשׁ תַּפּוּחַ? (כֵּן.)
• יֵשׁ חַלָּה? (לֹא.)
• יֵשׁ יַיִן? (לֹא.)
• יֵשׁ תַּפּוּחַ וְנֵרוֹת? (כֵּן.)
• יֵשׁ תַּפּוּחַ וְחַלָּה? (לֹא.)

• מִשְׁפָּחָה • Point to the chalkboard drawing of the family. Ask: אִמָּא בַּבַּיִת? (כֵּן.) הַיַּלְדָּה בַּבַּיִת? (כֵּן.)
Now circle all members of the family. Ask:
הַמִּשְׁפָּחָה בַּבַּיִת? (כֵּן.)

 **Put It Together** Call individual students to the board. Have them reply in full sentences to:

• הַמִּשְׁפָּחָה בַּבַּיִת? (כֵּן, הַמִּשְׁפָּחָה בַּבַּיִת.)
• יֵשׁ יַלְדָּה בַּבַּיִת? (כֵּן, יֵשׁ יַלְדָּה בַּבַּיִת.)
• אֵיפֹה אַבָּא? (הִנֵּה אַבָּא OR אַבָּא בַּבַּיִת.)

• טוֹב/טוֹבָה • Pretend to take a bite of the apple. Say: הַתַּפּוּחַ טוֹב! Pretend to take a piece of ḥallah. Say: חַלָּה טוֹבָה! Continue this way until students understand that טוֹב and טוֹבָה mean "good."

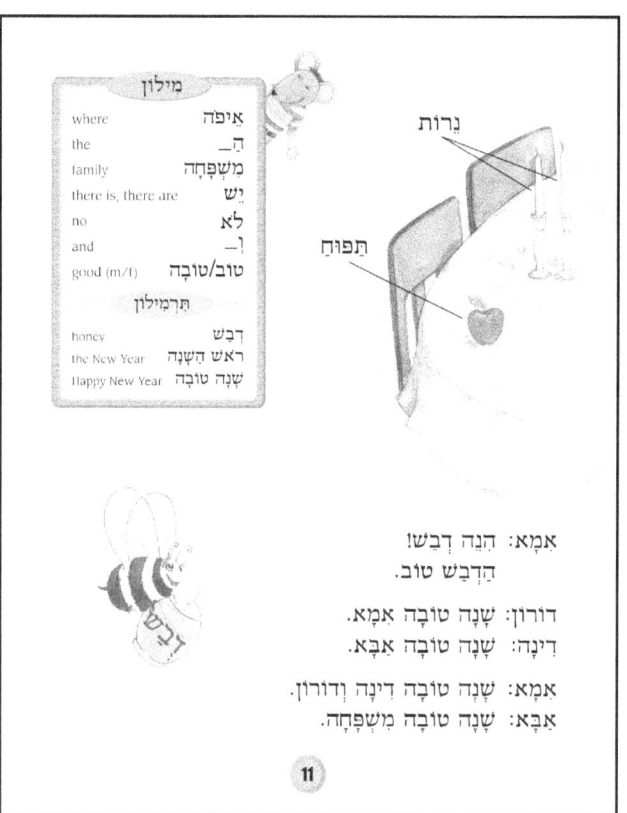

Chapter Story: אֵיפֹה הַדְּבַשׁ?
(pp. 10–11)

Ready for Reading Point to the picture of the bee on page 11. Ask a student to read the word inside the jar. (דְּבַשׁ) Ask: What does the title of the story mean? (*Where Is the Honey?*) You may wish to tell the class that the word for "bee" is דְּבוֹרָה.

Read Aloud! Read the entire story on pages 10–11 aloud.

Assign five students to read the parts of: narrator, אִמָּא, אַבָּא, דִּינָה, and דּוֹרוֹן. Ask students to use their hands, notebooks, or a sheet of paper to hide the story; tell them to reveal each line only as it is read. Have the narrator read the first two lines, then אַבָּא his first line. Ask the class: What are some possible answers to אַבָּא's question? (*Answers may include:* לֹא; כֵּן, הִנֵּה נֵרוֹת.) Continue this way for the next three pairs of lines.

When אַבָּא asks, יֵשׁ דְּבַשׁ?, have students reveal the rest of the page and continue normally through the end of page 11.

Ask: What does שָׁנָה טוֹבָה mean? (*Many students will know it as "Happy New Year," although it literally means "good [or happy] year."*)

Chapter 2

The Extra Mile Have groups of four students sit at the table and pretend to be the four characters in the story. Ask questions based on the story, including:

- For all characters: מִי בַּבַּיִת?
  (דּוֹרוֹן בַּבַּיִת, דִּינָה בַּבַּיִת...;
  דִּינָה וְדוֹרוֹן וְאִמָּא בַּבַּיִת...
  הַמִּשְׁפָּחָה בַּבַּיִת.)
- For אַבָּא: יֵשׁ נֵרוֹת? (כֵּן, יֵשׁ נֵרוֹת.)
- For דּוֹרוֹן: יֵשׁ חַלָּה? (כֵּן, יֵשׁ חַלָּה.)
- For אִמָּא: יֵשׁ נֵרוֹת וְיַיִן וְתַפּוּחַ?
  (כֵּן, יֵשׁ...)

Have each student wish the others a happy New Year. (For example, דּוֹרוֹן would say: שָׁנָה טוֹבָה אִמָּא; שָׁנָה טוֹבָה אַבָּא; שָׁנָה טוֹבָה דִּינָה.)

Greeting Cards (p. 12)

Have students complete the exercise on page 12 by writing the Hebrew for the person listed. Allow them to refer to the *milonim* on pages 4 and 5 for spellings. Check answers by having students read each card aloud.

Bring It to Life If you are teaching this chapter around Rosh Hashanah, have students create their own שָׁנָה טוֹבָה cards, using markers and construction paper. Tell your students to use רַק עִבְרִית—Hebrew only!

Word Match (p. 13)

Have students complete the two exercises on page 13 by writing the number of each item that is on the table next to its matching Hebrew word, then writing the Hebrew word below the matching picture. Check answers by having students show you their work.

>  **Game Box** Using 5" x 7" index cards, play "Concentration," as described on page 17.
>
> Have the class create 14 cards: 6 with the Hebrew words from page 13 and a "bonus" card with שָׁנָה טוֹבָה, plus 7 cards with illustrations of those words (you may wish to have students draw balloons and confetti for שָׁנָה טוֹבָה).
>
> Award 1 point for each matching pair, and 2 points for the "bonus" שָׁנָה טוֹבָה pair. You may wish to create a longer game by creating two sets of each word-illustration pair.

Mastering the Milon (p. 14)

• לְ___ • Point to אַבָּא and אִמָּא on the chalkboard, and say:

שָׁנָה טוֹבָה לְאִמָּא; שָׁנָה טוֹבָה לְאַבָּא...

Then, to individual students, say:

שָׁנָה טוֹבָה לְ [student's name];
שָׁנָה טוֹבָה לְ [student's name]...

Explain that like ___הַ and וְ___, לְ___ combines with the word that follows it.

Chapter Story: קוֹל שׁוֹפָר (p. 14)

 **Ready for Reading** Have a student read the title of the poem on page 14. Explain that this poem has lines that rhyme. Ask: What are some Hebrew words we know that rhyme with one another? (*Answers may include:* יַלְדָה, אַבָּא, אִמָּא, טוֹבָה, *etc.*)

> ♪ **Bring It to Life** If possible, invite your synagogue's cantor—or someone else who blows the *shofar*—to class. Have him or her blow the "*tu tu tu*" line that begins the poem!

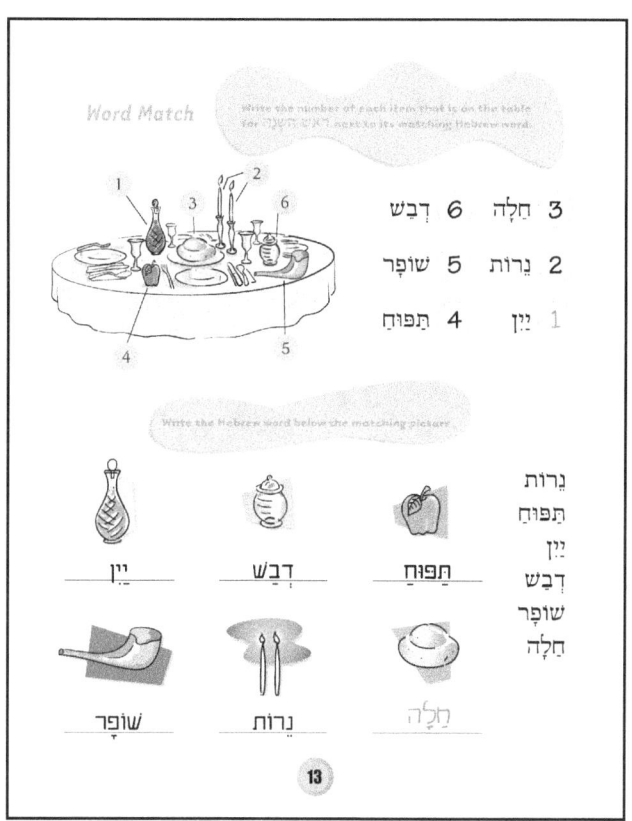

You may choose to assign each line, or each pair of lines, to individual students. Or have the class read the entire poem together.

A Special Voice (p. 15)

Put It Together Point to אִמָא and אַבָּא on page 14 and have students wish each of them שָׁנָה טוֹבָה individually, then together:

- שָׁנָה טוֹבָה לְאִמָא.
- שָׁנָה טוֹבָה לְאַבָּא.
- שָׁנָה טוֹבָה לְאִמָא וְאַבָּא.

Using the Photograph Have students read the caption to the photograph on page 15 aloud. Ask: What does it mean? (*Tu, tu, tu, the boy and girl have a shofar.*)

Challenge students to identify the boy, girl, and each shofar in the photograph, using הִנֵה.

(הִנֵה שׁוֹפָר; הִנֵה יַלְדָה; הִנֵה יֶלֶד.)

A Special Voice (p. 15)

Have your students complete the puzzle on page 15 by circling every third letter in each Hebrew line, then writing the circled letters in the blank spaces. Check answers by having students read the new Hebrew words, and their meaning, aloud.

Bring It to Life Using markers and poster board or construction paper, have students create their own "third-letter" puzzles. Students may use words or phrases from either of the first two chapters.

Remind your students to:
- Write one line of letters for each hidden word.
- Leave blank spaces for each hidden word.
- Leave a line to write the English solution to the puzzle.
- Use only letters—no vowels.

Once students have finished their puzzles, have them switch with a partner who will fill in the answers.

When everyone has finished, review the puzzles as a class, then display them on a bulletin board or classroom wall.

Shalom Ivrit 1 • Teacher's Edition

Chapter Story: הָעַכְבָּר בַּשׁוֹפָר

(p. 16)

Read Aloud! Read the entire poem aloud. Have students repeat each pair of lines twice. Be sure to stress the rhymes at the end of each pair of lines.

The Extra Mile After reading the poem, ask:

- אֵיפֹה גָר בָּר? (בָּר גָר בַּשׁוֹפָר.)
- מִי בַּשׁוֹפָר? (בָּר OR בָּר הָעַכְבָּר בַּשׁוֹפָר.)
- טוֹב לָעַכְבָּר בַּבַּיִת? (כֵּן, טוֹב לָעַכְבָּר בַּבַּיִת.)
- אִמָּא גָרָה בַּשׁוֹפָר? (לֹא, אִמָּא לֹא גָרָה בַּשׁוֹפָר.)
- אַבָּא גָר בַּשׁוֹפָר? (לֹא, אַבָּא לֹא גָר בַּשׁוֹפָר.)
- בָּר גָר בַּשׁוֹפָר? (כֵּן, בָּר גָר בַּשׁוֹפָר.)

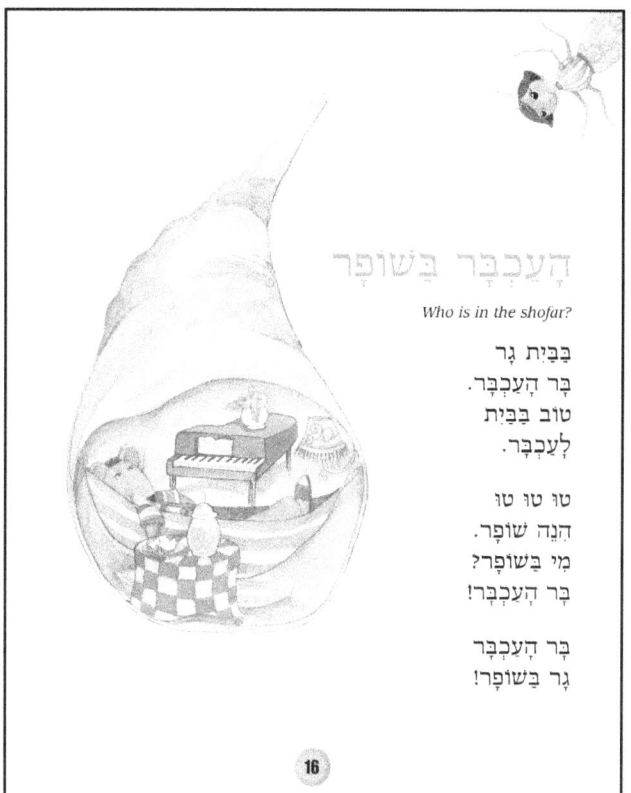

הָעַכְבָּר בַּשׁוֹפָר

Who is in the shofar?

בַּבַּיִת גָר
בָּר הָעַכְבָּר.
טוֹב בַּבַּיִת
לָעַכְבָּר.

טוּ טוּ טוּ
הִנֵּה שׁוֹפָר.
מִי בַּשׁוֹפָר?
בָּר הָעַכְבָּר!

בָּר הָעַכְבָּר
גָר בַּשׁוֹפָר!

16

Captain Grammar ‎לְ‏ is a handy prefix. It usually means "to," but can also mean "for"—as in טוֹב בַּבַּיִת לָעַכְבָּר — "It is good in the house *for* the mouse."

47 Chapter 2

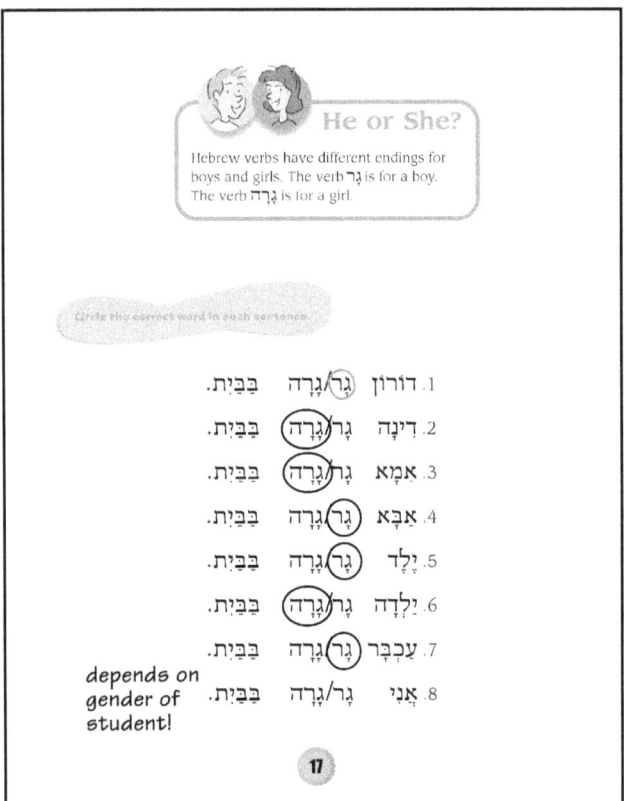

He or She? (p. 17)

Read the English directions together as a class. Have students complete the exercise by circling the correct word in each sentence.

 Captain Grammar Usually, Hebrew words that end with the syllable "ah" are feminine. But there are other feminine endings as well. You may wish to avoid establishing general gender rules with your students, and instead identify the gender of each word as you teach it.

 **Game Box** Review Chapter 2 by playing "Jeopardy!" as described on page 18.

Here are some sample questions for each category:

Read It!
Have students read:
- 1 point: The Hebrew side of Word Cards 14–21.
- 3 points: A complete greeting card from page 12.
- 5 points: One of the two 4-line stories on page 16. No mistakes allowed!

Know It!
Have students provide the Hebrew for:
- 1 point: The English side of Word Cards 14–21.
- 3 points: The word that means "family."
- 5 points: The sentence, "Bar the mouse lives in the house."

Say It!
On the chalkboard, draw a picture of a mother and son in a house. Ask:

- 1 point: אִמָא בַּבַּיִת? (כֵּן, אִמָא בַּבַּיִת.)
- 3 points: אַבָּא וְיַלְדָה בַּבַּיִת? (לֹא, אַבָּא וְיַלְדָה לֹא בַּבַּיִת.)
- 5 points: אִמָא וְהַיֶלֶד וְהַיַלְדָה בַּבַּיִת? (לֹא, אִמָא וְהַיֶלֶד וְהַיַלְדָה לֹא בַּבַּיִת.)

 **Looking Ahead** Explain to your students that they will soon join Doron, Dinah, and family in the sukkah. They'll learn words having to do with Sukkot, and also for weather conditions that might ruin a pleasant meal in the sukkah!

Tell your students that in the next chapter, they will also learn the words for "you"—אַתְּ for a girl and אַתָּה for a boy. Ask them to think of new Hebrew sentences they can create with these important new words.

Shalom Ivrit 1 • Teacher's Edition

Chapter 3

Lesson Objectives

Students will:
- Continue to build their everyday vocabulary, including words for weather conditions and articles of clothing.
- Understand that some Hebrew prefixes—such as לְ___ and ___הַ—may combine into a single prefix (in this case לַ___).

New Milon Words and Phrases

Core Vocabulary

you (m)	אַתָּה
you (f)	אַתְּ
grandfather	סַבָּא
grandmother	סַבְתָּא
also	גַם
children, boys	יְלָדִים
to the, for the	לְ___ , לַ___
goes, walks (m/f)	הוֹלֵךְ/הוֹלֶכֶת

Simḥat Torah-Related Vocabulary

Torah	תּוֹרָה
gift	מַתָּנָה

Other Useful Vocabulary

holiday	חַג
rain	גֶשֶׁם
cold	קַר
box	קוּפְסָה
coat	מְעִיל
hat	כּוֹבַע
umbrella	מִטְרִיָה

What We'll Need

- ❑ Text pages 18–25
- ❑ Word Cards 22–38
- ❑ Picture Cards 7–17
- ❑ Helpful props: a coat, a hat, an umbrella, and a ball

Where We Are

In Chapter 3, we meet Dinah and Doron's grandparents and join them (along with Bar) in the sukkah. We learn how little Bar manages to stay cool and dry even though it's cold and wet outside. Then we listen in as Doron's mother makes sure he has everything he needs for a walk on a rainy day.

Let's Review

Display Picture Cards 7–10. Point to each, saying:

הִנֵה הַחַלָה וְהַיַיִן וְהַנֵרוֹת וְהַתַפּוּחַ.

Then, call individual students to the table and ask:

- אֵיפֹה הַתַפּוּחַ? (הִנֵה הַתַפּוּחַ.)
- אֵיפֹה הַחַלָה וְהַנֵרוֹת? (הִנֵה...)
- אֵיפֹה הַיַיִן וְהַחַלָה וְהַתַפּוּחַ? (הִנֵה...)

Now place only the apple and ḥallah on the table:

- יֵשׁ תַפּוּחַ? (כֵּן, הִנֵה תַפּוּחַ.)
- יֵשׁ יַיִן? (לֹא.)
- יֵשׁ תַפּוּחַ וְחַלָה? (כֵּן, הִנֵה תַפּוּחַ וְחַלָה.)
- יֵשׁ תַפּוּחַ וְיַיִן? (לֹא.)

Introducing the Lesson

Ask students to look at the illustration on page 18. Have the boys in the class pretend to be Doron, and the girls pretend to be Dinah.

Ask individual students:

- אִמָא גָרָה בַּבַּיִת? (כֵּן, אִמָא גָרָה בַּבַּיִת.)
- אַבָּא גָר בַּבַּיִת? (כֵּן, אַבָּא גָר בַּבַּיִת.)

Point to a boy and ask: אַתָּה גָר בַּבַּיִת?
(Assist him with the answer: כֵּן, אֲנִי גָר בַּבַּיִת.)

Point to a girl and ask: אַתְּ גָרָה בַּבַּיִת?
(Assist her with the answer: כֵּן, אֲנִי גָרָה בַּבַּיִת.)

Continue this way until all students understand that אַתָּה means "you" for a boy, and אַתְּ means "you" for a girl.

Mastering the Milon (p. 19)

Display Picture Cards 11 and 12 on a bulletin board or the chalkboard ledge.

• **אַתָּה/אַתְּ** • Point to a boy in the class, and ask:

אַתָּה [student's name]? (כֵּן, אֲנִי _____.)

To a girl: אַתְּ _____? (כֵּן, אֲנִי _____.)

Point to a boy and use an incorrect name:

אַתָּה _____? (לֹא, אֲנִי _____.)

To a girl: אַתְּ _____? (לֹא, אֲנִי _____.)

Continue this way until students are comfortable with the correct usage of אַתָּה and אַתְּ, and can introduce themselves.

• **גַם** • Ask a girl in the class:

אַתְּ יַלְדָה? (כֵּן, אֲנִי יַלְדָה.)

Ask another girl: גַם אַתְּ יַלְדָה?

(Stress גַם as you would "also.") Ask: What do you think גַם means?

• **חַג** • Say: חַג הַפֶּסַח; חַג הַשָׁבוּעוֹת; חַג סֻכּוֹת

Continue this way until students understand that חַג means "holiday," say: חַג שָׂמֵחַ!

Ask: What does this expression mean? (*Many students will know that it means "happy holiday!"*)

 **Put It Together**

Say: חַג שָׂמֵחַ לְ_____ וְגַם
לְ_____;
חַג שָׂמֵחַ לְ_____ וְגַם לְ_____
וְגַם לְ_____.

Then have students each wish three classmates a happy holiday. (Ask them to incorporate לְ_____, וְ_____, and גַם into their sentences.) For example, a student may say:

חַג שָׂמֵחַ לְדָוִד וְגַם לְשָׂרָה וְגַם לְרִבְקָה.

• **סַבָּא** and **סַבְתָא** • Hold up Picture Cards 11 and 12. Raise card 11 and say: הִנֵה סַבְתָא.

Raise card 12, say: הִנֵה סַבָּא.

Show only card 12 and ask: סַבָּא? (כֵּן.) סַבְתָא? (לֹא.)

Continue until students understand that סַבָּא means "grandfather" and סַבְתָא means "grandmother."

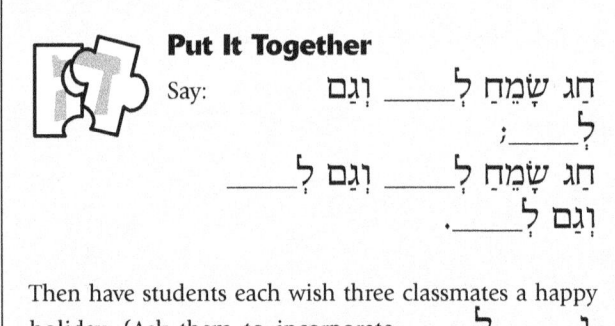

Chapter Story: בַּסוּכָּה (pp. 18–19)

 **Ready for Reading** Have a student read the story's Hebrew title and English question aloud. Ask: What are some things that we may find inside a Sukkah? (*fruit, leaves* or *s'chach, table and chairs, lulav and etrog,* etc.)

You may wish to point out the words for *lulav* and *etrog* in the *tarmilon* on page 19, so that students recognize them by sight.

Ask students to guess who the "surprise guest" might be. (*Many will predict that it's Bar.*)

 **Read Aloud!** Assign seven students to read the parts of: דּוֹרוֹן, דִּינָה, אִמָּא, אַבָּא, סַבְתָּא, סַבָּא, and בַּר. You may wish to have those students come to the front of the room and dramatize the reading as a play.

Have אִמָּא and אַבָּא read the first pair of lines.

• Ask אַבָּא: אַתָּה בַּבַּיִת? (כֵּן, אֲנִי בַּבַּיִת.)
• Ask אִמָּא: אֵיפֹה אַבָּא? (אַבָּא בַּבַּיִת.)

Have אִמָּא, דּוֹרוֹן, and דִּינָה read the next two pairs of lines.

• Ask דּוֹרוֹן: אַתָּה בַּסוּכָּה? (לֹא, אֲנִי לֹא בַּסוּכָּה.)
• Ask דִּינָה: אַתְּ בַּסוּכָּה? (לֹא, אֲנִי לֹא בַּסוּכָּה.)

Have אִמָּא, סַבָּא, סַבְתָּא, and בַּר read the remainder of the story.

• Ask אִמָּא: הַמִּשְׁפָּחָה בַּסוּכָּה? (לֹא, הַמִּשְׁפָּחָה לֹא בַּסוּכָּה.)
• Ask סַבָּא: אַתָּה בַּבַּיִת? (לֹא, אֲנִי לֹא בַּבַּיִת.)
• Ask סַבְתָּא: אַתְּ בַּסוּכָּה? (כֵּן, אֲנִי בַּסוּכָּה.)
• Ask עַכְבָּר: גַּם אַתָּה בַּסוּכָּה? (כֵּן, גַּם אֲנִי בַּסוּכָּה.)

 Captain Grammar Students may be confused by the expression גַּם אֲנִי—literally, "also I"—which is different than the English construction, "I [am] also." You may wish to explain this difference.

You may wish to incorporate גַּם אֲנִי (informally, "me, too") into your classroom routine.

סַבָּא: אֲנִי בַּסוּכָּה.
הִנֵּה לוּלָב.
סַבְתָּא: גַּם אֲנִי בַּסוּכָּה.
הִנֵּה אֶתְרוֹג.
עַכְבָּר: גַּם אֲנִי בַּסוּכָּה!
חַג שָׂמֵחַ!

מִילוֹן

אַתָּה — you (m)
אַתְּ — you (f)
סַבָּא — grandfather
סַבְתָּא — grandmother
גַּם — also
חַג — holiday

תַּרְמִילוֹן

סוּכָּה — sukkah
לוּלָב — lulav
אֶתְרוֹג — etrog
חַג שָׂמֵחַ — happy holiday

19

 **The Extra Mile** Assign seven students to pretend to be members of the family, as listed in "Read Aloud." Create two "stations" in the classroom: הַסוּכָּה and הַבַּיִת. Have דִּינָה, דּוֹרוֹן, אַבָּא, אִמָּא stand in הַבַּיִת. Have בַּר, סַבְתָּא, סַבָּא and stand in הַסוּכָּה.

Questions for family members:

• For אִמָּא: אֵיפֹה הַמִּשְׁפָּחָה? (הַמִּשְׁפָּחָה בַּבַּיִת.)
• For דּוֹרוֹן: אֵיפֹה דִּינָה? (הִנֵּה דִּינָה.)
• For דִּינָה: אֵיפֹה סַבָּא? (סַבָּא בַּסוּכָּה.)
• For אַבָּא: אֵיפֹה סַבָּא וְסַבְתָּא? (סַבָּא וְסַבְתָּא בַּסוּכָּה.)
• For סַבָּא: אַתָּה בַּבַּיִת? (לֹא, אֲנִי בַּסוּכָּה.)
• For סַבְתָּא: אַתְּ וְסַבָּא בַּסוּכָּה? (כֵּן, אֲנִי וְסַבָּא בַּסוּכָּה.)
• For בַּר: גַּם אַתָּה בַּסוּכָּה? (כֵּן, גַּם אֲנִי בַּסוּכָּה.)

Questions for other members of the class (have each student use וְ___ in the answer):

• מִי בַּבַּיִת? (אִמָּא וְאַבָּא וְדוֹרוֹן וְדִינָה בַּבַּיִת.)

▼

51

Chapter 3

עַכְבָּר בַּסוּכָּה

It's raining and it's cold. Everyone has left the sukkah except Bar. Why isn't Bar cold?

גֶּשֶׁם. קַר.
מִי בַּסוּכָּה?

הַמִּשְׁפָּחָה בַּסוּכָּה? לֹא.
הַיְלָדִים בַּסוּכָּה? לֹא.

מִי בַּסוּכָּה?
הָעַכְבָּר בַּסוּכָּה!

- סַבָּא וְסַבְתָּא בַּבַּיִת? (לֹא, סַבָּא וְסַבְתָּא לֹא בַּבַּיִת. OR לֹא, סַבָּא וְסַבְתָּא בַּסוּכָּה.)
- אֵיפֹה הַמִּשְׁפָּחָה? (הַמִּשְׁפָּחָה בַּבַּיִת. OR הַמִּשְׁפָּחָה בַּבַּיִת וְגַם בַּסוּכָּה.)

Mastering the Milon (p. 21)

• **יְלָדִים** • Point to a boy and say: הִנֵּה יֶלֶד.
To a girl, say: הִנֵּה יַלְדָּה.
Gesture to the entire class, say: הִנֵּה יְלָדִים.
Ask: אֵיפֹה הַיְלָדִים? (הִנֵּה הַיְלָדִים.)

• **לְ__ , לַ__** • Say, slowly: חַג שָׂמֵחַ לְ-הַ-יַלְדָּה.
Now say: חַג שָׂמֵחַ לַיַלְדָּה, with emphasis on לַ__. Repeat the second form. You may wish to write the two sentences on the board, with an equals sign between them.

Captain Grammar Hebrew uses contractions, just as English does. And just as in English, letters may drop out in order to communicate a message with fewer words and syllables. לְ__ and הַ__, for example, contract to become לַ__.

Put It Together Create a "human triangle," with three "corners": one boy, one girl, and one boy and one girl together. Have a student stand in the center of the triangle, and explain that the ball should be tossed to the "corner" you name. Sample directions:

לַיְלָדִים (ball should be tossed to the boy and girl)
לַיַלְדָּה (to the girl)
לַיֶּלֶד (to the boy)

Have a student "director" instruct the players. You may wish to challenge students to see how long they can play without tossing the ball to the incorrect "corner."

You may wish to either teach the following words using the suggestions provided, or distribute Word Cards 28, 29, and 32 to students, to pantomime for one another, using the Hebrew word and no other verbal clues!

Make sure your students understand the meaning of each of the following words before moving on:

• **גֶּשֶׁם** • Say: יֵשׁ גֶּשֶׁם בַּסוּכָּה!
Pantomime raindrops with your fingers. Partially open the umbrella and walk quickly, saying, גֶּשֶׁם, גֶּשֶׁם!

• **קַר** • Say "קררררר" as if saying, "brrrrrr," while pretending to keep yourself warm.

• **קוּפְסָה** • Point to various boxes in your classroom, or bring some in (crayon boxes, toy boxes, and lunch boxes are fine) and say: הִנֵּה קוּפְסָה. Point to other containers, such as a thermos, bookbag, or purse.
Ask: קוּפְסָה? (לֹא.)

Shalom Ivrit 1 • Teacher's Edition

Chapter Story: עַכְבָּר בַּסוּכָּה

(pp. 20–21)

 **Ready for Reading** Have a student read the title of the story and the English introduction. Have students look at the illustration on page 21 and ask: Why do you think Bar isn't cold? (*Students may guess that it's because Bar is in a box!*)

 **Read Aloud!** As you read the story aloud, keep in mind: The variety of sentences in this story may help familiarize students with a comfortable, conversational rhythm; be sure to stress the exclamation points and question marks!

Instead of having students read line by line, ask them to alternate reading full sentences. (One student reads גֶשֶׁם; another קַר; another מִי בַּסוּכָּה?; etc.) Read the entire story on pages 20–21 slowly, as a class.

Now have your students do a "quick read." Assign students the same sentences they read in the "slow read." Have them read as quickly as they can, while making sure that each word is clear and understandable.

 **The Extra Mile** Check comprehension with the following questions (you can ask these questions during the "slow read," or wait until the "quick read"):

- הַמִשְׁפָּחָה בַּסוּכָּה? (לֹא, הַמִשְׁפָּחָה לֹא בַּסוּכָּה.)
- הַיְלָדִים בַּסוּכָּה? (לֹא, הַיְלָדִים לֹא בַּסוּכָּה.)
- מִי בַּסוּכָּה? (בָּר בַּסוּכָּה.)
- בָּר בַּסוּכָּה? (כֵּן, בָּר בַּסוּכָּה.)
- קַר בַּסוּכָּה? (כֵּן, קַר בַּסוּכָּה.)
- טוֹב לַעַכְבָּר בַּסוּכָּה? (כֵּן, טוֹב לַעַכְבָּר בַּסוּכָּה.)

You may also wish to ask the questions above as "quick questions," to help students think and respond on their toes. You may even find students reporting that they are "thinking in Hebrew"—a good sign!

What's in the Sukkah? (p. 22)

Read the words inside the sukkah aloud as a class. Have your students complete the exercise by writing the six words on their correct lines.

> ♪ **Bring It to Life** If you are teaching this lesson around Sukkot, you may wish to bring in (or invite your synagogue's rabbi to bring in) a *lulav* and an *etrog*. Consider having students review the blessings for the *lulav*, and giving each student an opportunity to shake it.

Solve the Puzzle (p. 23)

Have students complete the puzzle by choosing the correct word from the list, then copying the words from the puzzle to complete each sentence. Review answers by asking students to read each sentence aloud and then provide the puzzle's solution (מִשְׁפָּחָה בַּסוּכָּה).

Game Box Play "מַה הַמִּילָה—What's the Word?," as described on page 17.

Explain to your students that this version will be called "מַה בַּסוּכָּה—What's in the Sukkah?"

Have a student choose from their textbook a member of the family or an object (or a tiny creature, of course) that may be found inside the sukkah. You may choose to have students draw from all three chapters, or limit words to those taught in this chapter.

The rest of the class should then ask questions that will help them guess מַה בַּסוּכָּה, such as:
- Is it a person or an object?
- Is it masculine or feminine?
- Is it bigger than a קוּפְסָה?
- Is it edible?

Allow each student, in turn, to ask one question. Have the rest of the class raise their hands if they would like to guess the word. If a student gives the correct answer, he or she provides the next clue. Each student may guess only once. The winner is the student with the most points after ten rounds.

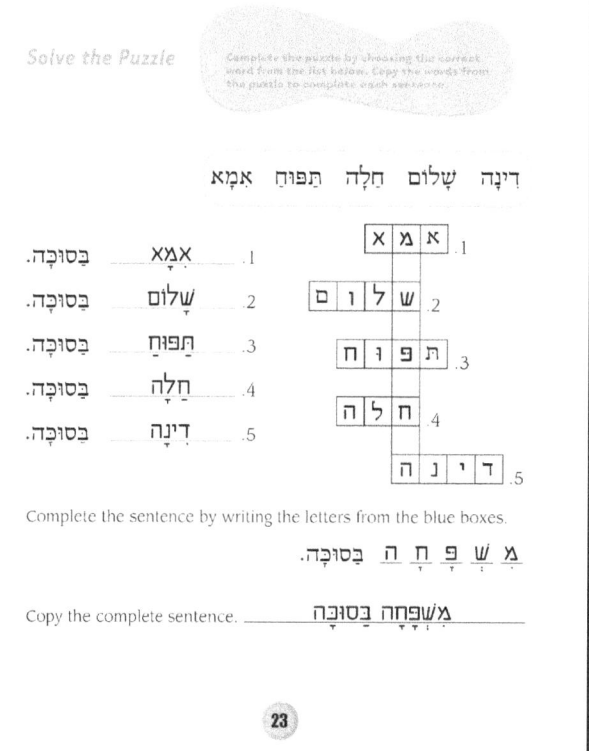

Mastering the Milon (p. 24)

• **תּוֹרָה** • Display Picture Card 17. Say: .הִנֵּה הַתּוֹרָה
Ask: ?מִי בַּתּוֹרָה (Adam and Eve, Abraham and Sarah, etc.)
Most students will be familiar with the word תּוֹרָה.

Our Tradition Ask: What do you think the word "תּוֹרָה" literally means? Explain to your students that not surprisingly, "תּוֹרָה" means "law" or "teach." Show your students how similar "תּוֹרָה" is to "מוֹרָה/מוֹרֶה"!

• **מַתָּנָה** • Place something that might be considered a gift (a toy, a book) into a box. Ask: ?מַתָּנָה בַּקּוּפְסָה
Look inside the box, take out the "gift."
Say: !כֵּן, מַתָּנָה בַּקּוּפְסָה. הִנֵּה מַתָּנָה טוֹבָה
Substitute various objects for the "gift." Continue this way until students understand that מַתָּנָה means "gift."

Chapter Story: תּוֹרָה–מַתָּנָה טוֹבָה (p. 24)

Read Aloud! Have four students each read a pair of lines aloud. You may wish to explain that שִׂמְחָה means "happiness" or "joy," and that שִׂמְחַת תּוֹרָה means "Joy of the Torah."

Bring It to Life Divide the class into three groups. Have each group create a melody based on this poem. Have each group sing its melody to the class.

Using the Photograph Direct your students' attention to the photo on page 24. Have a student read the caption aloud. Ask: What does the caption mean? (*Here is the Torah.*)

Ask your students if they have ever held or seen the Torah scroll before. See if you can arrange with the rabbi or school principal to receive an "up-close" tour of the Torah!

Mastering the Milon (p. 25)

Here's another list of words that may be fun for students to "teach" one another using Word Cards and pantomime.

Set a coat, hat, and umbrella (or Picture Cards 14–16) on a table at the front of the class.

- **מְעִיל** • Say: קַר בַּסוּכָּה, while showing that you are cold. Say: הִנֵּה מְעִיל!
Then, put on the coat.

- **כּוֹבַע** • Still wearing your coat, say:
קַר בַּסוּכָּה. הִנֵּה כּוֹבַע!
Then, put on the hat.

- **מִטְרִיָּה** • Say: גֶּשֶׁם בַּסוּכָּה.
Ah, הִנֵּה מִטְרִיָּה.
Then, lift the umbrella.

- **הוֹלֵךְ/הוֹלֶכֶת** • Walk around the circumference of your classroom. Say: אֲנִי הוֹלֵךְ/הוֹלֶכֶת
Ask: What do you think הוֹלֵךְ/הוֹלֶכֶת means? Keep walking until students understand that הוֹלֵךְ/הוֹלֶכֶת means "walks." Explain that the word may also mean "goes."

 **Put It Together** Place the coat, hat, and umbrella in different places around the classroom. Instruct individual students to act out the sentence you say. For example, say:

- דָּוִד הוֹלֵךְ לַכּוֹבַע.
- שָׂרָה הוֹלֶכֶת לַמִּטְרִיָּה.
- מִרְיָם הוֹלֶכֶת לַמְּעִיל וְגַם לַכּוֹבַע.

Chapter Story: גֶּשֶׁם (p. 25)

 **Ready for Reading** Have a student read the story's Hebrew title and English question aloud. Ask students to name three items that may come in handy on a cold, rainy day. (כּוֹבַע, מִטְרִיָּה, מְעִיל)

 **Read Aloud!** Explain to your students that the reading of גֶּשֶׁם will be a pretend audition for a Broadway play. Characters should read the passage dramatically, as if they were on stage—as emphatically or fearfully as the "script" dictates.

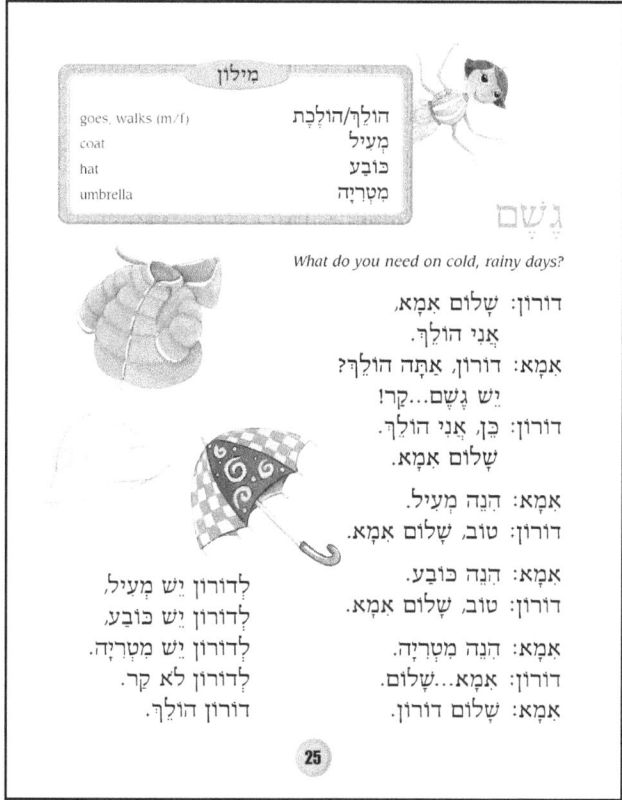

Ask for three volunteers (not everyone loves to ham it up!) to read the parts of דּוֹרוֹן, אִמָּא, and the narrator (who will read the final five lines of the story, in the left-hand column). You may choose to have each set of actors read the entire story, or only a few lines each.

 **The Extra Mile** Ask students the following questions:
In English:

- What would דּוֹרוֹן like to do? (הוֹלֵךְ)
- Which weather conditions cause אִמָּא to think that's a bad idea? (קַר, גֶּשֶׁם)
- What three items does אִמָּא insist דּוֹרוֹן take with him? (מִטְרִיָּה, כּוֹבַע, מְעִיל)

In Hebrew (explain that these questions take place once דּוֹרוֹן is bundled up):

- יֵשׁ לְדוֹרוֹן מְעִיל? (כֵּן, יֵשׁ לְדוֹרוֹן מְעִיל.)
- יֵשׁ לְדוֹרוֹן כּוֹבַע? (כֵּן, יֵשׁ לְדוֹרוֹן כּוֹבַע.)
- קַר לְדוֹרוֹן? (לֹא, לֹא קַר לְדוֹרוֹן.)

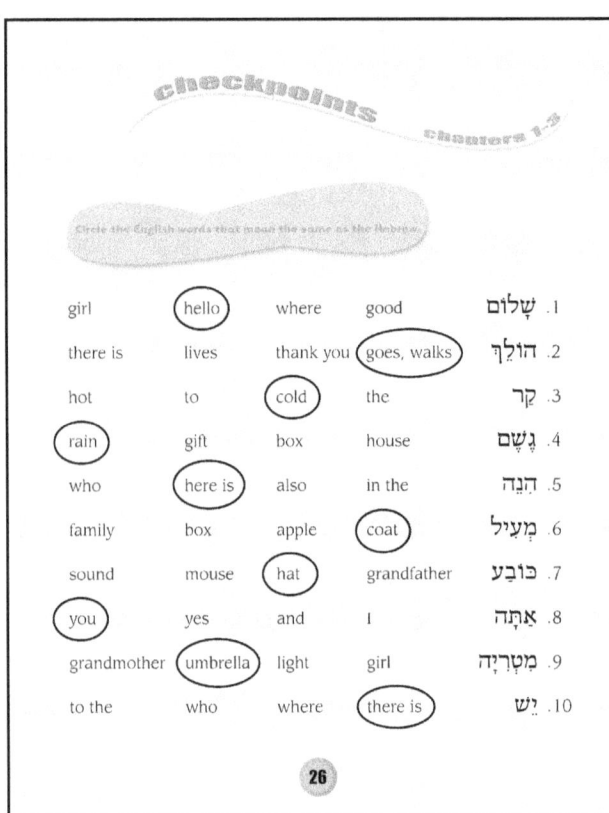

 **Looking Ahead** Tell your students that in the next chapter, they'll learn all sorts of new words: words for their pesky brothers and sisters, words for big and small, as well as the word for a very important object—cake!

Explain that they will soon learn the word for "maybe." Along with "yes" and "no," they will soon be able to answer questions in various ways. In preparation for the next lesson, ask your students to think of three questions in Hebrew that may take one of these three answers.

Checkpoint Completion (pp. 26–27)

Checkpoint 1

Have students complete Checkpoint 1 on page 26 by circling the English words that mean the same as the Hebrew.

Checkpoint 2

Have students complete Checkpoint 2 on page 27 by writing the English for the Hebrew words inside the raindrops.

Review answers by having students provide the English for each of the ten Hebrew words in Checkpoint 1, and each of the ten Hebrew words in Checkpoint 2. Instruct students to place a checkmark next to the answers that are correct, and an X next to the answers that are incorrect. Have them place a grade at the top of each page (for example, 7/10 or 9/10).

Review grades by checking each student's book.

Checkpoint Assessment

If possible, spend a few minutes with each student to review his or her work. Be sure to praise students for correct answers, and encourage them to find answers for incorrect ones.

For students who scored:
- 8–10 on either Checkpoint: praise them on a job well done (מְצוּיָן means "excellent").
- 6–7: See if there was a particular *milon* or chapter that the students found particularly troublesome. Encourage them to correct the words they missed by reviewing the *milonim* in which the words appeared.
- 5 or less: Review each incorrect answer with the students. If possible, have a teacher's aide work privately with them before moving on to the next lesson.

Keep your eyes out for words that your students consistently miss. You may wish to spend some time reviewing those words as a class.

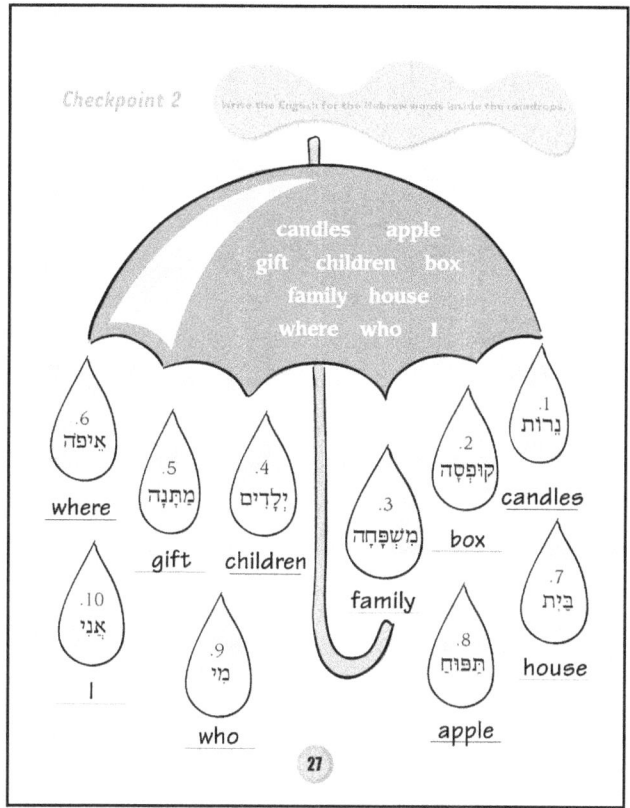

Dear Parent,

During the past few weeks, our class has learned words and phrases having to do with Rosh Hashanah, such as *d'vash* (honey) and *kol shofar* (sound of the shofar); and with Sukkot, such as *lulav, etrog,* and *ḥag sameaḥ* (happy holiday). We have also been working to build our core modern Hebrew vocabulary.

Here are some words your child has learned during the past few weeks, including ideas to incorporate these words into your daily conversations:

family	*mishpaḥah*	מִשְׁפָּחָה

Try calling the "mishpaḥah" to dinner!

no	*lo*	לֹא

Along with *kein* (yes), you can now answer everyday questions the Hebrew way!

grandfather	*saba*	סַבָּא
grandmother	*savta*	סַבְתָּא

Get into a new routine by calling Grandpa "Saba" or Grandma "Savta"!

coat	*m'il*	מְעִיל
hat	*kova*	כּוֹבַע
umbrella	*mitriyah*	מִטְרִיָּה

These words can come in handy, especially when it's miserable outside.

Thank you for helping us learn modern Hebrew!

B'Shalom,

Lesson Objectives

Students will:
- Understand how masculine and feminine forms of adjectives, including קָטָן/קְטַנָה, גָדוֹל/גְדוֹלָה, and שָׂמֵחַ/שְׂמֵחָה, work in Hebrew sentences.
- Significantly increase the potential for expression and conversation with רוֹצֶה/רוֹצָה and יֵשׁ לִי.

New Milon Words and Phrases

Core Vocabulary

I have	יֵשׁ לִי
brother	אָח
sister	אָחוֹת
big (m/f)	גָדוֹל/גְדוֹלָה
small (m/f)	קָטָן/קְטַנָה
what	מָה
everyone	כּוּלָם
next to	עַל־יַד
table	שׁוּלְחָן
wants (m/f)	רוֹצֶה/רוֹצָה
bread	לֶחֶם
maybe	אוּלַי
happy (m/f)	שָׂמֵחַ/שְׂמֵחָה
cries (m/f)	בּוֹכֶה/בּוֹכָה
or	אוֹ

Other Useful Vocabulary

cake	עוּגָה
ant	נְמָלָה
very small (f)	קְטַנְטַנָה

What We'll Need

❏ Text pages 28–35
❏ Word Cards 39–56
❏ Picture Cards 3, 4, 7, 10, 14–16, 18–20
❏ Helpful props: a small cake (cupcake), a large cake, and index cards

Where We Are

In Chapter 4, we meet a new gang: David, his big brother Dani, and their little sister, Lili "Lo, Lo." We listen in as David struggles to decide whether he's big or small as compared to his brother and sister.

We also meet another tiny creature, the petite *Malmalah han'malah*—Malmalah the Ant, and learn of her desire to share the family's food.

Let's Review

Display Picture Cards 14–16 on the chalkboard ledge. Draw a large sukkah on the chalkboard above the ledge. Tell students that this area is the *"sukkah."*

Provide a series of sentences for students to act out, such as:

- _____ הוֹלֵךְ/הוֹלֶכֶת לַכּוֹבַע בַּסוּכָּה.
  (*Student should walk to* כּוֹבַע *card.*)
- אֵיפֹה הַמִטְרִיָה וְהַמְעִיל? :Ask
  (*Student should point to cards specified and say:* הִנֵה...)
- _____ הוֹלֵךְ/הוֹלֶכֶת לְסַבְתָּא.
  Then: אַתָה/אַתְ בַּסוּכָּה? (כֵּן, אֲנִי בַּסוּכָּה.)
  קַר בַּסוּכָּה? (כֵּן, קַר בַּסוּכָּה, OR
  לֹא, לֹא קַר בַּסוּכָּה.)
- _____ הוֹלֵךְ/הוֹלֶכֶת לַמִטְרִיָה וְגַם לַמְעִיל בַּסוּכָּה.
  Then: אַתָה/אַתְ בַּסוּכָּה? (כֵּן, אֲנִי בַּסוּכָּה.)
  גֶשֶׁם בַּסוּכָּה? (כֵּן, גֶשֶׁם בַּסוּכָּה. OR
  לֹא, גֶשֶׁם לֹא בַּסוּכָּה.)
  סַבָּא וְסַבְתָּא בַּסוּכָּה?
  (כֵּן, סַבָּא וְגַם סַבְתָּא בַּסוּכָּה.)
  אֵיפֹה סַבָּא וְסַבְתָּא? (הִנֵה סַבָּא וְסַבְתָּא.)

You may wish to have students provide "הוֹלֵךְ/הוֹלֶכֶת" sentences for one another as well. Keep the Picture Cards on the board as you introduce the next lesson.

Introducing the Lesson

Pick up the כּוֹבַע Picture Card.
Say: יֵשׁ לִי הַכּוֹבַע.
Pick up the מִטְרִיָה card as well.
Say: יֵשׁ לִי הַכּוֹבַע וְגַם הַמִטְרִיָה.
Pick up the מְעִיל card, say:
יֵשׁ לִי הַכּוֹבַע וְגַם הַמִטְרִיָה וְגַם הַמְעִיל.
Continue this way until students understand that יֵשׁ לִי means "I have."

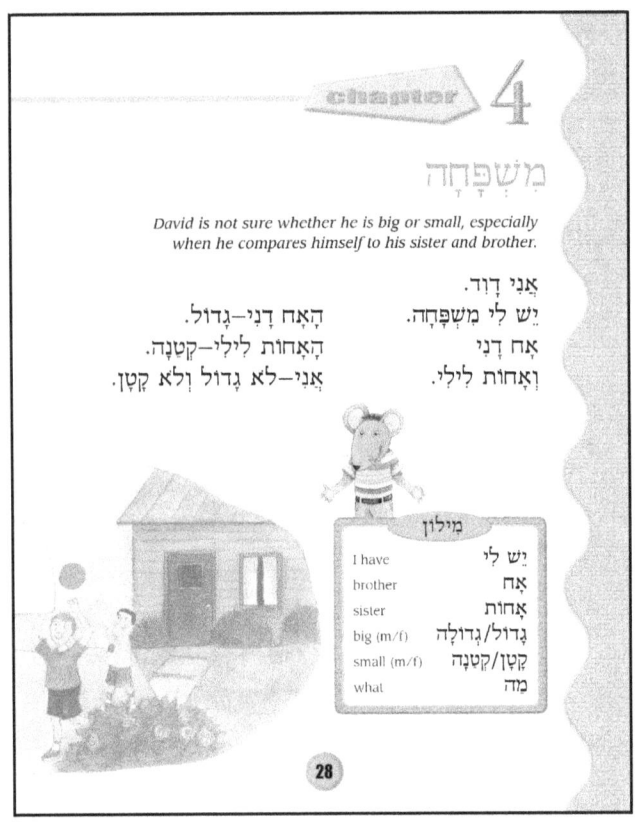

Have students come to the front of the room to pick up three objects, then announce what they have. For example, say:

הוֹלֵךְ/הוֹלֶכֶת לְסָבָא וְגַם לְסַבְתָּא, וְגַם ____ לַמְעִיל.

Student would then say:

יֵשׁ לִי סָבָא, יֵשׁ לִי סַבְתָּא, יֵשׁ לִי מְעִיל.

Pick up the small cake. In a quiet voice, say:

יֵשׁ לִי עוּגָה קְטַנָה.

Pick up the large cake. In a loud voice, say:

יֵשׁ לִי עוּגָה גְדוֹלָה.

Tell your students that in this chapter, they will learn adjectives—words that will help them describe objects.

Mastering the Milon (p. 28)

• יֵשׁ לִי • Have students name two family members using יֵשׁ לִי (יֵשׁ לִי אִמָא; יֵשׁ לִי סַבְתָּא, etc.)

>  **Captain Grammar** You may wish to explain to your students that יֵשׁ לִי, like אֲנִי, remains the same for boys and girls.

• אָח and אָחוֹת • Display Picture Cards 3 and 4.
Lift the יֶלֶד card and say: יֵשׁ לִי אָח.
Lift the יַלְדָה card, say: יֵשׁ לִי אָחוֹת.
Say: הַיֶלֶד אָח, וְהַיַלְדָה אָחוֹת.
Ask: What do you think אָח and אָחוֹת mean?

• גָדוֹל/גְדוֹלָה • On the chalkboard, have a student draw a small boy and a giant boy, a small girl and a giant girl. (Allow the student to be creative, even a little silly.) Point to the giant boy and say, in a deep, loud voice: יֶלֶד גָדוֹל!
Point to the giant girl and in the same voice say:

יַלְדָה גְדוֹלָה!

• קָטָן/קְטַנָה • Point to the small boy and say, in a squeaky, quiet voice: יֶלֶד קָטָן.
Point to the small girl, say: יַלְדָה קְטַנָה.
Continue this way, using small and giant עַכְבָּר, small and giant אִמָא, etc., until students understand the meaning (and gender differences) of both sets of words.

• מַה • Say to a student: שָׁלוֹם, ____.
When the student replies: שָׁלוֹם, מוֹרָה/מוֹרֶה,
place your hand to your ear, as if you did not hear, and ask:

מַה?

When student repeats answer, reply: מַה?
Continue this way until students understand that מַה means "what."

Chapter Story: מִשְׁפָּחָה (pp. 28–29)

 **Ready for Reading** Have a student read the Hebrew title and the English sentence aloud. Ask students to list all the members of הַמִשְׁפָּחָה that they know. (סַבְתָּא, סָבָא, אַבָּא, אִמָא, אָחוֹת גְדוֹלָה, אָח קָטָן, etc.)

>  **Captain Grammar** Unlike English, Hebrew does not use capital letters to designate people's names or other proper nouns. You may wish to explain this to your students so that "דָנִי," "לִילִי," and "דָוִד" don't look like strange words!

 **Read Aloud!** Have a boy read all seven lines on page 28. Ask:

• יֵשׁ לְדָוִד אָח? (כֵּן, יֵשׁ לְדָוִד אָח.)
• אָח קָטָן? (לֹא, אָח גָדוֹל.)
• יֵשׁ לְדָוִד אָחוֹת? (כֵּן, יֵשׁ לְדָוִד אָחוֹת.)
• אָחוֹת קְטַנָה? (כֵּן, אָחוֹת קְטַנָה.)
• דָוִד גָדוֹל? (לֹא, דָוִד לֹא גָדוֹל וְלֹא קָטָן.)

Now have a girl read all seven lines, changing David's name to

Shalom Ivrit 1 • Teacher's Edition

Sarah and the gender of all now-incorrect words. (The only words that should change are in the seventh line, which should read: אֲנִי–לֹא גְדוֹלָה וְלֹא קְטַנָּה.)

 **The Extra Mile** Now have students of either gender read all seven lines, while changing the gender of the siblings: Have דָּנִי become "דָּנִיאֵל," and לִילִי become "לִיאוֹ." Have the student change any now-incorrect words:
Third line: אָחוֹת דָּנִיאֵל.
Fourth line: וְאָח לִיאוֹ.
Fifth line: הָאָחוֹת דָּנִיאֵל–גְדוֹלָה.
Sixth line: הָאָח לִיאוֹ–קָטָן.
All other lines remain the same.

For the remainder of the story on page 29, assign 3 students to read the parts of דָּוִד, דָּנִי, and לִילִי. It might be fun to have the students dramatize the lines while standing before the class (in which case you'll also need to assign the part of אִמָּא, who has no lines).
Ask דָּנִי: דָּוִד גָדוֹל? (לֹא, דָּוִד קָטָן.)
Ask לִילִי: דָּוִד קָטָן? (לֹא, דָּוִד גָדוֹל.)

Big or Small? (p. 29)

Have students complete the exercise by drawing a line from the picture to the correct Hebrew phrase. Review the exercise aloud as a class. Have students explain why the alternate phrase is incorrect.

Challenge your students to draw lines from the incorrect phrase to its correct picture (all incorrect phrases have correct pictures available!).

 **Game Box**
Sibling Rivalry

Using 5" x 7" index cards, have students create the following Word Cards: אָח (two cards), אָחוֹת (two cards), גָדוֹל, קָטָן, גְדוֹלָה, and קְטַנָּה. Shuffle the cards and place them face down on a table. Divide the class into groups of four (ideally two girls and two boys each).

Instruct the class: each member of the group must take one of the following four parts—big brother, big sister, little brother, and little sister. ▶

▼
The object of the game is for all members of each group to, as quickly as they can:

1. Select the two cards that describe them (Big sister must find אָחוֹת and גְדוֹלָה, etc.).
2. Display their cards, in the correct order, to the class (אָחוֹת in the left hand, גְדוֹלָה in the right).
3. Introduce themselves, one at a time (by saying: אֲנִי אָחוֹת גְדוֹלָה, etc.).

Using a stopwatch or watch with a second hand, time each group. Explain that a 2-second penalty will be added to the team's score each time:
• a student holds an incorrect card
• a student holds the cards in the incorrect order
• a student introduces him or herself using incorrect words or pronunciation

The team that completes the challenge in the fewest total seconds is the winner.

 **Using the Photograph** Have students read the two photo captions on page 30 aloud. Ask individual students to answer each question by displaying his or her book to the class, then pointing and saying: אָחוֹת קָטָן, etc.

63 Chapter 4

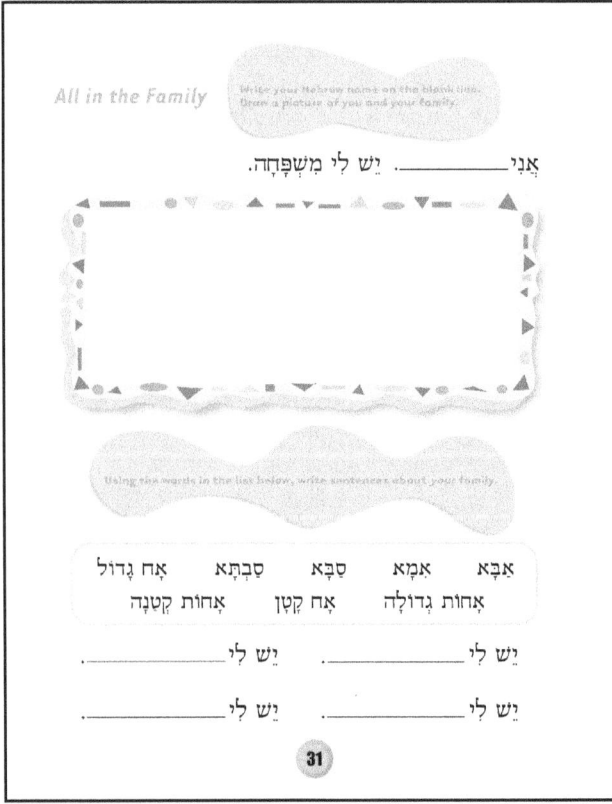

All in the Family (p. 31)

Have students write their Hebrew names in the space provided, then draw a picture of their families.

Ask students to present their drawings to the class, explaining what each member is by saying:

הִנֵּה אַבָּא וְהִנֵּה סַבָּא וְהִנֵּה אָח קָטָן...

(Have students "introduce" each sibling with both the noun and adjective.)

Have students choose up to four people from their family and list them in the spaces provided at the bottom of page 31. (Be sensitive to students who may not have four family members—explain that it's okay not to fill in all four.)

>  **Game Box** Play "מָצָאתִי!—I Found It!" as described on page 16. You may wish to have the "search area" be pages 28–31, or only page 31.
>
> Sample "מָצָאתִי" challenges:
> - Find the phrase that means "little sister."
>
>   (אָחוֹת קְטַנָּה)
>
> - Find the two words that mean "little."
>
>   (קְטַנָּה, קָטָן)
>
> - Find three words for people who are male.
>
>   (סַבָּא, אַבָּא, אָח)
>
> You may wish to ask a "bonus question," worth an extra point, after each correct response. For example:
>
> אַתָּה אָח גָּדוֹל? (כֵּן, אֲנִי אָח גָּדוֹל. OR
> לֹא, אֲנִי לֹא אָח גָּדוֹל.)

Mastering the Milon (p. 32)

- **כּוּלָם** • List the names of everyone in your class. Then say: לֹא כּוּלָם. List only a few members of the class, say: כּוּלָם! Continue this way until students understand that כּוּלָם means "everyone."

- **לֶחֶם** • Say:
  הַמּוֹצִיא לֶחֶם מִן הָאָרֶץ.
  Stress the word לֶחֶם. Ask: What do we say this blessing over? (*Many students will know that we say* hamotzi *over bread.*)

- **עוּגָה** • Display the small cake and the large cake. Point to the small cake and say—sadly—
  עוּגָה קְטַנָּה.
  Point to the large cake and say—excitedly—
  עוּגָה גְּדוֹלָה!
  Students will likely understand that עוּגָה means "cake."

- **רוֹצֶה/רוֹצָה** • Rub your hands together and say:
  אֲנִי רוֹצֶה/רוֹצָה עוּגָה!
  Ask individual students (be sure to use both forms):
  אַתָּה/אַתְּ רוֹצֶה/רוֹצָה עוּגָה?
  Continue this way until students understand that רוֹצֶה and רוֹצָה mean "want." (They eventually will!)

 **Bring It to Life** Depending on your synagogue's dietary rules, you may wish to enjoy the cake together. Be sure to recite the following blessing first, recited over baked goods:
בָּרוּךְ אַתָּה יְיָ, אֱלֹהֵינוּ מֶלֶךְ הָעוֹלָם,
בּוֹרֵא מִינֵי מְזוֹנוֹת.

Before serving each student, ask:
אַתָּה/אַתְּ רוֹצֶה/רוֹצָה עוּגָה?
Wait for a correct answer.
(כֵּן, אֲנִי רוֹצֶה/רוֹצָה עוּגָה.)

- **אוּלַי** • Rub your chin as if you are in deep thought and say:
  אוּלַי אֲנִי רוֹצֶה/רוֹצָה עוּגָה?
  אוּלַי דָּוִד אָח גָּדוֹל; אוּלַי לֶחֶם בַּבַּיִת...
  (stress אוּלַי as you would "maybe").

Why does the family call the little sister "Lili Lo, Lo"?

 **Put It Together** Remind students of the assignment from the end of the previous chapter. Have each student prepare to ask three "yes, no, maybe" questions. Suggestions for questions include:

- אַתָּה אָח גָּדוֹל? (כֵּן, אֲנִי אָח גָּדוֹל.)
- אַתָּה רוֹצֶה עוּגָה? (אוּלַי אֲנִי רוֹצֶה עוּגָה.)
- אַתָּה גָּר בַּסּוּכָּה? (לֹא, אֲנִי לֹא גָּר בַּסּוּכָּה.)

Divide the class into pairs. Have each student "interview" his or her partner by asking the prepared questions. Have students answer one another using complete sentences.

Now have each student "report" on their "interview" to the class. For example, a student might "report":

- שָׂרָה אָחוֹת גְּדוֹלָה.
- אוּלַי דָּנִיאֵל רוֹצֶה עוּגָה.
- דָּנִיאֵל לֹא גָּר בַּסּוּכָּה.

כּוּלָם אוֹכְלִים עוּגָה.
כּוּלָם שְׂמֵחִים.
לִילִי לֹא שְׂמֵחָה, לִילִי בּוֹכָה.

לִילִי: אֲנִי רוֹצָה עוּגָה. אֲנִי רוֹצָה עוּגָה.
דָּנִי: לִילִי לֹא, לֹא. לִילִי לֹא רוֹצָה...

לִילִי: אֲנִי רוֹצָה, אֲנִי רוֹצָה, כֵּן, כֵּן, כֵּן!

דָּוִד: לִילִי לֹא, לֹא אוֹ לִילִי כֵּן, כֵּן?

33

The Extra Mile Have students read the story again. Ask the class these questions after each group of lines:

Page 32:
Group 1: אֵיפֹה כּוּלָם? (כּוּלָם עַל-יַד הַשׁוּלְחָן.)
Group 2: לִילִי רוֹצָה לֶחֶם? (לֹא, לִילִי לֹא רוֹצָה לֶחֶם.)
Group 3: לִילִי רוֹצָה חַלָּה? (לֹא, לִילִי לֹא רוֹצָה חַלָּה.)
Group 4: לִילִי רוֹצָה תַּפּוּחַ? (לֹא, לִילִי לֹא רוֹצָה תַּפּוּחַ.)
Group 5: מָה לִילִי רוֹצָה? (אוּלַי לִילִי רוֹצָה עוּגָה. OR לִילִי רוֹצָה עוּגָה.)

Page 33:
Group 1: מָה כּוּלָם אוֹכְלִים? (כּוּלָם אוֹכְלִים עוּגָה.) לִילִי שְׂמֵחָה? (לֹא, לִילִי בּוֹכָה.)
Group 2: מָה לִילִי רוֹצָה? (לִילִי רוֹצָה עוּגָה.)

• שׁוּלְחָן • Knock on a table (not a desk) and say:
הִנֵּה שׁוּלְחָן.
Ask: הַשׁוּלְחָן גָּדוֹל? (כֵּן, הַשׁוּלְחָן גָּדוֹל.) OR (לֹא, הַשׁוּלְחָן לֹא גָּדוֹל.)

• עַל-יַד • Stand next to the table and say:
אֲנִי עַל-יַד הַשׁוּלְחָן.
Stand next to a student and say: אֲנִי עַל-יַד דָּנִיאֵל.
Continue this way until students understand that עַל-יַד means "near" or "next to." Explain that both meanings are appropriate.

Mastering the Milon (p. 33)

• שָׂמֵחַ/שְׂמֵחָה • Ask students: What is the holiday whose name means "joy of the Torah" or "happiness of the Torah"? (שִׂמְחַת תּוֹרָה) Point to the picture of David on page 32. Ask: דָּוִד שָׂמֵחַ? (כֵּן, דָּוִד שָׂמֵחַ.)
Point to the picture of Lili on page 33, ask:
לִילִי שְׂמֵחָה? (לֹא, לִילִי לֹא שְׂמֵחָה.)

• בּוֹכֶה/בּוֹכָה • Point to the picture of Lili on page 33. Ask:
מִי בּוֹכָה? אִמָּא בּוֹכָה? אַבָּא בּוֹכֶה? בַּר בּוֹכֶה? (לֹא, לִילִי בּוֹכָה.)

Make sure students understand that בּוֹכֶה and בּוֹכָה mean "cries," and not simply "sad" or "upset." Pretend to cry yourself, and say: אֲנִי בּוֹכֶה/בּוֹכָה.

Chapter Story: לִילִי לֹא, לֹא
(pp. 32–33)

 **Ready for Reading** Have a student read the Hebrew title and English question aloud. Ask your students: Do you have a nickname in your family? Have students answer:
אֲנִי [nickname] בַּבַּיִת.

 **Read Aloud!** This story is chock-full of brand-new vocabulary, so take care to read the entire story slowly, and with emphasis. You may wish to point to props or Picture Cards, including those for bread, ḥallah, an apple, cake, etc., as you read. Or appoint a student to display Picture Cards as you read those words.

Assign five students to read the parts of: the narrator, אִמָּא, לִילִי, דָּנִי, and דָּוִד. Explain that the story contains a familiar word in its plural form: שְׂמֵחִים. It also contains two unfamiliar words: אוֹכְלִים—"they eat," and אוֹ—"or." Have students read through the entire story.

He or She? (p. 34)

Have a student read the directions aloud. You may wish to explain that as a general rule, most Hebrew words have different endings for boys and girls.

Have students read each line and circle the word that best completes it.

> **Captain Grammar** For English-speaking students, the concept of "masculine" and "feminine" words can be confusing. As your students complete this exercise, explain that for this exercise, the word choice should "agree" with the word *before* it—the person doing the action—not the one after it. So in line 1, רוֹצָה should agree with לִילִי, not with עוּגָה.

Word Match (p. 34)

Have students complete the exercise individually by circling the correct English word. Have each student show you his or her completed work.

> **Game Box** Play "Tic-Tac-Toe on the Go," as described on page 17.
>
> For this version of the game, remove use Word Cards 39–53 and set them, Hebrew side showing, on the chalkboard ledge (or write those words on the board).
>
> Students earn "chairs" for their teams by choosing the correct word that completes the sentence you provide. For example, you might say to a student on one team:
>
> דָּוִד לֹא בּוֹכֶה; דָּוִד _____.
>
> That student must then choose the word שָׂמֵחַ from the chalkboard.
>
> If the student is correct, he or she may sit in any of the unoccupied tic-tac-toe chairs. That word is then removed from the chalkboard. If the student is incorrect, the turn moves to the opposite team, and the word remains on the board.
>
> The team that gets three in a row, in any direction, wins.

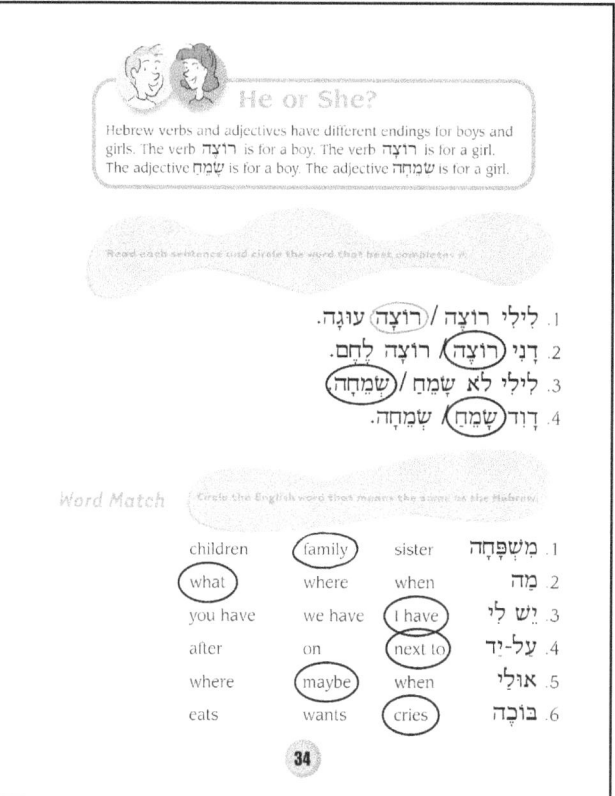

Mastering the Milon (p. 35)

• **נְמָלָה** • Point to the illustration of the ant on page 35. Say:

הִנֵּה נְמָלָה.

Ask: הַנְמָלָה גְדוֹלָה? (לֹא, הַנְמָלָה לֹא גְדוֹלָה.)

OR הַנְמָלָה קְטַנָּה.)

• **קְטַנְטַנָה** • Draw a girl, a mouse, and an ant (in proportion to one another) on the chalkboard. Point to the girl and say:

יַלְדָה גְדוֹלָה.

Point to the mouse and say: עַכְבָּר קָטָן.

Point to the ant and say: נְמָלָה קְטַנְטַנָה.

Vary the pitch of your voice to stress the differences in size.

Chapter Story: אֲנִי קְטַנְטַנָה (p. 35)

 **Ready for Reading** Have a student read the Hebrew title and English question. Ask: What are some things that מַלְמַלָה might like to eat? (לֶחֶם, עוּגָה, חַלָה)

 **Read Aloud!** Have your students alternate reading lines. It may be fun to have them read the poem in a high, squeaky voice, a voice they think מַלְמַלָה might have.

 **The Extra Mile** You may wish to ask the following as "quick questions," challenging students to keep up by raising their hands and providing the correct answer. Allow students to answer only once or only twice, in order to allow everyone a chance to answer.

• מַלְמַלָה נְמָלָה? (כֵּן, מַלְמַלָה נְמָלָה.)
• נְמָלָה גְדוֹלָה? (לֹא, נְמָלָה לֹא גְדוֹלָה.)
• נְמָלָה קְטַנְטַנָה? (כֵּן, נְמָלָה קְטַנְטַנָה.)
• יֵשׁ בַּבַּיִת לֶחֶם גָדוֹל? (לֹא, הַלֶחֶם קָטָן.)
• יֵשׁ בַּבַּיִת עוּגָה גְדוֹלָה?
   (לֹא, הָעוּגָה קְטַנָה.)
• יֵשׁ בַּבַּיִת חַלָה גְדוֹלָה?
   (כֵּן, הַחַלָה גְדוֹלָה.)
• נְמָלָה רוֹצָה חַלָה קְטַנְטַנָה?
   (לֹא, נְמָלָה לֹא רוֹצָה חַלָה קְטַנְטַנָה.)
• נְמָלָה רוֹצָה חַלָה גְדוֹלָה?
   (כֵּן, נְמָלָה רוֹצָה חַלָה גְדוֹלָה.)

 **Looking Ahead** Tell your students that in the next chapter, they will learn vocabulary that will come in handy in the classroom—such as words for quiet, write, chalkboard, notebook, and pencil.

Explain to your students that they will learn a tiny but important word that means "because." Have your students think of new sentences they may create with this helpful new word.

Chapter 5

Lesson Objectives

Students will:
- Further develop a base of vocabulary relating to their everyday lives, including עִפָּרוֹן, מַחְבֶּרֶת, and כִּסֵּא.
- Begin to comprehend and create more sophisticated sentences, with the addition of אֲבָל, כִּי, עַל, מְאֹד, and.

New Milon Words and Phrases

Core Vocabulary

comes (m/f)	בָּא/בָּאָה
quiet	שֶׁקֶט
new (m/f)	חָדָשׁ/חֲדָשָׁה
very	מְאֹד
on	עַל
because	כִּי
you have (m/f)	יֵשׁ לְךָ/יֵשׁ לָךְ
but	אֲבָל
I do not have	אֵין לִי
there is/are not	אֵין
sings (m/f)	שָׁר/שָׁרָה

Classroom-Related Vocabulary

class, classroom	כִּתָּה
teacher (m/f)	מוֹרֶה/מוֹרָה
writes (m/f)	כּוֹתֵב/כּוֹתֶבֶת
chalkboard	לוּחַ
chair	כִּסֵּא
notebook	מַחְבֶּרֶת
pencil	עִפָּרוֹן
book	סֵפֶר
closet	אָרוֹן

Other Useful Vocabulary

eyeglasses	מִשְׁקָפַיִם

What We'll Need

- ❑ Text pages 36–43
- ❑ Word Cards 57–77
- ❑ Picture Cards 3, 4, 19, 21
- ❑ Helpful props: a new and an old book, a notebook, a pencil, and a chair; markers and construction paper

Where We Are

In Chapter 5, we join David in his classroom and meet some of his classmates. Then we visit our old friend Doron as he realizes he's forgotten a thing or two on the way to school.

We then join מַלְמָלָה הַנְמָלָה as she continues her creative search for food—this time in David's classroom.

Let's Review

Have students draw four pictures on the chalkboard: a big and little brother, and a big and little sister, all of them happy (allow the students to be a bit silly!). Explain to students that they should follow the directions you provide.

- Say: _____ הוֹלֵךְ לְאָחוֹת גְּדוֹלָה.
  (Student should walk to the "big sister" drawing.)
- Ask: _____, אֵיפֹה אַתָּה?
  (אֲנִי עַל־יַד אָחוֹת גְּדוֹלָה.)
- Ask: אָחוֹת גְּדוֹלָה שְׂמֵחָה?
  (כֵּן, אָחוֹת גְּדוֹלָה שְׂמֵחָה.)
- Continue this way until students have reviewed all brother/sister–big/small combinations.

Have a student draw a picture of a cake on the chalkboard.

- Ask: מִי רוֹצֶה עוּגָה?
  (Students who want cake should raise their hands.)
- Ask a boy: _____, אוּלַי אַתָּה רוֹצֶה עוּגָה?
  (כֵּן, אֲנִי רוֹצֶה עוּגָה.)
- Ask a girl: _____, אוּלַי אַתְּ רוֹצָה עוּגָה?
  (כֵּן, אֲנִי רוֹצָה עוּגָה.)

Depending on your students' levels, you may wish to review all Word Cards from Chapters 1–4 (Word Cards 1–56) before beginning Chapter 5, as this chapter contains a fair amount of new vocabulary.

Introducing the Lesson

Have your students take a quick look at the three new *milonim* on pages 37, 38, and 43. Have them think of ways that the

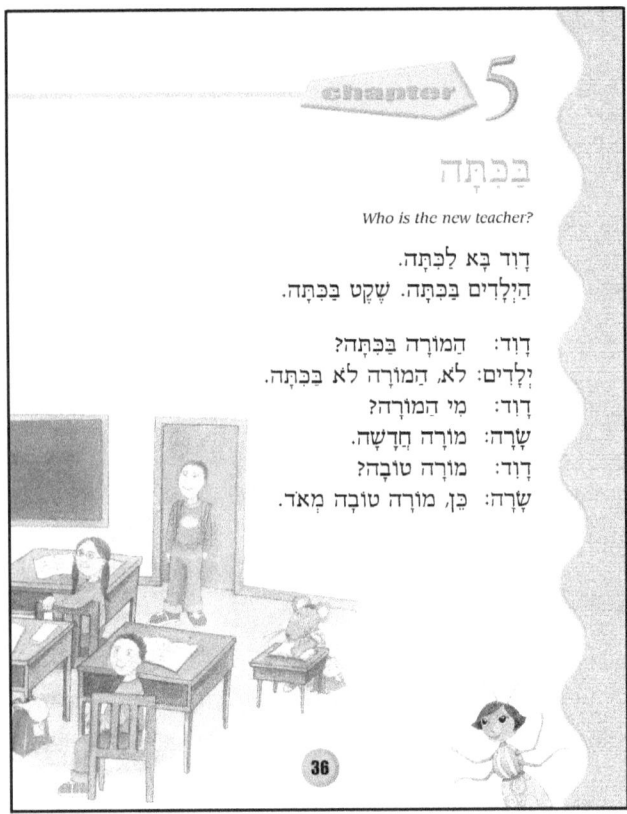

class might incorporate the new vocabulary into its everyday routine. List them on the board. Examples may include:
- Referring to a book, chair, pencil, etc., in Hebrew only.
- Referring to the class as כִּתָּה גְדוֹלָה, or another name the class agrees upon.
- When the class is noisy, using שֶׁקֶט to call the class to order.

Place Word Cards 39 and 68 (יֵשׁ לְךָ/יֵשׁ לָךְ, יֵשׁ לִי) on the chalkboard ledge. Allow students to refer to these cards during this exercise.

Call a boy and a girl to the front of the class. Give a book to the boy and a notebook to the girl. Hold a pencil in your hand.

- Hold up the pencil and say: יֵשׁ לִי עִפָּרוֹן.
- To the boy, ask: יֵשׁ לְךָ סֵפֶר? _____, (כֵּן, יֵשׁ לִי סֵפֶר.)
- To the girl: יֵשׁ לָךְ מַחְבֶּרֶת? _____, (כֵּן, יֵשׁ לִי מַחְבֶּרֶת.)
- Look at your pencil, shake your head, and say: יֵשׁ לִי עִפָּרוֹן, אֲבָל אֵין לִי סֵפֶר.
- Ask the girl: יֵשׁ לָךְ סֵפֶר? (לֹא, אֵין לִי סֵפֶר.)
- Ask the boy: יֵשׁ לְךָ סֵפֶר? (כֵּן, יֵשׁ לִי סֵפֶר.)

Mastering the Milon (p. 37)

- **כִּתָּה** • Have a student step outside the classroom. Say:
_____ לֹא בַּכִּתָּה.

Have him or her reenter the classroom. Say:
_____ בַּכִּתָּה.

Ask: _____ בַּכִּתָּה? (כֵּן, _____ בַּכִּתָּה.)

Explain that כִּתָּה not only means "classroom," but may refer to the class itself.

- **בָּא/בָּאָה** • Have a girl step outside the classroom, then reenter.
Say: _____ בָּאָה לַכִּתָּה.
Have a boy do the same. Say: _____ בָּא לַכִּתָּה.
Explain that בָּאָה and בָּא mean "comes" (and not "enter").

- **מוֹרָה/מוֹרֶה** • Point to yourself and say:
אֲנִי מוֹרֶה/מוֹרָה.
You may wish to have students call you _____ מוֹרָה.

Put It Together Enter the classroom and greet the class. Have a student "narrate" your entrance.
- Narrator: הַמּוֹרֶה/הַמּוֹרָה בָּא/בָּאָה לַכִּתָּה.
- Say: שָׁלוֹם, כִּתָּה.
- Class: שָׁלוֹם, מוֹרֶה/מוֹרָה.

Have a student of the opposite gender "play" the teacher, repeat.

- **שֶׁקֶט** • Tell the class to be perfectly quiet. Whisper:
שֶׁקֶט בַּכִּתָּה.
Ask: What do you think שֶׁקֶט means?

- **חָדָשׁ/חֲדָשָׁה** • Lift a book that is brand new, say: חָדָשׁ!
Lift a book that is old and tattered, say: לֹא חָדָשׁ.
Explain that חֲדָשָׁה is used for things that are feminine.

- **מְאֹד** • Have a student draw three girls on the chalkboard—one small, one large, one very large. Point to the small girl and say: יַלְדָּה קְטַנָּה.
The large: יַלְדָּה גְדוֹלָה.
The very large: יַלְדָּה גְדוֹלָה מְאֹד.

Stress מְאֹד as you would "very."

• **כּוֹתֵב/כּוֹתֶבֶת** • Call a boy and girl to the chalkboard. Have the boy write on the board. As he does, say:

_____ כּוֹתֵב.

Have the girl write her name, say:

_____ כּוֹתֶבֶת.

Continue this way until students understand that כּוֹתֵב/כּוֹתֶבֶת means "writes."

• **עַל** • Place Picture Cards 3, 4, and 19 on a table. Point to each and say:

הַיֶּלֶד עַל הַשּׁוּלְחָן; הַיַּלְדָּה עַל הַשּׁוּלְחָן; הָעוּגָה עַל הַשּׁוּלְחָן.

Place the עוּגָה card on a student's head. Say:

עוּגָה עַל _____.

• **לוּחַ** • Draw a picture of a boy on the chalkboard, say:

הַיֶּלֶד עַל הַלּוּחַ.

Draw a picture of a girl, say: הַיַּלְדָּה עַל הַלּוּחַ.

Draw a cake, say: הָעוּגָה עַל הַלּוּחַ.

(You may wish to make it clear that לוּחַ in this chapter refers to a chalkboard, but it may also refer to a calendar, a bulletin board, or another display board.)

Put It Together Call three students to the front of the class. Ask each to pretend to write on a table, the chalkboard, and a box. Have other students describe what the three are doing. Answers may include:

• דָּוִד כּוֹתֵב עַל הַלּוּחַ.
• שָׂרָה כּוֹתֶבֶת עַל הַשּׁוּלְחָן.
• דָּנִיאֵל כּוֹתֵב עַל הַקּוּפְסָה.

To add a bit of fun, have a new group of three students pretend to write on a boy, a girl, and an ant!

• **כִּי** • Point to the picture of Bar on page 36. Say:

בַּר קָטָן כִּי בַּר עַכְבָּר.

Point to the picture of Malmalah on the same page, say:

מַלְמָלָה קְטַנָּה כִּי מַלְמָלָה נְמָלָה.

Ask: What do you think כִּי means?

Chapter Story: בַּכִּתָּה (pp. 36–37)

Ready for Reading Read the story aloud. As you do, write כִּתָּה טוֹבָה when the teacher in the story does. Erase it when you have finished reading.

Explain that טוֹבִים, which appears at the end of the story, means "good" when talking about more than one thing.

Say: יַלְדָּה טוֹבָה; יְלָדִים טוֹבִים.

Read Aloud! Assign 4 students to read the parts of הַמּוֹרָה, שָׂרָה, דָּוִד, and the narrator. Instruct the rest of the class to read the lines for יְלָדִים together.

The Extra Mile Ask the following questions to review the story:

• אֵיפֹה הַיְלָדִים? (הַיְלָדִים בַּכִּתָּה.)
• יֵשׁ שֶׁקֶט בַּכִּתָּה? (כֵּן, יֵשׁ שֶׁקֶט בַּכִּתָּה.)
• מָה כּוֹתֶבֶת הַמּוֹרָה עַל הַלּוּחַ? (הַמּוֹרָה כּוֹתֶבֶת "כִּתָּה טוֹבָה" עַל הַלּוּחַ.)
• עַל מָה כּוֹתֶבֶת הַמּוֹרָה? (הַמּוֹרָה כּוֹתֶבֶת עַל הַלּוּחַ.)

 **Captain Grammar** You may wish to explain to your students that word order in Hebrew is different than in English. For example, in English we say, "What does the teacher write on?" In Hebrew we say, "On what writes the teacher?" Assure your students that as they continue to progress, this will sound more natural.

Mastering the Milon (p. 38)

• כִּסֵּא • Sit in a chair.

Say: אֲנִי עַל הַכִּסֵּא.

Point to individual students and say:

_____ עַל הַכִּסֵּא...

Continue this way until students understand that כִּסֵּא means "chair."

• מַחְבֶּרֶת • Pretend to write in a notebook.

Say: יֵשׁ לִי מַחְבֶּרֶת. אֲנִי כּוֹתֶבֶת בַּמַּחְבֶּרֶת.

Make sure students understand that מַחְבֶּרֶת means "notebook," and not any book.

• סֵפֶר • Hold up the textbook.

Say: יֵשׁ לִי סֵפֶר.

Point to different books around the room.

Say: הִנֵּה סֵפֶר, הִנֵּה סֵפֶר...

Place the textbook on a table.

Ask: אֵיפֹה יֵשׁ סֵפֶר? (יֵשׁ סֵפֶר עַל הַשׁוּלְחָן.)

Have students each locate a book and say: הִנֵּה סֵפֶר.

• יֵשׁ לְךָ/יֵשׁ לָךְ • Pick up a book. Say: יֵשׁ לִי סֵפֶר.

Hand the book to a boy. Say: יֵשׁ לְךָ סֵפֶר.

Ask: יֵשׁ לְךָ סֵפֶר? (כֵּן, יֵשׁ לִי סֵפֶר.)

Hand the book to a girl. Say: יֵשׁ לָךְ סֵפֶר.

Ask: יֵשׁ לָךְ סֵפֶר? (כֵּן, יֵשׁ לִי סֵפֶר.)

• עִפָּרוֹן • Pick up a pencil. Say: יֵשׁ לִי עִפָּרוֹן.

Ask a boy with a pencil:

יֵשׁ לְךָ עִפָּרוֹן? (כֵּן, יֵשׁ לִי עִפָּרוֹן.)

Ask a girl: יֵשׁ לָךְ עִפָּרוֹן? (כֵּן, יֵשׁ לִי עִפָּרוֹן.)

 **Put It Together** Place three chairs around a table. Call students to the table by pointing to each chair and say:

אֲנִי רוֹצֶה/רוֹצָה _____ עַל הַכִּסֵּא...

Distribute a notebook, a book, and a pencil to the three students.

• Ask each student:

מַה יֵּשׁ לְךָ/לָךְ? (יֵשׁ לִי מַחְבֶּרֶת; יֵשׁ לִי סֵפֶר; יֵשׁ לִי עִפָּרוֹן.)

• Ask the student with the notebook:

יֵשׁ לְךָ/לָךְ מַחְבֶּרֶת? (כֵּן, יֵשׁ לִי מַחְבֶּרֶת.)

• Ask the student with the pencil:

יֵשׁ לְךָ/לָךְ עִפָּרוֹן? (כֵּן, יֵשׁ לִי עִפָּרוֹן.)

• Ask the student with the book:

יֵשׁ לְךָ/לָךְ עִפָּרוֹן? (לֹא, יֵשׁ לִי סֵפֶר.)

To other students:

• יֵשׁ לְ_____ עִפָּרוֹן? (כֵּן, יֵשׁ לְ_____ עִפָּרוֹן.)

• יֵשׁ לְ_____ סֵפֶר? (לֹא, יֵשׁ לְ_____ עִפָּרוֹן.)

• מַה יֵּשׁ עַל הַשּׁוּלְחָן? (יֵשׁ סֵפֶר וְעִפָּרוֹן עַל הַשּׁוּלְחָן.)

Shalom Ivrit 1 • Teacher's Edition

Take as much time with this exercise as you feel the class requires. There are not only many new vocabulary words, but the increased use of יֵשׁ and לְ_____ may take some practice for students to become accustomed to.

• **מִשְׁקָפַיִם** • If you wear glasses, point to them and say:

יֵשׁ לִי מִשְׁקָפַיִם.

Individually, to a student with glasses:

יֵשׁ לְ_____ מִשְׁקָפַיִם; יֵשׁ לְ_____ מִשְׁקָפַיִם.

Continue this way until students understand that מִשְׁקָפַיִם are "glasses."

• **אֵין לִי** • Hold a notebook. Say: יֵשׁ לִי מַחְבֶּרֶת.

Give the notebook to a student, show your empty hands and say:

אֵין לִי מַחְבֶּרֶת; יֵשׁ לְךָ/לָךְ מַחְבֶּרֶת.

Take the notebook back, repeat. Continue this way until students understand that אֵין לִי means "I do not have."

• **אֲבָל** • Hold up a notebook. Say:

יֵשׁ לִי מַחְבֶּרֶת, אֲבָל אֵין לִי עִפָּרוֹן;
יֵשׁ לִי מַחְבֶּרֶת, אֲבָל אֵין לִי סֵפֶר.

Stress אֲבָל as you would "but."

Put It Together Hold a notebook in your hand. Say:

יֵשׁ לִי מַחְבֶּרֶת, אֲבָל אֵין לִי עִפָּרוֹן.

Call up two students, one with a notebook and no pencil, one with a pencil and no notebook. Have each explain why he or she can't write:

1. יֵשׁ לִי מַחְבֶּרֶת, אֲבָל אֵין לִי עִפָּרוֹן.
2. יֵשׁ לִי עִפָּרוֹן, אֲבָל אֵין לִי מַחְבֶּרֶת.

Have different pairs of students "perform" the same scenario. You may wish to use מִשְׁקָפַיִם and סֵפֶר as well.

• **אָרוֹן** • Place a book and notebook in a closet.
Open the closet and ask: מַה בָּאָרוֹן?
Take out the book, say: סֵפֶר בָּאָרוֹן!
The notebook: מַחְבֶּרֶת בָּאָרוֹן!

Our Tradition Two words in this סֵפֶר—מִילוֹן and אָרוֹן—may be found in your synagogue's sanctuary. You may wish to show your class the אָרוֹן קֹדֶשׁ—The Holy Ark, and the סֵפֶר תּוֹרָה—the Scroll (or Books) of the Torah.

Chapter Story: דּוֹרוֹן בַּכִּתָּה (p. 38)

Ready for Reading Have students list all the things they need בַּכִּתָּה. (סֵפֶר, מַחְבֶּרֶת, כִּסֵּא, עִפָּרוֹן)

Read Aloud! Assign two students to read the parts of דּוֹרוֹן and מוֹרָה. Have the other students in the class hold up each item as דּוֹרוֹן and מוֹרָה mention them (except for the chair, of course; you may wish to have the class rise when it's mentioned!).

The Extra Mile Have the class stand in a circle. Hand a notebook and a pencil to a student. Have the student write his or her name. The student should say:

יֵשׁ לִי מַחְבֶּרֶת וְעִפָּרוֹן.

Instruct the next student in the circle to say:

אֵין לִי מַחְבֶּרֶת וְעִפָּרוֹן; יֵשׁ לְךָ/לָךְ מַחְבֶּרֶת וְעִפָּרוֹן?

The first student should reply,

כֵּן, יֵשׁ לִי מַחְבֶּרֶת וְעִפָּרוֹן.

and pass the notebook and pencil. The second student then signs his or her name.

Continue this way, until everyone around the circle has signed the notebook.

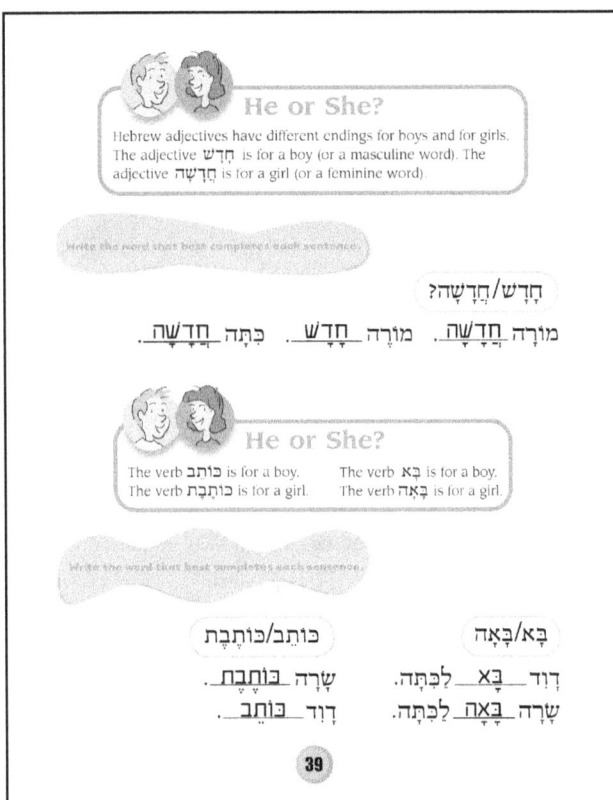

He or She? (p. 39)

Have students write the word that best completes each sentence in the two exercises. Check student answers by having students read each sentence aloud.

If you feel the class can use more gender practice, write the following sentences on the board. Have your students complete the sentences in a notebook:

גָּדוֹל/גְּדוֹלָה

סֵפֶר _____. (גָּדוֹל)
עוּגָה _____. (גְּדוֹלָה)
יַלְדָּה _____. (גְּדוֹלָה)
לֶחֶם _____. (גָּדוֹל)

רוֹצֶה/רוֹצָה

רִבְקָה _____ עוּגָה. (רוֹצָה)
דָּנִיאֵל _____ מִטְרִיָּה. (רוֹצֶה)
שָׂרָה _____ לֶחֶם. (רוֹצָה)

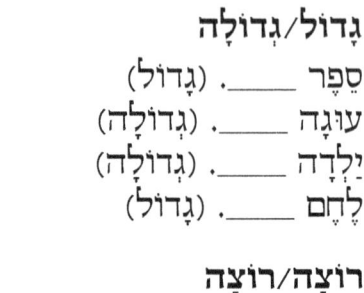

Conversation Corner Divide students into groups of three. Have students "converse" using the following formula:

1. אֲנִי [name].
2. יֵשׁ לִי _____ וְקָטָן/גָּדוֹל [sibling relation, including].
   OR אֵין לִי אָח אוֹ אָחוֹת.
3. יֵשׁ לְךָ אָח אוֹ אָחוֹת?

If students have more than one sibling, have them mention only one.

Picture Match 1 (p. 40)

Have students complete the exercise by placing a checkmark next to the sentence that describes each picture. Check answers by having students read all three sentences in each puzzle, then specifying which answer is correct.

**Bring It to Life** Using markers and construction paper, assign each student (or pairs of students) to draw illustrations for each of the *incorrect* sentences on page 40.

Write numbers on the illustrations, then display them on the chalkboard or bulletin board. Using their textbooks and pencils, students should write the number of the illustration inside the parentheses next to each sentence. Review the answers as a class.

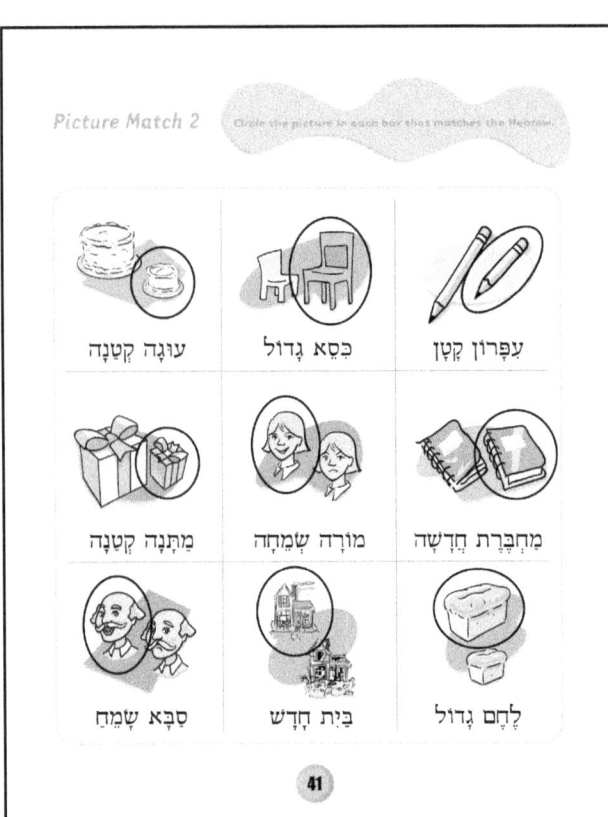

Picture Match 2 (p. 41)

Have students complete the exercise by circling the picture in each box that matches the Hebrew. Check student answers by having them read each description, then describing the correct picture (*"the happy grandfather," etc.*).

 **Game Box** Play "Hebrew Baseball," as described on page 16. You may choose to base the questions on all of Chapter 5, or only the exercises on pages 40–41.

Sample questions include:

- For a single: Show a new book, say:

סֵפֶר _____.

(*any masculine adjective*—גָּדוֹל, קָטָן, חָדָשׁ)

- For a double: Show a pencil. Instruct the batter to describe it using its name and an adjective

(עִפָּרוֹן קָטָן, עִפָּרוֹן חָדָשׁ...)

- For a triple: Write gibberish on the chalkboard. Have the batter describe what you are doing.

(הַמּוֹרֶה/הַמּוֹרָה כּוֹתֵב/כּוֹתֶבֶת עַל הַלּוּחַ.)

- For a home run: Hand a notebook to the batter. Instruct the student to describe his or her situation by using: "I have," "I don't have," "but," and at least seven words total.

(יֵשׁ לִי מַחְבֶּרֶת, אֲבָל אֵין לִי סֵפֶר...)

You may wish to allow students to steal second base by answering a question within five seconds. For example: Name three objects found in the classroom.

Chapter Story: נְמָלָה בַּכִּתָּה (p. 42)

Ready for Reading Have a student read the Hebrew title and English sentence aloud. Ask: What are some foods we know to offer our little visitor?

(לֶחֶם, חַלָה, עוּגָה, תַּפּוּחַ)

Review the list of plurals in the *tarmilon*. Point out that the pronunciation of some words change in their plural forms. For example, תַּפּוּחַ becomes תַּפּוּחִים.

The Extra Mile Using a stopwatch or watch with a seconds hand, time students as they read the poem. See who can read the fastest and most accurately—a mistake costs 2 seconds!

When students are finished reading, ask a "bonus" round of questions. Subtract 2 seconds from the student's score for each correct answer. Sample questions include:

- מִי בַּכִּתָּה? (נְמָלָה בַּכִּתָּה OR מַלְמַלָה בַּכִּתָּה.)
- יֵשׁ סְפָרִים בַּכִּתָּה? (כֵּן, יֵשׁ סְפָרִים בַּכִּתָּה.)
- יֵשׁ עוּגוֹת בַּכִּתָּה? (לֹא, אֵין עוּגוֹת בַּכִּתָּה.)
- יֵשׁ חַלוֹת בַּכִּתָּה? (כֵּן, יֵשׁ חַלוֹת בַּכִּתָּה.)

An unexpected, hungry guest visits the classroom.

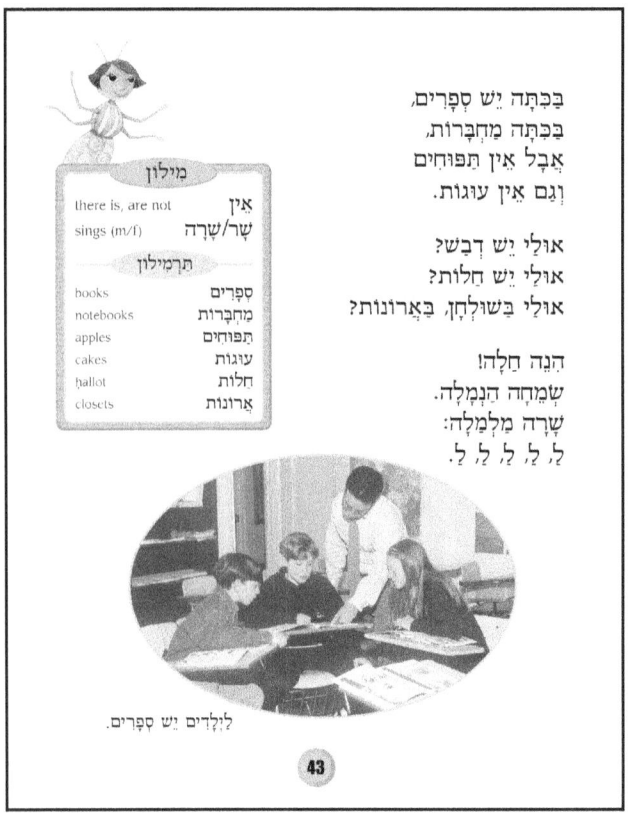

Mastering the Milon (p. 43)

• **אֵין** • Place a book on the table.
Say: יֵשׁ סֵפֶר.
Remove the book, say: אֵין סֵפֶר.
Repeat with various objects until students understand that אֵין means "there is not."

• **שָׁר/שָׁרָה** • Have a boy and a girl make believe they are famous opera singers. They will perform their famous song, consisting of one note and one word. Have the boy sing, שָׁר! and the girl sing, שָׁרָה!

 **Using the Photograph** Direct your students' attention to the photo on page 43. Have a student read the caption aloud. Ask: What does the caption mean? (*The students have books*.)

Ask the following questions about the photograph:

• יֵשׁ יְלָדִים בַּכִּתָּה? (כֵּן, יֵשׁ יְלָדִים בַּכִּתָּה.)
• יֵשׁ מוֹרָה בַּכִּתָּה? (לֹא, יֵשׁ מוֹרֶה בַּכִּתָּה.)
• הַיַלְדָה כּוֹתֶבֶת בַּסֵפֶר?
 (לֹא, הַיַלְדָה לֹא כּוֹתֶבֶת בַּסֵפֶר.)

 **Looking Ahead** Explain to your students that in the next chapter, they'll learn vocabulary having to do with Shabbat. Ask them to think of Shabbat words they already know.

(בְּרָכָה, שַׁבָּת שָׁלוֹם, נֵרוֹת, חַלָה)

Tell your students that they will learn the words מְנוּחָה, something that takes place on Shabbat, and עֲבוֹדָה, something that takes place every other day of the week. What do they think these words mean?

Shalom Ivrit 1 • Teacher's Edition

Lesson Objectives

Students will:

- Practice incorporating gendered verbs into sentences, with the addition of אוֹהֵב/אוֹהֶבֶת, עוֹבֵד/עוֹבֶדֶת and אוֹכֵל/אוֹכֶלֶת.
- Synthesize their knowledge of prepositions עַל, עַל־יַד, and בְּ by determining where they belong in given sentences.

New Milon Words and Phrases

Core Vocabulary

nice, pretty (m/f)	יָפֶה/יָפָה
likes, loves (m/f)	אוֹהֵב/אוֹהֶבֶת
eats (m/f)	אוֹכֵל/אוֹכֶלֶת
day	יוֹם

Shabbat-Related Vocabulary

a peaceful Shabbat	שַׁבָּת שָׁלוֹם
flower(s)	פֶּרַח, פְּרָחִים
Shabbat	שַׁבָּת
blessing	בְּרָכָה
rest	מְנוּחָה
tired (m/f)	עָיֵף/עֲיֵפָה
work	עֲבוֹדָה
works (m/f)	עוֹבֵד/עוֹבֶדֶת

What We'll need

- ❏ Text pages 44–51
- ❏ Word Cards 78–89
- ❏ Picture Cards 7, 9, 10, 18 and 19
- ❏ Helpful props: fresh flowers (or photograph of flowers), brand-new pencil, old pencil

Where We Are

In Chapter 6, we join Doron and his family as they share Shabbat dinner together. We learn that our little friend Bar enjoys Shabbat as well.

We also discover that another little friend looks forward to resting on Yom Shabbat—tiny Malmalah!

Let's Review

Review vocabulary from the previous chapter by giving your students a "tour" of the classroom.

- Pick up a notebook and say: יֵשׁ לִי מַחְבֶּרֶת.
  Ask a girl:
  _____, יֵשׁ לָךְ מַחְבֶּרֶת? (כֵּן, יֵשׁ לִי מַחְבֶּרֶת.)
- Pick up a pencil and say: יֵשׁ לִי עִפָּרוֹן.
  Ask a boy:
  _____, יֵשׁ לְךָ עִפָּרוֹן? (כֵּן, יֵשׁ לִי עִפָּרוֹן.)
- Point to your (or a student's) glasses. Say:
  יֵשׁ לִי (לְךָ/לָךְ) מִשְׁקָפַיִם.
  To a student without glasses:
  יֵשׁ לְךָ/לָךְ מִשְׁקָפַיִם? (לֹא, אֵין לִי מִשְׁקָפַיִם.)
- Ask a student to place a book into the closet.
  Ask: אֵיפֹה הַסֵּפֶר? (הַסֵּפֶר בָּאָרוֹן.)

Have students raise their hands to complete these sentences:

- While writing on the chalkboard, say:
  אֲנִי כּוֹתֵב/כּוֹתֶבֶת עַל _____. (הַלּוּחַ)
- Have a student write her name in a notebook, say:
  שָׂרָה כּוֹתֶבֶת בַּ_____. (מַחְבֶּרֶת)
- Display a brand-new book, say:
  הִנֵּה סֵפֶר _____. (חָדָשׁ)

Introducing the Lesson

Place Word Cards 2, 82, and 86 on the chalkboard ledge. Point to each new word as you say it for the first time.

Pretend to be shoveling, hammering, or doing some other form of physical work. Say: אֲנִי עוֹבֵד/עוֹבֶדֶת!
Pretend to be resting, say:
אָהָה...אֲנִי אוֹהֵב/אוֹהֶבֶת מְנוּחָה.

Remind your students of the question from the end of the previous session: What do מְנוּחָה and עֲבוֹדָה mean? Work and rest!

- Tell your students that in this chapter, they will learn new words having to do with Shabbat.
- Say: (Have class respond, שַׁבָּת שָׁלוֹם!) שַׁבָּת שָׁלוֹם!
- Say: שַׁבָּת לֹא יוֹם עֲבוֹדָה. שַׁבָּת יוֹם מְנוּחָה.
- Say: אֲנִי אוֹהֵב/אוֹהֶבֶת מְנוּחָה בְּשַׁבָּת.
  Ask: What do you think אוֹהֵב/אוֹהֶבֶת means?

Mastering the Milon (p. 44)

• שַׁבָּת and שַׁבָּת שָׁלוֹם • Many students will recognize Shabbat and its familiar greeting. To a student, say:

שַׁבָּת שָׁלוֹם _____. (שַׁבָּת שָׁלוֹם, מוֹרֶה/מוֹרָה.)

Have each student wish you a שַׁבָּת שָׁלוֹם.

Bring it to Life Teach the melody to "Shabbat Shalom" (or invite your synagogue's cantor to teach the song). The words are easy: It's just "Shabbat" and "shalom"!

• יָפֶה and יָפָה • Hold up a brand-new pencil, say:

עִפָּרוֹן יָפֶה!

Hold up an old, stubby pencil, say: עִפָּרוֹן לֹא יָפֶה!

Explain that יָפָה is the feminine form of the word. Explain that the word can mean "pretty" or "nice," but only when talking about physical things such as a sunny day or a smiling face, not how friendly people are.

• פֶּרַח/פְּרָחִים • Display the fresh flowers (or a drawing of flowers on the chalkboard) to the class. Hold a flower up and say:

פֶּרַח יָפֶה!

Hand the flower to a student, ask:

יֵשׁ לְךָ/לָךְ פֶּרַח יָפֶה? (כֵּן, יֵשׁ לִי פֶּרַח יָפֶה.)

Put It Together Ask students to name objects that we might see on Shabbat, along with adjectives that describes them. Have them use the singular form of each object. Answers may include:

• פֶּרַח יָפֶה
• חַלָּה גְּדוֹלָה
• מִשְׁפָּחָה שְׂמֵחָה

Chapter Story: שַׁבָּת שָׁלוֹם (p. 44)

Ready for Reading Have a student read the Hebrew title and translate the English question into Hebrew.

(מַה יֵשׁ עַל הַשֻּׁלְחָן לְשַׁבָּת?)

Have students think of objects that may be found on the Shabbat table (without looking at the story!). List them in Hebrew on the board.

Explain to your students that חַלּוֹת is the plural form of חַלָּה.

Read Aloud! Have students alternate reading lines. Challenge them to read the entire poem with a smooth, continuous rhythm.

The Extra Mile Ask the following questions, either after the entire poem or after each stanza:

Stanza 1:

• מִי בַּבַּיִת?
(אַבָּא בַּבַּיִת; אִמָּא בַּבַּיִת; כֻּלָּם בַּבַּיִת...)
• טוֹב בַּבַּיִת? (כֵּן, טוֹב בַּבַּיִת.)

Stanza 2:

• מָה יֵשׁ עַל הַשֻּׁלְחָן?
• (יֵשׁ נֵרוֹת עַל הַשֻּׁלְחָן; חַלּוֹת עַל הַשֻּׁלְחָן; יַיִן עַל הַשֻּׁלְחָן...)
• יָפֶה בַּבַּיִת? (כֵּן, יָפֶה בַּבַּיִת.)

Stanza 3:

• יֵשׁ שָׁלוֹם בַּבַּיִת? (כֵּן, יֵשׁ שָׁלוֹם בַּבַּיִת.)

Shalom Ivrit 1 • Teacher's Edition

Yes or No? (p. 45)

Have students complete the exercise individually by writing כֵּן or לֹא in the spaces provided.

Review answers by having students read each sentence, then saying whether it is כֵּן or לֹא.

Then restate each sentence as a question. For example:

אַבָּא בַּבַּיִת?; סַבְתָּא בַּבַּיִת?; הָעִפָּרוֹן עַל הַשׁוּלְחָן?...

Have students respond using full sentences.

(כֵּן, אַבָּא בַּבַּיִת; לֹא, סַבְתָּא לֹא בַּבַּיִת...)

Word Match (p. 45)

Have your students complete the exercise by circling the Hebrew word that means the same as the English. Check answers by having students read each Hebrew/English pair aloud.

Game Box Play this version of "Scrambled!" as described on page 18.

Give each student a blank sheet of paper and a pencil. Challenge the students to create three short Hebrew sentences in five minutes, using the words in "Word Match." (Tell your students that בְּ means "in" and אֲרוֹנוֹת is the plural form of אָרוֹן.)

Sample sentences include:

- שָׁלוֹם, אָחוֹת.
- מִי טוֹב?
- הִנֵּה פְּרָחִים.
- כֵּן, יֵשׁ נֵרוֹת.

After the time has expired, have each student read one sentence aloud. Determine whether the sentence makes sense, based on gender and number. (אָחוֹת חָדָשׁ and אֲנִי נֵרוֹת, for example, don't count.) Have all students with the same sentence cross theirs out.

Students receive points for unique sentences, based on the number of words in the sentence:

2 words	1 point
3 words	2 points
4 words	3 points

The student with the most points at the end of the game is the winner.

81

Chapter 6

מִי בַּבַּיִת בְּשַׁבָּת?

What does Bar like about Shabbat?

מִי בַּבַּיִת?
הַיְלָדִים בַּבַּיִת.
הַמִּשְׁפָּחָה בַּבַּיִת.
גַּם עַכְבָּר בַּבַּיִת!

עַכְבָּר: כֵּן, אֲנִי בַּבַּיִת!
אֲנִי אוֹהֵב חַלָּה.
אֲנִי אוֹהֵב יַיִן.
אֲנִי אוֹהֵב פְּרָחִים.
אֲנִי אוֹהֵב אֶת הַשַּׁבָּת!

הָעַכְבָּר שָׁר: אֲנִי בַּר הָעַכְבָּר.
אֲנִי בַּבַּיִת גָּר.
בַּבַּיִת לֹא קַר.

בְּשַׁבָּת אֲנִי שָׁר!
אֲנִי שָׁר בְּרָכָה.
אֲנִי אוֹכֵל חַלָּה.

מִילוֹן
likes, loves (m/f)	אוֹהֵב/אוֹהֶבֶת
blessing	בְּרָכָה
eats (m/f)	אוֹכֵל/אוֹכֶלֶת

46

Mastering the Milon (p. 46)

Tell your students that this short *milon* contains verbs that will allow them to create many new sentences with words they already know.

• **אוֹהֵב/אוֹהֶבֶת** • Say:

אֲנִי אוֹהֵב/אוֹהֶבֶת מְנוּחָה בְּשַׁבָּת; אֲנִי אוֹהֵב/אוֹהֶבֶת חַלָּה; אֲנִי אוֹהֵב/אוֹהֶבֶת עוּגָה.

Stress אוֹהֵב/אוֹהֶבֶת as you would "like" or "love."

Ask a student: ‗‗‗‗‗, אַתָּה/אַתְּ אוֹהֵב/אוֹהֶבֶת עוּגָה? (כֵּן, אֲנִי אוֹהֵב/אוֹהֶבֶת עוּגָה.)

 Captain Grammar Your students may find it interesting that Hebrew uses one word for both "like" and "love." You may wish to ask your students: How can we tell whether someone truly loves something, or just kind of likes something? (*People will stress the word differently; the context in which it appears in a sentence; etc.*)

• **בְּרָכָה** • Point to the בְּרָכָה Word Card (83). Say or sing:

בָּרוּךְ אַתָּה יְיָ, אֱלֹהֵינוּ מֶלֶךְ הָעוֹלָם...

Ask: What is a בְּרָכָה?

• **אוֹכֵל/אוֹכֶלֶת** • Display Picture Cards of various foods (7, 9, 10, 18, 19). Pretend to eat them, saying:

אֲנִי אוֹכֵל/אוֹכֶלֶת תַּפּוּחַ,
אֲנִי אוֹכֵל/אוֹכֶלֶת עוּגָה,
אֲנִי אוֹכֵל/אוֹכֶלֶת לֶחֶם...

Ask a student to pretend to eat.

Ask: ‗‗‗‗‗, אַתָּה/אַתְּ אוֹכֵל/אוֹכֶלֶת תַּפּוּחַ? (כֵּן, אֲנִי אוֹכֵל/אוֹכֶלֶת תַּפּוּחַ.)

 **Put It Together** Have students each name two foods they eat. For example:

• אֲנִי אוֹכֵל תַּפּוּחַ וְחַלָּה.
• אֲנִי אוֹכֶלֶת לֶחֶם וְעוּגָה.

Have students each name a food they like and a food they do not like. For example:

• אֲנִי אוֹהֵב תַּפּוּחַ, אֲבָל אֲנִי לֹא אוֹהֵב חַלָּה.
• אֲנִי אוֹהֶבֶת עוּגָה, אֲבָל אֲנִי לֹא אוֹהֶבֶת לֶחֶם.

Chapter Story: מִי בַּבַּיִת בְּשַׁבָּת? (p. 46)

 **Ready for Reading** Read the Hebrew title and English question aloud. Ask your students to think of words that describe why Bar might like Shabbat. (שָׁלוֹם, חַלָּה, פְּרָחִים, etc.)

Explain to your students that the word אֶת in the ninth line of the story has no English translation—it's a "helper word," used in certain sentences. We won't be working with אֶת just yet!

 **Read Aloud!** Encourage your students to have some fun with Bar's poem about Shabbat. You may wish to:

- Have each student read a line in his or her best "squeaky mouse" voice.
- Give a student all the food Picture Cards, ready to hold up the one that's mentioned.
- Have the singers in the class come up with their own melody for the poem's third stanza, הָעַכְבָּר שָׁר.

You may wish to invite a younger class into yours to watch the "play." Even if the little ones don't understand the Hebrew, they'll enjoy matching pictures to words and seeing the "big kids" having fun with Hebrew.

Shalom Ivrit 1 • Teacher's Edition

 **The Extra Mile** Review Bar's poem with the following questions:

• הַיְלָדִים בַּבַּיִת? (כֵּן, הַיְלָדִים בַּבַּיִת.)
• הַמִשְׁפָּחָה בַּבַּיִת? (כֵּן, הַמִשְׁפָּחָה בַּבַּיִת.)
• גַם עַכְבָּר בַּבַּיִת? (כֵּן, גַם עַכְבָּר בַּבַּיִת.)
• הָעַכְבָּר אוֹהֵב חַלָה וְיַיִן?
  (כֵּן, הָעַכְבָּר אוֹהֵב חַלָה וְיַיִן.)
• קַר לָעַכְבָּר? (לֹא, לֹא קַר לָעַכְבָּר.)
• מַה שָׁר הָעַכְבָּר? (הָעַכְבָּר שָׁר בְּרָכָה.)

He or She? (p. 47)

Tell students to look at the fourth word in the list of word choices. Have a student read it aloud. (Beigel.) Ask: What do you think the word means? (*a bagel, of course!*)

 **Captain Grammar** Your students may find it interesting—or even funny—to see the Hebrew word for bagel. You may wish to tell your students that many Hebrew words are borrowed from English—such as טֶלֶוִיזְיָה, בָּנָנָה, and רַדְיוֹ.

Have students complete the exercise by circling the correct verb in each line, then writing it in the blank space. Check answers by having students read each complete sentence aloud.

 **Conversation Corner** Divide students into pairs. Have them share their family's favorite foods with one another. Here are three new foods to choose from:

pizza	=	פִּיצָה
chicken	=	עוֹף
Chinese food	=	אֹכֶל סִינִי

A student might say:

• אַבָּא אוֹכֵל עוּגָה.
• אִמָא אוֹכֶלֶת בֵּייגֶל.
• הָאָחוֹת אוֹכֶלֶת תַפּוּחַ.

Have each student "report" what they learned about their partner to the class by saying,

אָח גָדוֹל אוֹכֵל פִּיצָה, סַבְתָּא אוֹכֶלֶת חַלָה...

Where Is It? (p. 48)

Have students complete the exercise by filling in the correct prepositions.

For extra practice, ask students about the relationships of people and objects in the classroom to one another. For example:

- Place a book in the closet and ask:

אֵיפֹה הַסֵפֶר? (הַסֵפֶר בָּאָרוֹן.)
- אֵיפֹה דָוִד?
(דָוִד עַל הַכִּסֵא; דָוִד עַל־יַד דָנִיאֵל...)
- אֵיפֹה אֲנִי? (אַתְּ עַל־יַד הַלוּחַ; אַתְּ בַּכִּתָּה...)

He or She? (p. 49)

Have students complete the exercise by writing the appropriate form of the verb אוֹהֵב/אוֹהֶבֶת. They should notice quickly that it's the same form of the verb for every food in every instance!

> **Bring it to Life** List all six foods from "He or She?" on the chalkboard. Take a poll to see which foods are the class favorites. Depending on your synagogue's dietary rules, you may wish to have a *Shalom Ivrit* party featuring the winners!

> **Game Box**
> **Check, Please!**
>
> Have students draw the six foods mentioned in "He or She?" on page 49 (פִּיצָה, תַּפּוּחַ, בְּנָנָה, בֵּייגֶל, חַלָּה, עוּגָה). Give your students five minutes to memorize the list of likes and dislikes in the right-hand column on the page.
>
> Set six "place cards" with the names of the characters from "He or She?" around a table. Have student "servers," one at a time, pretend to deliver their orders.
>
> The server should say:
>
> - שָׁלוֹם, דּוֹרוֹן. אַתָּה אוֹכֵל פִּיצָה.
>   (The server places the drawing of pizza in front of Doron.)
> - שָׁלוֹם, דִּינָה. אַתְּ אוֹכֶלֶת תַּפּוּחַ.
>   (The server places the drawing of an apple in front of Dinah.)
> - Etc.
>
> Each student receives a "shekel" tip for every order that is correct. Students lose a "shekel" for an incorrect "meal" or verb form. The student with the highest "tip" is the winner.

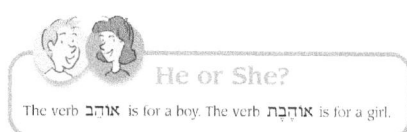

He or She?

The verb אוֹהֵב is for a boy. The verb אוֹהֶבֶת is for a girl.

Complete each sentence only if you like to eat that food. Write אוֹהֵב if you are a boy. Write אוֹהֶבֶת if you are a girl.

1. דּוֹרוֹן אוֹכֵל פִּיצָה. אֲנִי _depends on gender of student_ פִּיצָה.
2. דִּינָה אוֹכֶלֶת תַּפּוּחַ. אֲנִי _depends on gender of student_ תַּפּוּחַ.
3. אִמָּא אוֹכֶלֶת בְּנָנָה. אֲנִי _depends on gender of student_ בְּנָנָה.
4. אַבָּא אוֹכֵל בֵּייגֶל. אֲנִי _depends on gender of student_ בֵּייגֶל.
5. דָּוִד אוֹכֵל חַלָּה. אֲנִי _depends on gender of student_ חַלָּה.
6. לִילִי אוֹכֶלֶת עוּגָה. אֲנִי _depends on gender of student_ עוּגָה.

Sample descriptions include:

- שָׂרָה עוֹבֶדֶת.
- דָּוִד עָיֵף.
- דָּנִיאֵל אוֹהֵב מְנוּחָה.

• **יוֹם** • Say: יוֹם כִּפּוּר, יוֹם שַׁבָּת, יוֹם טוֹב.

Ask: What do you think יוֹם means?

Chapter Story: יוֹם שַׁבָּת, יוֹם מְנוּחָה (p. 50)

 **Ready for Reading** Read the Hebrew title aloud. Ask a student what the title means. (*Day of Shabbat, Day of Rest*)

Review the two words in the *tarmilon*: כָּל יוֹם—every day, and סְבִיבוֹן!)—spins (like a מִסְתּוֹבֵב/מִסְתּוֹבֶבֶת.

 **Read Aloud!** Have four students come to the front of the class. Explain that they are "agents" for the famous Malmalah, and they are reporting to the press on her latest doings. Have them each read a pair of lines aloud.

Challenge the students to read smoothly and with correct pronunciation.

Mastering the Milon (p. 50)

Display Words Cards 85–89 on the chalkboard ledge. Allow students to refer to them as they learn these new words.

• **עוֹבֵד/עוֹבֶדֶת** • Pretend to be shoveling, cutting wood, sawing, or doing some other physical work.

Say: אֲנִי עוֹבֵד/עוֹבֶדֶת.

Ask a student: _____, אַתָּה/אַתְּ עוֹבֵד/עוֹבֶדֶת?

(כֵּן, אֲנִי עוֹבֵד/עוֹבֶדֶת.)

Continue this way until students understand that עוֹבֵד/עוֹבֶדֶת mean "work."

• **עֲבוֹדָה** • Continue "working." Happily, say:

אֲנִי אוֹהֵב/אוֹהֶבֶת עֲבוֹדָה!

Change from one "task" to another.

Again, say: אֲנִי אוֹהֵב/אוֹהֶבֶת עֲבוֹדָה!

> **Captain Grammar** This may be the first time your students observe first-hand the close resemblance between Hebrew verbs and nouns. You may wish to explain that the Hebrew words are built from שׁוֹרָשִׁים, or roots. That's why עֲבוֹדָה and עוֹבֵד/עוֹבֶדֶת look and sound so similar.

• **עָיֵף/עֲיֵפָה** • Yawn, tired from your work, then sit down.

Say: אֲנִי עָיֵף/עֲיֵפָה!

Ask a student: _____, אַתָּה/אַתְּ עָיֵף/עֲיֵפָה?

(לֹא, אֲנִי לֹא עָיֵף/עֲיֵפָה.)

Ask: What do you think עָיֵף/עֲיֵפָה means?

• **מְנוּחָה** • Still sitting, now recline.

Say, אָהּ...מְנוּחָה! אֲנִי אוֹהֵב/אוֹהֶבֶת מְנוּחָה!

> **Put It Together** Have three students come to the front of the room. Have one pretend to work, one pretend to be tired, and one pretend to rest. Have them describe themselves:
> - Worker: אֲנִי עוֹבֵד/עוֹבֶדֶת!
> - Tired student: אֲנִי עָיֵף/עֲיֵפָה!
> - Resting student: אָהּ...מְנוּחָה!
>
> Have three students play these same parts, now without speaking. Have their classmates guess what they are doing (using אוֹהֵב/אוֹהֶבֶת for the resting student).

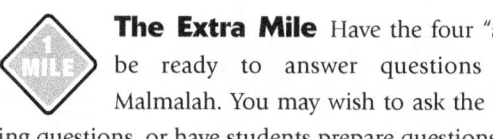 **The Extra Mile** Have the four "agents" be ready to answer questions about Malmalah. You may wish to ask the following questions, or have students prepare questions:

- מַלְמַלָה עֲיֵפָה? (לֹא, מַלְמַלָה לֹא עֲיֵפָה.)
- מַה מַלְמַלָה אוֹהֶבֶת? (מַלְמַלָה אוֹהֶבֶת עֲבוֹדָה.)
- מַלְמַלָה עוֹבֶדֶת כָּל יוֹם? (כֵּן, מַלְמַלָה עוֹבֶדֶת כָּל יוֹם.)
- מַלְמַלָה עוֹבֶדֶת בְּיוֹם שַׁבָּת? (לֹא, מַלְמַלָה לֹא עוֹבֶדֶת בְּיוֹם שַׁבָּת.)

 **Using the Photograph** Have students look at the photograph on page 51. Have a student read the caption aloud. Ask: What does the caption mean? (*Ḥallah, wine, and candles are on the table.*) Ask your students:

- חַלָה עַל הַשׁוּלְחָן? (כֵּן, חַלָה עַל הַשׁוּלְחָן.)
- יַיִן וְנֵרוֹת עַל הַשׁוּלְחָן? (כֵּן, יַיִן וְנֵרוֹת עַל הַשׁוּלְחָן.)
- פְּרָחִים עַל הַשׁוּלְחָן? (לֹא, פְּרָחִים לֹא עַל הַשׁוּלְחָן.)

He, She, or They? (p. 51)

Have a student read the English directions aloud.

 Captain Grammar You may wish to remind students that the ending ים makes masculine words plural, and is also the ending used for groups of more than one person, as long as at least one of them is a boy!

Have students complete the exercise on page 51 by choosing the correct English meaning for each verb and writing it in the space provided.

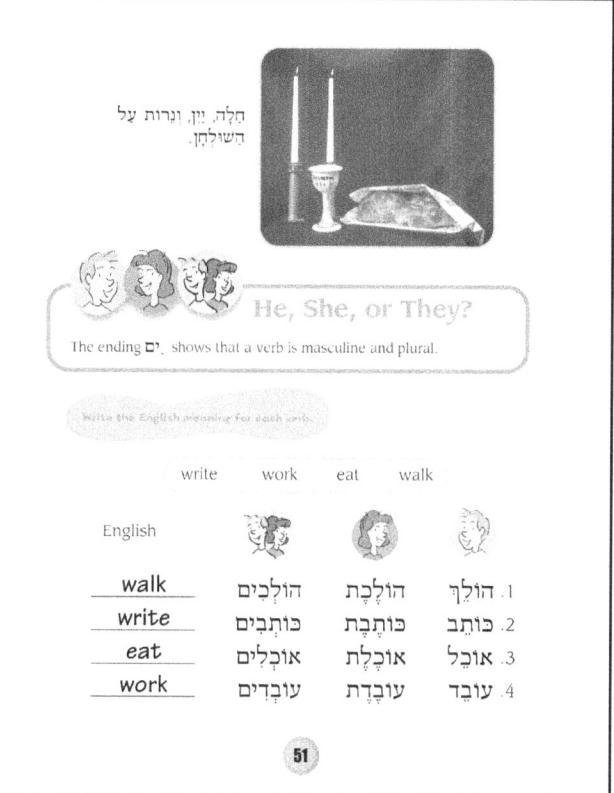

 **Game Box**
Listen Up!

Have the class rise, either by their desks or in an open area. Draw from the twelve Hebrew words on page 51 as your "Listen Up!" directions.

Call out one of the twelve words. Depending on the number and gender of the word, those students should pretend to engage in that activity. For example, for forms of הוֹלֵךְ: all the boys (הוֹלֵךְ), all the girls (הוֹלֶכֶת), or the entire class (הוֹלְכִים) should pretend to walk, either in place or in a circle. For forms of כּוֹתֵב, all appropriate students should pretend to write, etc.

Read words quickly and keep your eyes open for students who "oops!" You may wish to have a student aide, or a student "referee" help determine who should be "out." Those students who are "out" should be seated.

The student or students who are still standing are the winners.

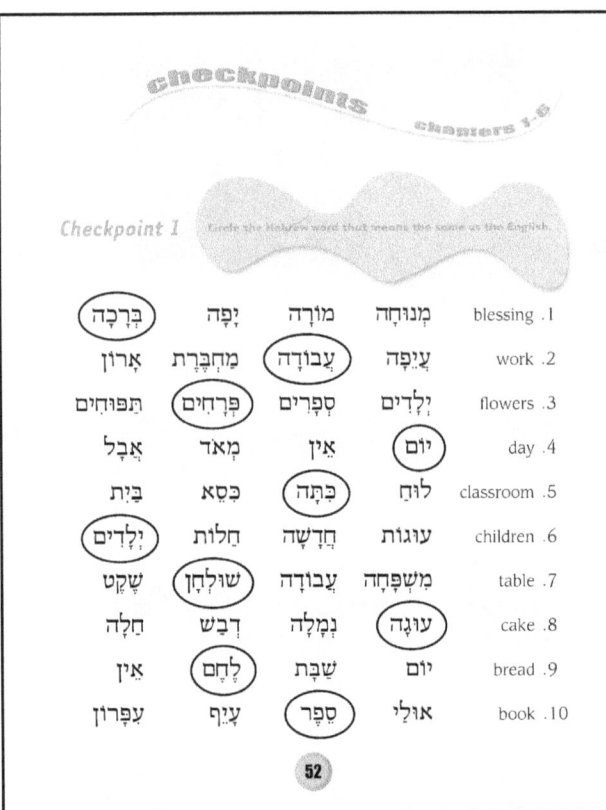

Looking Ahead Explain to your students that in the next chapter, they'll learn vocabulary having to do with Ḥanukkah, including words that will help them to understand the Ḥanukkah blessings.

Tell your students that Ḥanukkah is חַג הָאוֹר. Ask: What do they think אוֹר means?

Checkpoints Completion (pp. 52–55)
Checkpoint 1
Have students complete the exercise by circling the Hebrew word that means the same as the English.

Checkpoint 2
Have students complete the exercise by writing the Hebrew word that matches the English in each blank lens.

Continue with Checkpoints 3 and 4 on the next page.

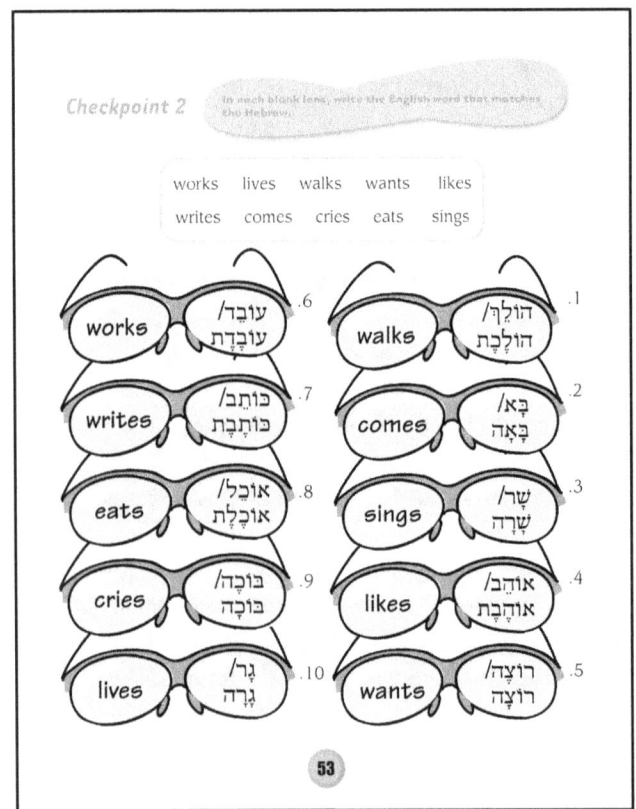

Shalom Ivrit 1 • Teacher's Edition

Checkpoint 3

Have students complete the exercise by connecting each noun to its matching adjective and writing the English meaning of the adjective in the empty box.

Checkpoint 4

Have students complete the exercise by choosing the correct Hebrew word from the list and writing it in the blank space.

Review answers by having students provide the answers for each question in Checkpoints 1–4. Instruct students to place a checkmark next to the answers that are correct, and an X next to the answers that are incorrect. Have them place a grade at the top of each page (for example, 7/10, 9/10, or 5/7).

Review grades by checking each student's book.

Checkpoint Assessment

If possible, spend a few minutes with each student to review his or her work. Be sure to praise students for correct answers and encourage them to find answers for incorrect ones.

For students who scored (on Checkpoints 1, 2, or 4):
- 8–10 on any Checkpoint: praise them on a job well done (מְצוּיָן means "excellent").
- 6–7: See if there was a particular *milon* or chapter that the students found particularly troublesome. Encourage them to correct the words they missed by reviewing the *milonim* in which the words appeared.
- 5 or less: Review each incorrect answer with the students. If possible, have a teacher's aide work privately with them before moving on to the next lesson.

For Checkpoint 3, adjust the grading scale to students who scored: 6–7, 4–5, and 3 or lower.

Keep your eyes out for words that your students consistently miss. You may wish to spend some time reviewing those words as a class.

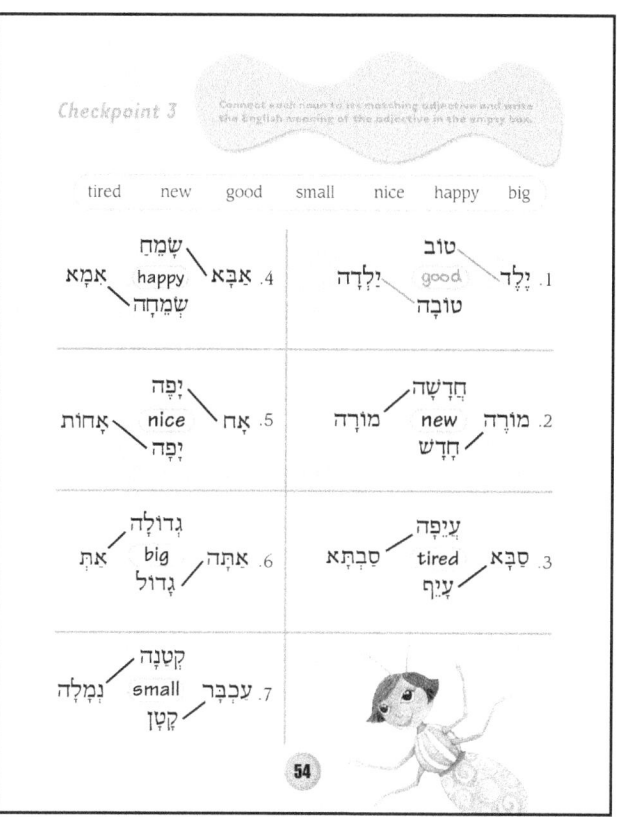

Chapter 6

Dear Parent,

During the past few weeks, our class has learned Hebrew words and phrases for items found in the classroom, such as *seifer* (book), *maḥberet* (notebook), and *iparon* (pencil); and words having to do with Shabbat, such as *brachah* (blessing) and *Shabbat shalom* (a peaceful Shabbat). We have also been working to build our core modern Hebrew vocabulary.

Here are some words your child has learned during the past few weeks, including ideas to incorporate these words into your daily conversations:

chair	*kiseh*	כִּסֵא
table	*shulḥan*	שׁוּלְחָן

Ask your child to sit in the *kiseh* by the *shulḥan*.

bread	*leḥem*	לֶחֶם
cake	*ugah*	עוּגָה

Include some Hebrew names for food in your mealtime routine!

quiet	*sheket*	שֶׁקֶט

Just in case things get a bit noisy at home.

Thank you for helping us learn modern Hebrew!

B'Shalom,

Lesson Objectives

Students will:
- Comprehend and create a greater variety of sentences and phrases, with the addition of שֶׁל.
- Continue to understand a greater variety of everyday verbs, with the addition of נוֹתֵן/נוֹתֶנֶת, עוֹשֶׂה/עוֹשָׂה, and אוֹמֵר/אוֹמֶרֶת.

New Milon Words and Phrases

Core Vocabulary

today	הַיּוֹם
of, belonging to	שֶׁל
we have	יֵשׁ לָנוּ
makes, does (m/f)	עוֹשֶׂה/עוֹשָׂה
gives (m/f)	נוֹתֵן/נוֹתֶנֶת
says (m/f)	אוֹמֵר/אוֹמֶרֶת
head	רֹאשׁ

Ḥanukkah-Related Vocabulary

light	אוֹר
first	רִאשׁוֹן
lights (m/f)	מַדְלִיק/מַדְלִיקָה
candle(s)	נֵר/נֵרוֹת

Other Useful Vocabulary

warm	חַם

What We'll need

- ☐ Text pages 56–63
- ☐ Word Cards 49, 57, 73, 84, 87, 89, and 90–101
- ☐ Helpful props: a Ḥanukkiah, Ḥanukkah candles, and a dreidel

Where We Are

In Chapter 7, we join David and his family as they light the ḥanukkiah and celebrate Ḥanukkah together.

We then find a dizzy Bar Ha'achbar in—of all places—a dreidel.

Let's Review

Remove Word Cards 84, 87, and 89. Call three students to the front of the class and give each a card.

Have each student, in turn, ask, מָה אֲנִי? and pantomime his or her word(s) for the class. Have the class respond in full sentences. Sample responses include:

- דָּוִד עָיֵף. You may wish to follow up by asking:
  דָּוִד רוֹצֶה מְנוּחָה? (כֵּן, דָּוִד רוֹצֶה מְנוּחָה.)
- שָׂרָה עוֹבֶדֶת. Follow up with:
  שָׂרָה אוֹהֶבֶת עֲבוֹדָה?
  (כֵּן, שָׂרָה אוֹהֶבֶת עֲבוֹדָה. OR לֹא, שָׂרָה לֹא אוֹהֶבֶת עֲבוֹדָה.)
- דָּנִי אוֹכֵל. Follow up:
  מָה דָּנִיאֵל אוֹכֵל? (דָּנִיאֵל אוֹכֵל תַּפּוּחַ, דָּנִיאֵל אוֹכֵל עוּגָה...)

Continue by asking your students the following "quick questions":

- אֵיפֹה ____ ? (____ עַל הַכִּסֵּא, ____ בַּכִּתָּה, ____ עַל־יַד הַשּׁוּלְחָן...)
- מִי אוֹהֵב עוּגָה? (אֲנִי אוֹהֵב/אוֹהֶבֶת עוּגָה; ____ אוֹהֵב/אוֹהֶבֶת עוּגָה...)
- מָה יֵשׁ עַל הַשּׁוּלְחָן? (יֵשׁ מַחְבֶּרֶת עַל הַשּׁוּלְחָן, יֵשׁ סֵפֶר עַל הַשּׁוּלְחָן...)
- אֵיפֹה הָעִפָּרוֹן? (הִנֵּה הָעִפָּרוֹן, הָעִפָּרוֹן בָּאָרוֹן, הָעִפָּרוֹן עַל הַשּׁוּלְחָן...)

Introducing The Lesson

Place Word Cards 90–93, 95, and 98 on the chalkboard ledge. Point to each new word as you introduce it.

Set up the ḥanukkiah on a table.
- Say: הִנֵּה חֲנוּכִּיָּה.
  Hold up a candle and say: הִנֵּה נֵר.
  Place the candle in the *shamash* holder.
- Point downward to indicate "today" and say:
  הַיּוֹם חֲנוּכָּה!
- Place the first-night candle in the Ḥanukkiah and continue:
  הַיּוֹם יוֹם רִאשׁוֹן שֶׁל חֲנוּכָּה.
  Point to a candle, say: נֵר עוֹשֶׂה אוֹר.
  Gesture toward the wick, indicating a flame, and stress אוֹר. Remind your students that Ḥanukkah is also called חַג הָאוֹר. Ask: What do you think אוֹר means?

Who lights the first Ḥanukkah candle?

חַג חֲנוּכָּה בָּא!
חֲנוּכָּה חַג יָפֶה.
חֲנוּכָּה חַג שָׂמֵחַ.
חֲנוּכָּה חַג הָאוֹר.

56

 **Put It Together** Remove Word Cards 92–95. Call a student to the *ḥanukkiah*. Have the student light the first-night candle with the *shamash*.

- Say: _____ מַדְלִיק/מַדְלִיקָה נֵר.

  Place those two Word Cards, in order, on the chalkboard ledge.

- Say: _____ מַדְלִיק/מַדְלִיקָה נֵר רִאשׁוֹן.

  Add the רִאשׁוֹן Word Card to the ledge.

- Say: _____ מַדְלִיק/מַדְלִיקָה נֵר רִאשׁוֹן שֶׁל חֲנוּכָּה.

  Add שֶׁל to the ledge.

Leaving the *ḥanukkiah* set up, segue directly into the review of the *milon* on page 57.

Mastering the Milon (p. 57)

• **אוֹר** • Switch off and on the lights in the classroom.
Say: יֵשׁ אוֹר בַּכִּתָּה!
Light the *shamash* on the Ḥanukkiah.
Say: יֵשׁ אוֹר בַּחֲנוּכִּיָה!

>  **Our Tradition** The Torah tells us that אוֹר was the very first thing God created. יְהִי אוֹר!—Let there be light!, God said.
>
> It may be fun to turn on the classroom lights at the beginning of each class and have the class respond: וַיְהִי אוֹר!

• **הַיוֹם** • Point downward, indicating "today." Look out the window and say: הַיוֹם יוֹם יָפֶה.
OR הַיוֹם לֹא יָפֶה.
Smile, say: הַיוֹם אֲנִי שָׂמֵחַ/שְׂמֵחָה.
Yawn, say: הַיוֹם אֲנִי עָיֵף/עֲיֵפָה.
Continue this way until students understand that הַיוֹם means "today."

• **נֵר/נֵרוֹת** • Lift a candle and say: הִנֵּה נֵר.
Lift two candles, say: הִנֵּה נֵרוֹת.
Lift one, repeat: נֵר; lift two, repeat: נֵרוֹת.

• **רִאשׁוֹן** • Point to the first-night candle in the *ḥanukkiah* and say: הַנֵּר הָרִאשׁוֹן.
Point to the first book in a shelf or stack, say: הַסֵּפֶר הָרִאשׁוֹן.
Ask: What do you think רִאשׁוֹן means?

• **שֶׁל** • Point to the *ḥanukkiah* and say: הִנֵּה חֲנוּכִּיָה שֶׁל חֲנוּכָּה.
Lift a book from a student's desk, say: הַסֵּפֶר שֶׁל _____.
Point to yourself, say: אֲנִי הַמוֹרֶה/הַמוֹרָה שֶׁל הַכִּתָּה.
Explain that שֶׁל may mean either "of" or "belonging to."

• **מַדְלִיק/מַדְלִיקָה** • Light the *shamash*.
Say: אֲנִי מַדְלִיק/מַדְלִיקָה נֵר.

Shalom Ivrit 1 • Teacher's Edition

Chapter Story: חֲנוּכָּה (pp. 56–57)

Ready for Reading Explain to your students that בְּרָכוֹת, שָׁרִים, מַדְלִיקִים are plural forms of words they already know. Also explain that לְהַדְלִיק means "to light."

Read Aloud! Have a student read the four introductory lines on page 56.

- Ask: חֲנוּכָּה חַג יָפֶה? (כֵּן, חֲנוּכָּה חַג יָפֶה.)
- Ask: חֲנוּכָּה חַג שָׂמֵחַ? (כֵּן, חֲנוּכָּה חַג שָׂמֵחַ.)
- הַיּוֹם חֲנוּכָּה?

(*If it is during Ḥanukkah:* כֵּן, הַיּוֹם חֲנוּכָּה; *if not:* לֹא, הַיּוֹם לֹא חֲנוּכָּה.)

Assign five students to read the parts of the narrator, דָּנִי, לִילִי, דָּוִד, and אִמָּא on page 57.

- Ask דָּנִי: אַתָּה מַדְלִיק נֵר רִאשׁוֹן?
(כֵּן, אֲנִי מַדְלִיק נֵר רִאשׁוֹן.)
- Ask לִילִי: אַתְּ מַדְלִיקָה נֵר רִאשׁוֹן?
(כֵּן, אֲנִי מַדְלִיקָה נֵר רִאשׁוֹן.)
- Ask דָּוִד: אַתָּה רוֹצֶה לְהַדְלִיק נֵר רִאשׁוֹן?
כֵּן, אֲנִי רוֹצֶה לְהַדְלִיק נֵר רִאשׁוֹן?
- Ask אִמָּא: מִי מַדְלִיק נֵר רִאשׁוֹן?
(כּוּלָּם! OR כּוּלָּם מַדְלִיקִים נֵר רִאשׁוֹן.)

Have a student read the five closing lines on page 57.

- Ask דָּנִי: אַתָּה שָׂמֵחַ? (כֵּן, אֲנִי שָׂמֵחַ.)
- Ask דָּוִד: אַתָּה שָׂמֵחַ? (כֵּן, אֲנִי שָׂמֵחַ.)
- Ask לִילִי: אַתְּ שְׂמֵחָה? (כֵּן, אֲנִי שְׂמֵחָה.)
- Ask other students:
מִי שָׁרִים בְּרָכוֹת שֶׁל חֲנוּכָּה?
(כּוּלָּם שָׁרִים בְּרָכוֹת שֶׁל חֲנוּכָּה.)

הַמִּשְׁפָּחָה בַּבַּיִת.
הַיּוֹם יוֹם רִאשׁוֹן שֶׁל חֲנוּכָּה.

דָּנִי: אֲנִי מַדְלִיק נֵר רִאשׁוֹן!

לִילִי: לֹא, לֹא!
אֲנִי מַדְלִיקָה נֵר רִאשׁוֹן!

דָּוִד: גַּם אֲנִי רוֹצֶה לְהַדְלִיק נֵר.

דָּנִי: אֲנִי אָח רִאשׁוֹן,
אֲנִי מַדְלִיק נֵר רִאשׁוֹן.

אִמָּא: דָּוִד, הִנֵּה חֲנוּכִּיָּה.
לִילִי, הִנֵּה חֲנוּכִּיָּה.
דָּנִי, הִנֵּה חֲנוּכִּיָּה.

כּוּלָּם שְׂמֵחִים.
דָּנִי, דָּוִד, וְלִילִי
מַדְלִיקִים נֵר רִאשׁוֹן.
כּוּלָּם שָׁרִים בְּרָכוֹת
שֶׁל חֲנוּכָּה.

מִילוֹן

light	אוֹר
today	הַיּוֹם
first (m)	רִאשׁוֹן
of, belonging to	שֶׁל
lights (m/f)	מַדְלִיקִים/מַדְלִיקוֹת
candle(s)	נֵר/נֵרוֹת

תַּרְמִילוֹן

Hanukkah	חֲנוּכָּה
to light	לְהַדְלִיק
Hanukkah menorah	חֲנוּכִּיָּה
light (pl)	מַדְלִיקִים
sing (pl)	שָׁרִים
blessings	בְּרָכוֹת

The Extra Mile Ask students in the class:
מִי מַדְלִיק נֵר רִאשׁוֹן בַּבַּיִת?
אַתְּ? אַתָּה? אָח? אָחוֹת?

Provide a sample answer:
אָחוֹת קְטַנָּה מַדְלִיקָה נֵר רִאשׁוֹן.

Other answers may include:
- אֲנִי מַדְלִיק נֵר רִאשׁוֹן.
- סַבְתָּא מַדְלִיקָה נֵר רִאשׁוֹן.

Ask: מִי רוֹצָה לְהַדְלִיק נֵר רִאשׁוֹן?
(אֲנִי רוֹצֶה/רוֹצָה לְהַדְלִיק נֵר רִאשׁוֹן.)

Picture Match Check (✓) the words that describe the picture.

( ) 1. חַג הַסוּכּוֹת
(✓) 2. חַג חֲנוּכָּה
( ) 3. חַג שִׂמְחַת תּוֹרָה

( ) 1. דָוִד רוֹצֶה נֵר.
( ) 2. דָוִד אוֹכֵל נֵר.
(✓) 3. דָוִד מַדְלִיק נֵר.

( ) 1. הַיוֹם יוֹם קַר.
( ) 2. הַיוֹם יוֹם חֲנוּכָּה.
(✓) 3. הַיוֹם יוֹם יָפֶה.

(✓) 1. אוֹר בַּבַּיִת.
( ) 2. אוֹר בַּכִּתָּה.
( ) 3. אוֹר בָּאָרוֹן.

58

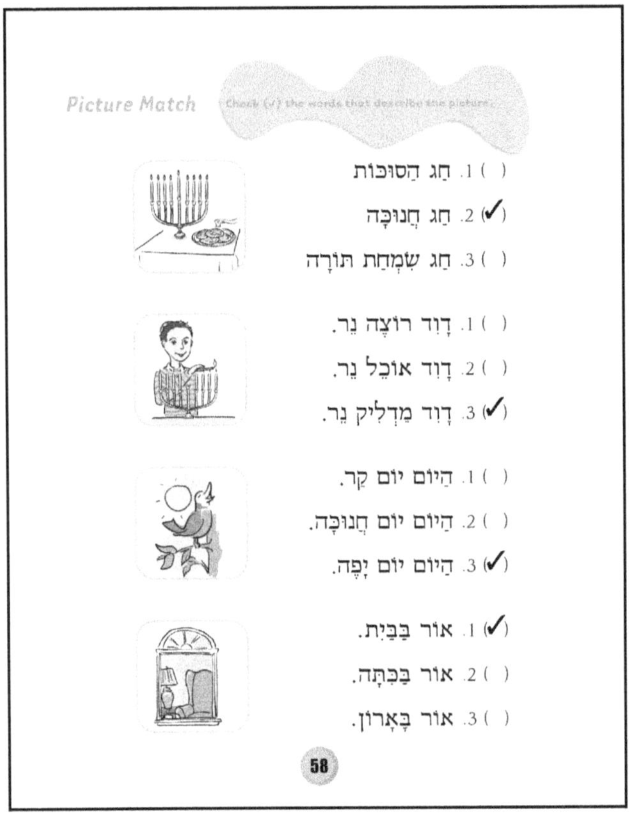

Picture Match (p. 58)

Have students place a checkmark in the box that describes the picture. Review answers by having students read all three choices aloud, then choose the number of the correct sentence.

Bring It to Life Have students write a short story using all four correct sentences from the exercise on page 58 and at least three new sentences. For example, a student may write:

הַיוֹם יוֹם יָפֶה. יֵשׁ אוֹר בַּכִּתָּה.
הַיוֹם חַג חֲנוּכָּה. יֵשׁ חֲנוּכִּיָה עַל הַשׁוּלְחָן.
דָוִד לֹא עוֹבֵד. דָוִד מַדְלִיק נֵר. חֲנוּכָּה שָׂמֵחַ!

You may wish to have students illustrate their stories. Display the illustrations and have students read their stories to the class.

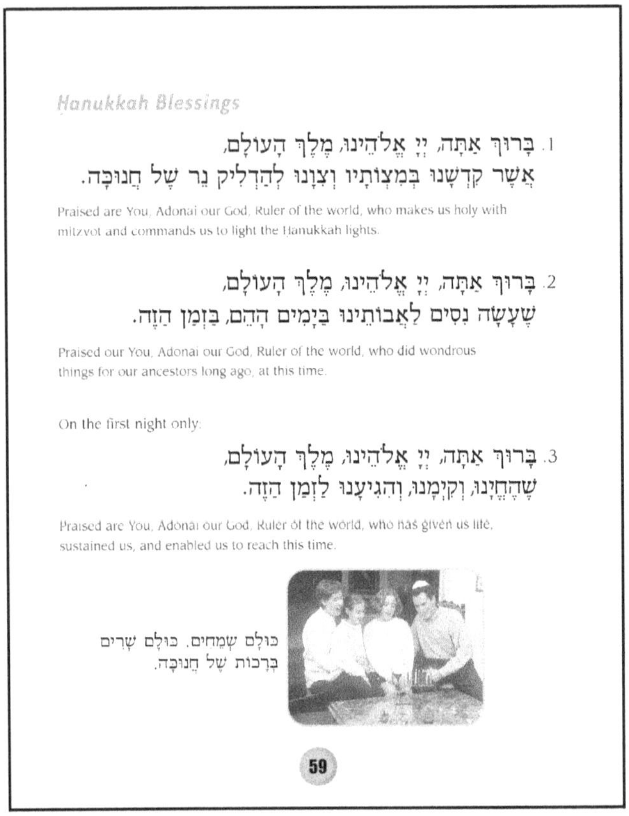

Ḥanukkah Blessings

1. בָּרוּךְ אַתָּה, יְיָ אֱלֹהֵינוּ, מֶלֶךְ הָעוֹלָם,
אֲשֶׁר קִדְּשָׁנוּ בְּמִצְוֹתָיו וְצִוָּנוּ לְהַדְלִיק נֵר שֶׁל חֲנוּכָּה.

Praised are You, Adonai our God, Ruler of the world, who makes us holy with mitzvot and commands us to light the Ḥanukkah lights.

2. בָּרוּךְ אַתָּה, יְיָ אֱלֹהֵינוּ, מֶלֶךְ הָעוֹלָם,
שֶׁעָשָׂה נִסִּים לַאֲבוֹתֵינוּ בַּיָמִים הָהֵם, בַּזְּמַן הַזֶּה.

Praised our You, Adonai our God, Ruler of the world, who did wondrous things for our ancestors long ago, at this time.

On the first night only:

3. בָּרוּךְ אַתָּה, יְיָ אֱלֹהֵינוּ, מֶלֶךְ הָעוֹלָם,
שֶׁהֶחֱיָנוּ, וְקִיְּמָנוּ, וְהִגִּיעָנוּ לַזְּמַן הַזֶּה.

Praised are You, Adonai our God, Ruler of the world, who has given us life, sustained us, and enabled us to reach this time.

כּוּלָם שְׂמֵחִים. כּוּלָם שָׁרִים
בְּרָכוֹת שֶׁל חֲנוּכָּה.

59

Ḥanukkah Blessings (p. 59)

Your students may be surprised to discover how many words in the familiar Ḥanukkah blessings they already know!

Review the words in the Ḥanukkah blessings that your students have learned so far. Have students find words they know in the blessings, then list them on the board. The words are:

- אַתָּה
- לְהַדְלִיק
- נֵר
- שֶׁל
- בַּיָמִ(ים)

(Explain to your students that בַּיָמִים means "in those days," from the word יוֹם!)

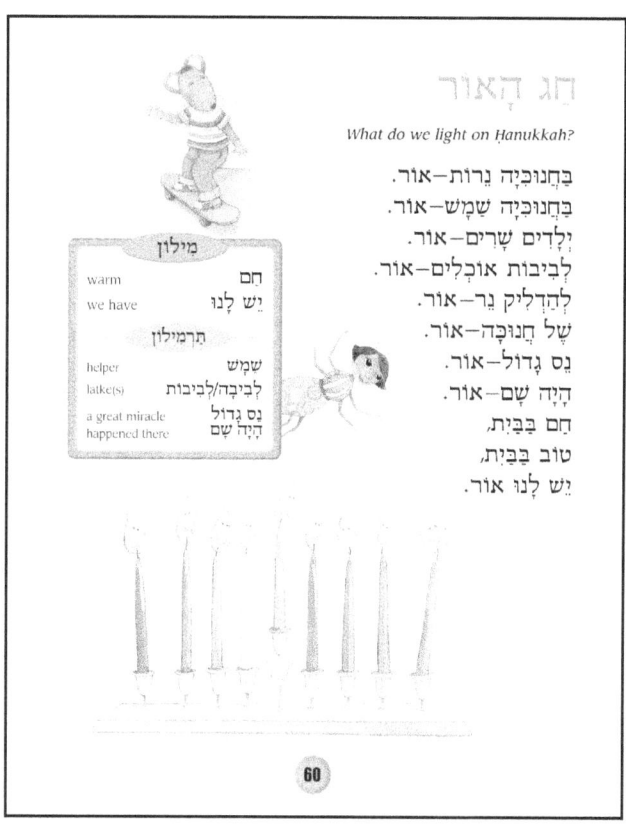

חַג הָאוֹר

What do we light on Ḥanukkah?

בַּחֲנוּכִּיָּה נֵרוֹת–אוֹר.
בַּחֲנוּכִּיָּה שַׁמָּשׁ–אוֹר.
יְלָדִים שָׁרִים–אוֹר.
לְבִיבוֹת אוֹכְלִים–אוֹר.
לְהַדְלִיק נֵר–אוֹר.
שֶׁל חֲנוּכָּה–אוֹר.
נֵס גָּדוֹל–אוֹר.
הָיָה שָׁם–אוֹר.
חַם בַּבַּיִת,
טוֹב בַּבַּיִת,
יֵשׁ לָנוּ אוֹר.

מִילוֹן

warm	חַם
we have	יֵשׁ לָנוּ

תַּרְמִילוֹן

helper	שַׁמָּשׁ
latke(s)	לְבִיבָה/לְבִיבוֹת
a great miracle happened there	נֵס גָּדוֹל הָיָה שָׁם

 **Using the Photograph** Ask students to each make a Hebrew list of objects they recognize in the photo on page 59. Have them only use words that they've learned so far! (*Answers may include:* חֲנוּכִּיָּה, יַלְדָּה, יֶלֶד, אַבָּא, אִמָּא, נֵרוֹת, שׁוּלְחָן, אוֹר.)

Mastering the Milon (p. 60)

• חַם • Fan yourself, using your hand or a sheet of paper. Say:

חַם בַּכִּתָּה! חַם הַיּוֹם!

Ask: What do you think חַם means?

• יֵשׁ לָנוּ • Lift a book. Say:

יֵשׁ לִי סֵפֶר.

Point to a student's book and say:

_____, יֵשׁ לְךָ/לָךְ סֵפֶר.

Gesture to the entire class, including yourself, say:

יֵשׁ לָנוּ סְפָרִים.

Ask: What do you think יֵשׁ לָנוּ means?

 **Put It Together** Set Word Cards 49, 57, and 73 on the chalkboard ledge. Have students create sentences using all four forms of יֵשׁ לְ, using these three words. For example, a student may say:

• יֵשׁ לִי כִּתָּה; יֵשׁ לְךָ כִּתָּה; יֵשׁ לָךְ כִּתָּה; יֵשׁ לָנוּ כִּתָּה.
• יֵשׁ לִי לֶחֶם; יֵשׁ לְךָ לֶחֶם; יֵשׁ לָךְ לֶחֶם; יֵשׁ לָנוּ לֶחֶם.
• יֵשׁ לִי סֵפֶר; יֵשׁ לְךָ סֵפֶר; יֵשׁ לָךְ סֵפֶר; יֵשׁ לָנוּ סְפָרִים.

It may be fun to have the class raise their volume each time they say אוֹר, starting with a whisper, then finishing with a loud, hearty, אוֹר! to symbolize the fully lit *hanukkiah*.

The Extra Mile Ask a series of "quick questions":

• מַה יֵּשׁ בַּחֲנוּכִּיָּה? (יֵשׁ נֵרוֹת בַּחֲנוּכִּיָּה.)
• מַה שָׁרִים יְלָדִים? (יְלָדִים שָׁרִים בְּרָכוֹת.)
• מַה אוֹכְלִים יְלָדִים? (יְלָדִים אוֹכְלִים לְבִיבוֹת.)

Chapter Story: חַג הָאוֹר (p. 60)

 **Ready for Reading** Many of your students will already know the words שַׁמָּשׁ (helper), לְבִיבוֹת (latkes), and the phrase נֵס גָּדוֹל הָיָה שָׁם (a great miracle happened there).

 **Read Aloud!** Assign students to alternate reading the lines of the poem on page 60. Have the class finish each of the first eight lines by saying אוֹר together. Then have the class read the last three lines in unison.

Latke Puzzle (p. 61)

Have students complete the latke puzzle by writing the Hebrew word next to its English meaning. (All words may be found inside the *l'vivot*.)

Instruct students to write those letters with numbers beneath them on the line at the bottom of the page.

You may wish to turn the Latke Puzzle into a race. Have students who are finished turn their books over and call "אֲנִי לְבִיבָה"! The first three students (with the correct answers!) are the winners. Be sure to tell your students not to announce the bottom answer before everyone has finished!

Bring It to Life Write the words נֵס גָּדוֹל הָיָה שָׁם on the board. Ask students to look at the first letter of each word. Ask: Where do we find these letters on Ḥanukkah? (*on the s'vivon, or dreidel, of course.*)

Ask: How do you think the *s'vivon* is different in Israel than it is here? (*S'vivonim in Israel say* נֵס גָּדוֹל הָיָה פֹּה—*a great miracle happened here!*)

You may wish to bring in *s'vivonim* and have a class championship in celebration of Ḥanukkah.

Sample questions, in ascending order of difficulty, include:

1. What's the Hebrew word for [object from chapter]?
2. What's the Hebrew word(s) for [verb from chapter]?
3. Holding up object, ask in Hebrew: [object]? (כֵּן, [object])
4. Ask: יֵשׁ לָנוּ [object in classroom] בַּכִּתָּה? (כֵּן, יֵשׁ לָנוּ [object] בַּכִּתָּה.)
5. Place [object] on a table, ask: מָה יֵשׁ עַל הַשֻּׁלְחָן? (יֵשׁ [object] עַל הַשֻּׁלְחָן.)
6. Place [two objects] in the closet, ask: מָה בָּאָרוֹן? (יֵשׁ [object] וְ[object] בָּאָרוֹן.)
7. Ask: אַתָּה/אַתְּ אוֹהֵב/אוֹהֶבֶת לְהַדְלִיק נֵרוֹת שֶׁל חֲנוּכָּה? (כֵּן, אֲנִי אוֹהֵב/אוֹהֶבֶת לְהַדְלִיק נֵרוֹת שֶׁל חֲנוּכָּה.)
8. Say: Recite the first Ḥanukkah blessing.

You may wish to allow each student a "free latke pass" or allow each to "fry a friend" by asking someone else for an answer.

Game Box
Latke Walk

Write large numbers 1–8 on index cards or sheets of paper. Lay them down in a "walkway" across the classroom floor.

Explain to your students that it is the night before Ḥanukkah, and they are inside a greasy frying pan with eight sizzling latkes. The only way to avoid becoming latkes themselves is by safely stepping across all eight. They do this by correctly answering eight questions.

You may wish to do one of the following:

- Prepare questions beforehand, based on your class level. (Order the questions in ascending order of difficulty.)
- Have students each prepare 3–5 questions, to be shuffled together.
- Use the following sample questions.

Mastering the Milon (p. 62)

• **רֹאשׁ** • Point to your head and say:

הָרֹאשׁ שֶׁל הַמּוֹרֶה/הַמּוֹרָה.

Point to your students' heads, say:

רֹאשׁ שֶׁל ____; רֹאשׁ שֶׁל ____...

 **Captain Grammar** In Hebrew, even more so than English, each word may have many different meanings. רֹאשׁ, for example, may mean "head," "top," "leader," or "beginning," as in רֹאשׁ הַשָּׁנָה—literally, Head (Beginning) of the New Year.

• **עוֹשֶׂה/עוֹשָׂה** • Pretend to be frying latkes.

Say: אֲנִי עוֹשֶׂה/עוֹשָׂה לְבִיבוֹת.

Have students pretend to fry latkes.

Say: ____ עוֹשֶׂה/עוֹשָׂה לְבִיבוֹת;
____ עוֹשֶׂה/עוֹשָׂה לְבִיבוֹת...

Explain that עוֹשֶׂה and עוֹשָׂה mean "do" as well as "make."

• **נוֹתֵן/נוֹתֶנֶת** • Give the dreidel to a student and say:

אֲנִי נוֹתֵן/נוֹתֶנֶת סְבִיבוֹן לְ____.

Then have the students pass the dreidel around the classroom and narrate as they go. For example:

אֲנִי נוֹתֵן סְבִיבוֹן לְשָׂרָה.
אֲנִי נוֹתֶנֶת סְבִיבוֹן לְרִבְקָה;
אֲנִי נוֹתֶנֶת סְבִיבוֹן לְדָנִיאֵל...

• **אוֹמֵר/אוֹמֶרֶת** • Refer students back to the dialogue on page 57.

Say: דָּנִי אוֹמֵר, "אֲנִי מַדְלִיק נֵר רִאשׁוֹן";
לִילִי אוֹמֶרֶת, "לֹא, לֹא!"

Continue this way until students understand that אוֹמֵר and אוֹמֶרֶת mean "says." Explain that אוֹמֵר is the masculine form of the word.

Put It Together Divide the class into groups of three. Have two students in each group engage in the following short skit, with the third student narrating:

• Student 1 pretends to fry latkes. The narrator says:

____ עוֹשֶׂה/עוֹשָׂה לְבִיבוֹת.

• Student 1 gives latkes to Student 2. Narrator:

____ נוֹתֵן/נוֹתֶנֶת לְבִיבוֹת לְ____.

• Student 2 says, "טוֹב!" Narrator:

____ אוֹמֵר/אוֹמֶרֶת, "טוֹב!"

You may wish to give each student the opportunity to narrate the skit. It may be fun to time each group, to see which can perform it the most quickly (with no mistakes!).

Chapter Story: הָעַכְבָּר בַּסְבִיבוֹן

(pp. 62–63)

 **Ready for Reading** Ask students to create sentences that describe their own Ḥanukkah experiences. Students may say:

אֲנִי מַדְלִיקָה נֵרוֹת; אָח גָדוֹל שָׁר בְּרָכוֹת; אַבָּא עוֹשֶׂה לְבִיבוֹת...

Explain to your students that סְבִיבוֹן is the Hebrew name for a *dreidel*, which is actually a Yiddish word. Explain that מַתָּנוֹת is plural for מַתָּנָה, and that אוֹמְרִים is plural for אוֹמֵר/אוֹמֶרֶת.

 **Read Aloud!** Tell your students that they will read the four paragraphs of "הָעַכְבָּר בַּסְבִיבוֹן" differently:

- The first paragraph should be read slowly, one line per student, as the Ḥanukkah scene is set.
- The second paragraph should be read quickly by one student, in a hurried tone, as the search for Achbar takes place.
- The third paragraph should be read energetically by one student except for the words that follow אוֹמְרִים, which should be read by the entire class in unison.
- The fourth paragraph should be read by one student, playing an exhausted, squeaky-voiced Bar, dizzy from his ride in the s'vivon!

Encourage your students to have fun with this long, playful story.

הָעַכְבָּר מִסְתּוֹבֵב...
הַיְלָדִים אוֹמְרִים: "נִי" — נֵס!
הָעַכְבָּר מִסְתּוֹבֵב...
הַיְלָדִים אוֹמְרִים: "גִּי" — גָּדוֹל!
הָעַכְבָּר מִסְתּוֹבֵב...
הַיְלָדִים אוֹמְרִים: "הֵי" — הָיָה!
הָעַכְבָּר מִסְתּוֹבֵב...
הַיְלָדִים אוֹמְרִים: "שִׁי" — שָׁם!

הָעַכְבָּר אוֹמֵר:
"שִׁי" — שֶׁקֶט!
הַסְבִיבוֹן מִסְתּוֹבֵב,
הַבַּיִת מִסְתּוֹבֵב,
הַשֻׁלְחָן מִסְתּוֹבֵב,
הָרֹאשׁ מִסְתּוֹבֵב,
אֲנִי עָיֵף!

63

▼
- אַתְ אוֹהֵב/אוֹהֶבֶת מַתָּנוֹת?
(כֵּן, אֲנִי אוֹהֵב/אוֹהֶבֶת מַתָּנוֹת.)

 **Looking Ahead** Explain to your students that the next chapter will include a tour through the days of the week, including a review of what God created during the very *first* week.

Have your students think about the names of the days of the week in English. Ask: What do all these words have in common? (*The word "day"*) Have them think about the Hebrew word that is included in all the *Hebrew* days of the week.

 **The Extra Mile** You may wish to have your students close their books before asking the following review questions:

- מִי שָׁרָה בְּרָכוֹת? (אִמָּא שָׁרָה בְּרָכוֹת.)
- מִי מַדְלִיקִים נֵרוֹת? (יְלָדִים מַדְלִיקִים נֵרוֹת.)
- מִי עוֹשֶׂה לְבִיבוֹת? (אַבָּא עוֹשֶׂה לְבִיבוֹת.)
- אֵיפֹה בַּר הָעַכְבָּר? (בַּר הָעַכְבָּר בַּסְבִיבוֹן.)

Continue by asking:

- אַתָּה/אַתְ גָר/גָרָה בַּסְבִיבוֹן?
(לֹא, אֲנִי לֹא גָר/גָרָה בַּסְבִיבוֹן.)
- אַתָּה/אַתְ עוֹשֶׂה/עוֹשָׂה לְבִיבוֹת?
(כֵּן, אֲנִי עוֹשֶׂה/עוֹשָׂה לְבִיבוֹת OR
לֹא, אֲנִי לֹא עוֹשֶׂה/עוֹשָׂה לְבִיבוֹת.)

◀

Lesson Objectives

- Students will:
- Continue to develop ease in reading more complex combinations of gendered nouns and verbs.
- Understand the use of _____ וְ in a series of objects.

New Milon Words and Phrases

Core Vocabulary

all, every	כָּל
week	שָׁבוּעַ

Other Useful Vocabulary

Sunday	יוֹם רִאשׁוֹן
Monday	יוֹם שֵׁנִי
Tuesday	יוֹם שְׁלִישִׁי
Wednesday	יוֹם רְבִיעִי
Thursday	יוֹם חֲמִישִׁי
Friday	יוֹם שִׁשִּׁי
Shabbat, Saturday	יוֹם שַׁבָּת
created (m)	בָּרָא
God	אֱלֹהִים

What We'll need

- ❑ Text pages 64–71
- ❑ Word Cards 102–112
- ❑ Picture Cards 22–27
- ❑ Helpful props: a month-by-month calendar, markers and construction paper, six buttons or pennies for each student

Where We Are

In Chapter 8, we hear Dinah's list of creative excuses for missing school—every day of the week! We also review the order of God's creation of the world.

Let's Review

Have a student draw *l'vivot* on two index cards. Have students pass the *l'vivot* to one another using the following formula:

1. Student 1 announces he or she is making *l'vivot*.

(אֲנִי עוֹשֶׂה/עוֹשָׂה לְבִיבוֹת.)

2. Student 1 offers *l'vivot* to Student 2.

(אַתָּה/אַתְּ רוֹצֶה/רוֹצָה לְבִיבוֹת?)

3. Student 1 announces delivery of *l'vivot*.

(אֲנִי נוֹתֵן/נוֹתֶנֶת לְבִיבוֹת לְ_____.)

4. Student 2 acknowledges receipt of *l'vivot*.

(יֵשׁ לִי לְבִיבוֹת.)

When everyone has received the *l'vivot*, say:

(יֵשׁ לָנוּ לְבִיבוֹת!)

Introducing the Lesson

Display Word Cards 104–110 on the chalkboard ledge. Point to each day of the week as you introduce it.

Point to a Jewish calendar page with a full month layout.

- Point to Sunday and say:

בְּיוֹם רִאשׁוֹן, אֲנִי אוֹכֵל/אוֹכֶלֶת עוּגָה.

- To Monday, say:

בְּיוֹם שֵׁנִי, אֲנִי עוֹבֵד/עוֹבֶדֶת כָּל הַיּוֹם.

- To Tuesday, say:

בְּיוֹם שְׁלִישִׁי, אֲנִי עוֹבֵד/עוֹבֶדֶת כָּל הַיּוֹם.

- To Wednesday, say:

בְּיוֹם רְבִיעִי, אֲנִי עוֹבֵד/עוֹבֶדֶת...

- To Thursday, say:

בְּיוֹם חֲמִישִׁי, אֲנִי עוֹבֵד/עוֹבֶדֶת...

- To Friday, say:

בְּיוֹם שִׁשִּׁי, אֲנִי עוֹבֵד/עוֹבֶדֶת...

- To Saturday, say:

בְּיוֹם שַׁבָּת, אֲנִי לֹא עוֹבֵד/עוֹבֶדֶת. יוֹם שַׁבָּת יוֹם מְנוּחָה!

Review each day of the week by pointing to it on the calendar, saying it in Hebrew, and having students repeat.

Ask students to list three or four days of the week on their own!

Mastering the Milon (p. 65)

• **כָּל** • List the names of each of your students, then say:

כָּל הַיְלָדִים, כָּל הַכִּתָּה!

Ask: What do you think כָּל means?

• **יוֹם רִאשׁוֹן** • Draw a ḥanukkiah containing a first-night candle on the board. Point to the candle and say:

הַנֵּר הָרִאשׁוֹן.

Point to Sunday on the calendar, say: יוֹם רִאשׁוֹן.

Point to the first book in a stack or in a bookshelf, say:

הַסֵּפֶר הָרִאשׁוֹן.

 Captain Grammar Tell your students that in order to say, "On Tuesday" or "On Sunday," we add the prefix _____בְּ—which usually means "in," but can also be used for "on"—to the name of the day.

For the teaching of יוֹם שֵׁנִי through יוֹם שִׁישִׁי, point to each day on the calendar and ask individual students:

מָה אַתָּה/אַתְּ עוֹשֶׂה/עוֹשָׂה בְּיוֹם _____ ?

Have them answer in complete sentences. Explain that the answers may be true or "creative."

Sample answers include:

- בְּיוֹם שֵׁנִי, אֲנִי כּוֹתֵב בַּכִּתָּה.
- בְּיוֹם שְׁלִישִׁי, אֲנִי שָׁר.
- בְּיוֹם חֲמִישִׁי, אֲנִי עוֹשָׂה חַלָּה.
- בְּיוֹם שִׁישִׁי, אֲנִי מַדְלִיקָה נֵרוֹת.

• **יוֹם שַׁבָּת** • Have students think of Hebrew words that are important on Yom Shabbat. Answers may include: מְנוּחָה, חַלָּה, and נֵרוֹת.

• **שָׁבוּעַ** • Point to the calendar and repeat each day of the week. Circle the entire row of days and say: שָׁבוּעַ.

Circle the next week, repeat: שָׁבוּעַ.

Continue this way until students understand that שָׁבוּעַ means "week."

 **Bring It to Life** Sing (or invite your synagogue's cantor in to sing) "*Shavua Tov*" with the class. Explain that this song is sung during Havdalah, after Shabbat ends. Ask: What do the words of this song mean? (*A good week*)

Put It Together Have students name a food they eat every day of the week, then a food they eat only on a specific day of the week. They should include כָּל and שָׁבוּעַ in their answers. (Again, explain that "creative" answers are okay.)

Sample answers include:

- כָּל הַשָּׁבוּעַ, אֲנִי אוֹכֶלֶת לֶחֶם, אֲבָל בְּיוֹם שִׁישִׁי, אֲנִי אוֹכֶלֶת תַּפּוּחַ.
- כָּל הַשָּׁבוּעַ אֲנִי אוֹכֵל עוּגָה, אֲבָל בְּיוֹם רִאשׁוֹן, אֲנִי אוֹכֵל פִּיצָה.

Chapter Story: דִינָה שְׂמֵחָה

(pp. 64–65)

 **Ready for Reading** This is an ideal time to review some "oldies" that are included in the chapter story: Display Word Cards 35 and 52 on the chalkboard ledge (הוֹלֵךְ/הוֹלֶכֶת and שָׂמֵחַ/שְׂמֵחָה). Ask: What do these words mean? (*goes, walks; happy*)

Challenge students to create two sentences that include both words. (The sentences must be related to one another!) Sample answers include:

- אֲנִי הוֹלֶכֶת לַכִּתָּה; אֲנִי שְׂמֵחָה.
- דָוִד לֹא שָׂמֵחַ. הַמִשְׁפָּחָה הוֹלֶכֶת לַכִּתָּה!

Have a student read the Hebrew title and English sentence aloud. Ask your students to think of 1–3 word excuses—in Hebrew, of course—why they might not be able to go to school. (*Answers may include:* אֵין לִי מִשְׁקָפַיִם, קַר, גֶשֶׁם, *etc.*)

 **Read Aloud!** Assign three students to read the parts of: דִינָה, the narrator, and אַבָּא. (Or assign a different דִינָה for each day of the week.) Tell the class that they will announce the names of the days together. Read the entire story.

 **The Extra Mile** Read the entire story together a second time. This time, after each excuse is given, ask דִינָה:

אַתְ לֹא הוֹלֶכֶת לַכִּתָּה?!

Have דִינָה (or each דִינָה) provide reasons in complete sentences:

- יוֹם רִאשׁוֹן: לֹא, אֵין כִּתָּה בְּיוֹם רִאשׁוֹן.
- יוֹם שֵׁנִי: לֹא, גֶשֶׁם בְּיוֹם שֵׁנִי.
- יוֹם שְׁלִישִׁי: לֹא, קַר בְּיוֹם שְׁלִישִׁי.
- יוֹם רְבִיעִי: לֹא, חַם בְּיוֹם רְבִיעִי.
- יוֹם חֲמִישִׁי: לֹא, אֵין לִי מִשְׁקָפַיִם בְּיוֹם חֲמִישִׁי.
- יוֹם שִׁשִּׁי: לֹא, אֲנִי עֲיֵפָה בְּיוֹם שִׁשִּׁי.
- יוֹם שַׁבָּת: לֹא, אֵין כִּתָּה בְּיוֹם שַׁבָּת *OR* יוֹם שַׁבָּת יוֹם מְנוּחָה!

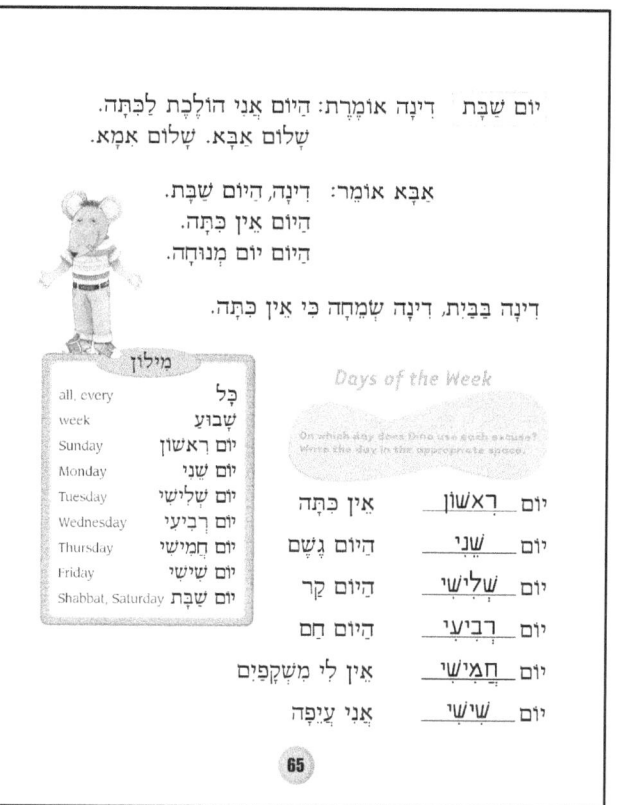

Days of the Week (p. 65)

Have students complete the exercise by filling in the days in their appropriate spaces. Review answers by having students each read a day and its corresponding excuse aloud.

Have students come up with their own creative excuses for missing school and write them on the board. Encourage them to be silly—as long as they use רַק עִבְרִית—Hebrew only! Sample answers include:

- בְּיוֹם שִׁשִּׁי, אֲנִי לֹא הוֹלֵךְ לַכִּתָּה. אֵין לִי עִפָּרוֹן.
- בְּיוֹם שְׁלִישִׁי, אֲנִי לֹא הוֹלֵךְ לַכִּתָּה. אֲנִי עָיֵף.
- בְּיוֹם חֲמִישִׁי, אֲנִי לֹא הוֹלֶכֶת לַכִּתָּה. אֲנִי אוֹכֶלֶת עוּגָה גְדוֹלָה.

Take a class vote to determine the most creative excuse. Remind them that they'd better not try to use the excuse with you!

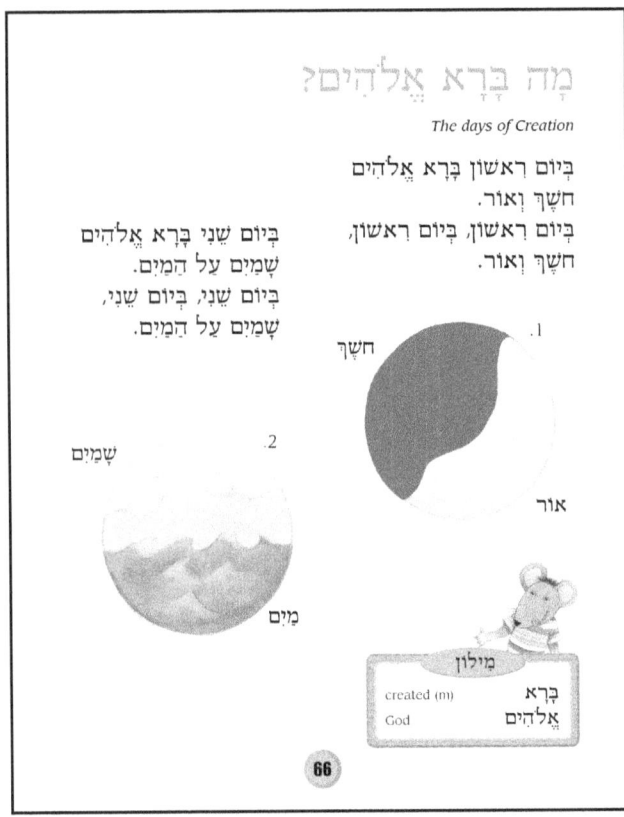

Mastering the Milon (p. 66)

• **אֱלֹהִים** • Many students will know אֱלֹהִים from their prayer study. Ask: מָה נוֹתֵן אֱלֹהִים?
Answers may include: אֱלֹהִים נוֹתֵן תּוֹרָה; אֱלֹהִים נוֹתֵן לֶחֶם; etc.; any correctly phrased answer is acceptable!

Our Tradition Your students may find it interesting that אֱלֹהִים looks like a plural form. But if there is only one God, why use the plural? Explain that one answer our ancient rabbis give is that the word אֱלֹהִים refers to the many aspects of God (love, justice, etc.).

• **בָּרָא** • Say:

אֱלֹהִים בָּרָא פְּרָחִים; אֱלֹהִים בָּרָא גֶשֶׁם; אֱלֹהִים בָּרָא אוֹר.

Ask: What do you think בָּרָא means?

Put It Together Have students list three things that God made. The lists may include anything they wish. Answers may include:

- אֱלֹהִים בָּרָא אִמָּא וְאַבָּא.
- אֱלֹהִים בָּרָא לוּחַ וְסֵפֶר וּמַחְבֶּרֶת.
- אֱלֹהִים בָּרָא אוֹר.

Chapter Story: מָה בָּרָא אֱלֹהִים (pp. 66–69)

Ready for Reading Congratulate your students on an important step: They are now reading a story based on actual words and phrases from the Torah!

Spend some time teaching the words surrounding the days of Creation. You may wish to display Picture Cards 22–27 on the chalkboard ledge and refer to them as you teach each word:

• **אוֹר** and **חֹשֶׁךְ** • Flick the classroom lights off.
Say: חֹשֶׁךְ!
Then on again: אוֹר!
Say: אֱלֹהִים בָּרָא (lights off) חֹשֶׁךְ וְ (on) אוֹר!

• **שָׁמַיִם** and **מַיִם** • Point to the picture of the sea and sky on page 66. Pretend to be swimming and say: מַיִם.
Pretend to be flying, say: שָׁמַיִם!
Explain that שָׁמַיִם means "sky", not "clouds" or "air."

• **עֵצִים** and **פְּרָחִים** • Point to the picture of the trees on page 67, say: עֵצִים.
(Students should already know פְּרָחִים.)

• **שֶׁמֶשׁ, יָרֵחַ** and **כּוֹכָבִים** • Have students draw a daytime and a nighttime sky on the chalkboard (or, if time allows, on construction paper with markers). Have them label the sun, moon, and stars in Hebrew. Ask:

אֵיפֹה הַשֶׁמֶשׁ? אֵיפֹה הַיָרֵחַ? אֵיפֹה הַכּוֹכָבִים?
(בַּשָׁמַיִם!)

• **צִיפּוֹרִים** and **דָגִים** • Point to the picture of the birds and fish on page 68. Ask individual students:

מָה אַתָּה/אַתְּ אוֹהֵב/אוֹהֶבֶת–
דָגִים אוֹ צִיפּוֹרִים?

• **אֲנָשִׁים** and **חַיוֹת** • Point to the picture of the animals and people on page 68. Explain that אֲנָשִׁים are people, while חַיוֹת refers to all other land animals.

 **Read Aloud!** Assign students to read the first two lines of each paragraph. Have the entire class "respond" with the remaining lines in each paragraph.

 **The Extra Mile** Have students read the story again. This time, ask "quick questions" after each paragraph:

1. מַה בָּרָא אֱלֹהִים בְּיוֹם רִאשׁוֹן?
(בְּיוֹם רִאשׁוֹן בָּרָא אֱלֹהִים חֹשֶׁךְ וְאוֹר.)

2. מַה בָּרָא אֱלֹהִים בְּיוֹם שֵׁנִי?
(בְּיוֹם שֵׁנִי בָּרָא אֱלֹהִים מַיִם וְשָׁמַיִם.)

3. מַה בָּרָא אֱלֹהִים בְּיוֹם שְׁלִישִׁי?
(בְּיוֹם שְׁלִישִׁי בָּרָא אֱלֹהִים פְּרָחִים וְעֵצִים.)

Ask a student:

אַתָּה/אַתְּ אוֹהֵב/אוֹהֶבֶת עֵצִים?
(כֵּן, אֲנִי אוֹהֵב/אוֹהֶבֶת עֵצִים.)

4. מַה בָּרָא אֱלֹהִים בְּיוֹם רְבִיעִי?
(בְּיוֹם רְבִיעִי אֱלֹהִים בָּרָא שֶׁמֶשׁ, יָרֵחַ, וְכוֹכָבִים.)

Ask: מַה עוֹשָׂה הַשֶּׁמֶשׁ?
(הַשֶּׁמֶשׁ עוֹשָׂה אוֹר.)

5. מַה בָּרָא אֱלֹהִים בְּיוֹם חֲמִישִׁי?
(בְּיוֹם חֲמִישִׁי בָּרָא אֱלֹהִים דָּגִים וְצִפֳּרִים.)

Ask: אֵיפֹה יֵשׁ דָּגִים?

(You may need to coach students to:
(יֵשׁ דָּגִים בַּמַּיִם.)
אֵיפֹה יֵשׁ צִפֳּרִים?
(יֵשׁ צִפֳּרִים בַּשָּׁמַיִם.)

6. מַה בָּרָא אֱלֹהִים בְּיוֹם שִׁשִּׁי?
(בְּיוֹם שִׁשִּׁי בָּרָא אֱלֹהִים חַיוֹת וַאֲנָשִׁים.)

Ask: יֵשׁ לְךָ/לָךְ אֲנָשִׁים בַּבַּיִת?
(כֵּן, יֵשׁ לִי אֲנָשִׁים בַּבַּיִת.)

7. מַה יֵשׁ בְּיוֹם שַׁבָּת? (בְּיוֹם שַׁבָּת יֵשׁ מְנוּחָה. OR בְּיוֹם שַׁבָּת יֵשׁ שָׁלוֹם.)

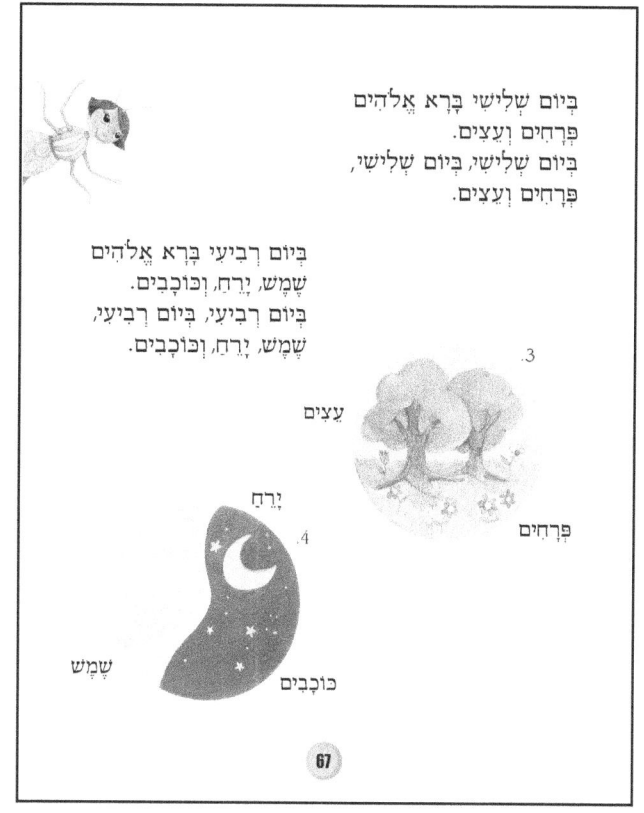

בְּיוֹם שְׁלִישִׁי בָּרָא אֱלֹהִים
פְּרָחִים וְעֵצִים.
בְּיוֹם שְׁלִישִׁי, בְּיוֹם שְׁלִישִׁי,
פְּרָחִים וְעֵצִים.

בְּיוֹם רְבִיעִי בָּרָא אֱלֹהִים
שֶׁמֶשׁ, יָרֵחַ, וְכוֹכָבִים.
בְּיוֹם רְבִיעִי, בְּיוֹם רְבִיעִי,
שֶׁמֶשׁ, יָרֵחַ, וְכוֹכָבִים.

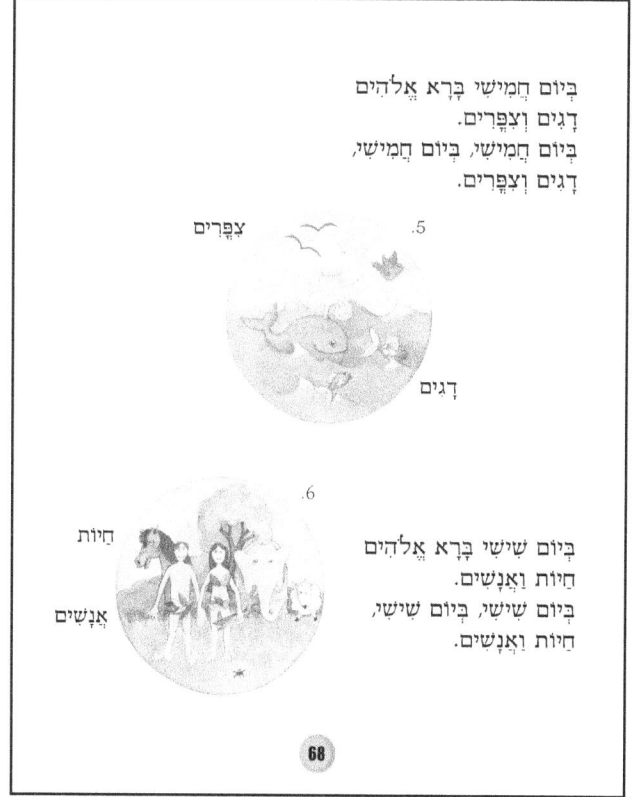

בְּיוֹם חֲמִישִׁי בָּרָא אֱלֹהִים
דָּגִים וְצִפֳּרִים.
בְּיוֹם חֲמִישִׁי, בְּיוֹם חֲמִישִׁי,
דָּגִים וְצִפֳּרִים.

בְּיוֹם שִׁשִּׁי בָּרָא אֱלֹהִים
חַיוֹת וַאֲנָשִׁים.
בְּיוֹם שִׁשִּׁי, בְּיוֹם שִׁשִּׁי,
חַיוֹת וַאֲנָשִׁים.

יוֹם שַׁבָּת, יוֹם שַׁבָּת,
יוֹם מְנוּחָה.
יוֹם שַׁבָּת, יוֹם שַׁבָּת,
יוֹם מְנוּחָה.
שַׁבָּת שָׁלוֹם!

כּוּלָם שָׁרִים "שַׁבָּת שָׁלוֹם."

69

 Bring It to Life Using markers (or watercolors) and construction paper, have students draw their own artistic version of what was created on each day.

You may wish to have each student draw all six days, or divide the class into six groups to work on a single day together. Have students label each object with its Hebrew name.

 Using the Photograph Have students look at the photo on page 69 and ask:

- מָה עַל הַשׁוּלְחָן? (פְּרָחִים וְנֵרוֹת וְיַיִן וְחַלָה עַל הַשׁוּלְחָן.)
- מִי שָׁר "שַׁבָּת שָׁלוֹם"? (יֶלֶד שָׁר; אִמָא שָׂרָה; אַבָּא שָׁר...)

 **Game Box** Play "מָצָאתִי—I Found It!" as described on page 16. Tell your students that this game will be based on "מַה בָּרָא אֱלֹהִים?" on pages 66–69.

You may wish to include an extra bonus question (see below) as well. Bonus questions are available only to the student who answers the initial question and must be answered in Hebrew.

Sample questions, in ascending levels of difficulty, include:

- Find the word that means "darkness." (חֹשֶׁךְ) Bonus point: What was created on the same day as darkness? (אוֹר)
- What three "celestial" objects did God create? (כּוֹכָבִים, יָרֵחַ, שֶׁמֶשׁ) Bonus: Which was created first, light or the sun? (אוֹר)
- מַה בָּרָא אֱלֹהִים בְּיוֹם שְׁלִישִׁי? (פְּרָחִים וְעֵצִים.) Bonus: פֶּרַח עוֹשֶׂה תַפּוּחַ? (לֹא, פֶּרַח לֹא עוֹשֶׂה תַפּוּחַ.)
- מַה גָר בַּמַיִם? (דָגִים.) Bonus: מַה גָר בַּשָׁמַיִם? (צִפֳּרִים.)
- מָה עוֹשֶׂה אֱלֹהִים בְּיוֹם שַׁבָּת? (מְנוּחָה.) Bonus: אֱלֹהִים בָּרָא חַיוֹת בְּיוֹם שַׁבָּת? (לֹא, אֱלֹהִים לֹא בָּרָא חַיוֹת בְּיוֹם שַׁבָּת.)

You may wish to play a version of the game in which students create questions for one another. Award an extra point to students who "stump" the rest of the class.

The student with the most points at the end of the game is the winner.

Shalom Ivrit 1 • Teacher's Edition

God's World (p. 70)

Have students complete the exercise by writing the Hebrew word under its matching picture. Review answers by pointing to each picture and having students say the Hebrew words.

> **Game Box**
> **Creation Bingo**
>
> Have students draw a 3 x 3 chart (see page 70 of the pupil edition) on a sheet of paper. Ask them to create quick sketches of the nine objects in the chart *in any order they choose.* Distribute six buttons or pennies to each student.
>
> Call names of objects listed on page 70, one at a time. Have students place markers on the correct pictures as they are called. The first student to connect three in a row, in any direction, calls "Bingo!" and receives a point.
>
> The first student with three points is the winner.

Chapter 8

Days of the Week (p. 71)

Have students complete the exercise by writing the number for each day of the week. Review answers by having seven students announce each day, in order, beginning with יוֹם רִאשׁוֹן.

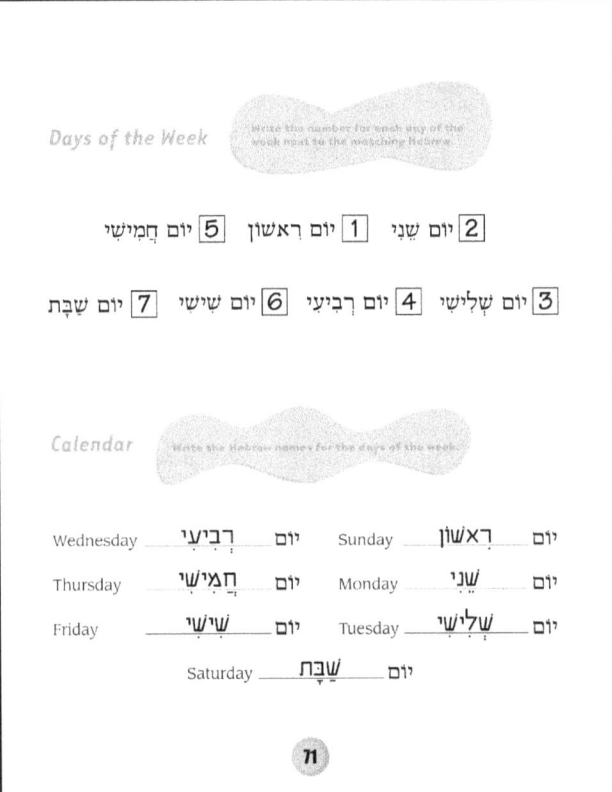

> **Game Box**
> **All Mixed Up!**
>
> Shuffle Picture Cards 22–27. Hand the cards to a student. Explain that you will provide a series of "Creation objects," and that the student should arrange the cards on the chalkboard ledge in the correct order.
>
> For example, if you say: אוֹר, שֶׁמֶשׁ, דָּגִים, the student should place Picture Cards 22, 25, then 26 on the board.
>
> Using a stopwatch or a watch with a second hand, time each student. Subtract three seconds for incorrect cards, or cards out of order.
>
> The student with the fewest number of seconds is the winner.

Calendar (p. 71)

Have students complete the exercise by writing the Hebrew names for each day of the week. Check student answers by calling on each student to read the entire list.

> **Bring It to Life** Give students 8½" x 11" sheets of paper, and ask them to create their own "weekly planners." Have students create a grid, as pictured to the left, then fill in the planner with their schedule for the upcoming week. Allow students to use English in the schedule (אֲנִי עוֹשֶׂה/עוֹשָׂה) column, but encourage them to use as much Hebrew as possible. Suggestions include:
>
> • כִּתָּה הַיּוֹם.
> • אֲנִי עוֹבֶדֶת בַּבַּיִת.
> • חַג חֲנוּכָּה.

Looking Ahead

Explain to your students that in the next chapter they will learn words having to do with Tu B'Shevat—the birthday of the trees.

Tell students that *"yom huledet"* means "birthday" in Hebrew. Ask your students to think about how we might say "happy birthday" in Hebrew.

Lesson Objectives

Students will:

- Develop strength in conversational skills with the addition of לְךָ/לָךְ and עִם.
- Practice incorporating possessives with an increased use of the prefix ‎לְ‎ּ‎.

New Milon Words and Phrases

Core Vocabulary

morning	בּוֹקֶר
thank you	תּוֹדָה
night	לַיְלָה
joy, happiness	שִׂמְחָה
stands (m/f)	עוֹמֵד/עוֹמֶדֶת
eyes	עֵינַיִם
with	עִם
to you (m/f)	לְךָ/לָךְ

Tu B'Shevat–Related Vocabulary

tree(s)	עֵץ/עֵצִים
birthday	יוֹם הוּלֶדֶת
fruit (pl)	פֵּרוֹת

Other Useful Vocabulary

party	חֲגִיגָה

What We'll need

- ❑ Text pages 72–79
- ❑ Word Cards 113–124
- ❑ Picture Cards 10, 18, and 19
- ❑ Helpful props: markers, poster board, and construction paper

Where We Are

In Chapter 9, we celebrate three birthdays. First, Tu B'Shevat—the birthday of the trees. Then we join Bar Ha'achbar, the host of a very unusual birthday party. Last but not least, we listen in as Lili and Saba decide on a birthday gift together.

Let's Review

Conduct a "student pantomime" to review God's creations and the days of the week from the previous chapter.

For each day of the week, ask:

מַה בָּרָא אֱלֹהִים בְּ [day of the week]?

Provide "performers" with index cards containing works of Creation written on them. Students provide clues by pantomiming or drawing their objects for their classmates.

Answers for each day are:

1. בְּיוֹם רִאשׁוֹן בָּרָא אֱלֹהִים חֹשֶׁךְ וְאוֹר.
2. בְּיוֹם שֵׁנִי בָּרָא אֱלֹהִים מַיִם וְשָׁמַיִם.
3. בְּיוֹם שְׁלִישִׁי בָּרָא אֱלֹהִים פְּרָחִים וְעֵצִים.
4. בְּיוֹם רְבִיעִי בָּרָא אֱלֹהִים שֶׁמֶשׁ, יָרֵחַ, וְכוֹכָבִים.
5. בְּיוֹם חֲמִישִׁי בָּרָא אֱלֹהִים דָּגִים וְצִפֳּרִים.
6. בְּיוֹם שִׁשִּׁי בָּרָא אֱלֹהִים חַיּוֹת וַאֲנָשִׁים.
7. יוֹם שַׁבָּת יוֹם מְנוּחָה.

Introducing the Lesson

Remove Picture Cards 18 and 19.

- Hand Picture Card 18 to a boy and say:

  אֲנִי נוֹתֵן/נוֹתֶנֶת לְךָ לֶחֶם.

  Extend your hand for the student to return the לֶחֶם to you. Say: תּוֹדָה!

- Hand Picture Card 19 to a girl, say:

  אֲנִי נוֹתֵן/נוֹתֶנֶת לָךְ עוּגָה.

  Extend your hand for the student to return the עוּגָה, say: תּוֹדָה!

- Repeat with each member of the class.

Invite pairs of students to rise (you may wish to invite students of the same gender, to avoid giggles). Say:

עוֹמֵד עִם _____ ; עוֹמֶדֶת עִם _____.

Continue to have pairs of students rise. Once students understand that עִם means "with," have classmates narrate the "standing" pairs.

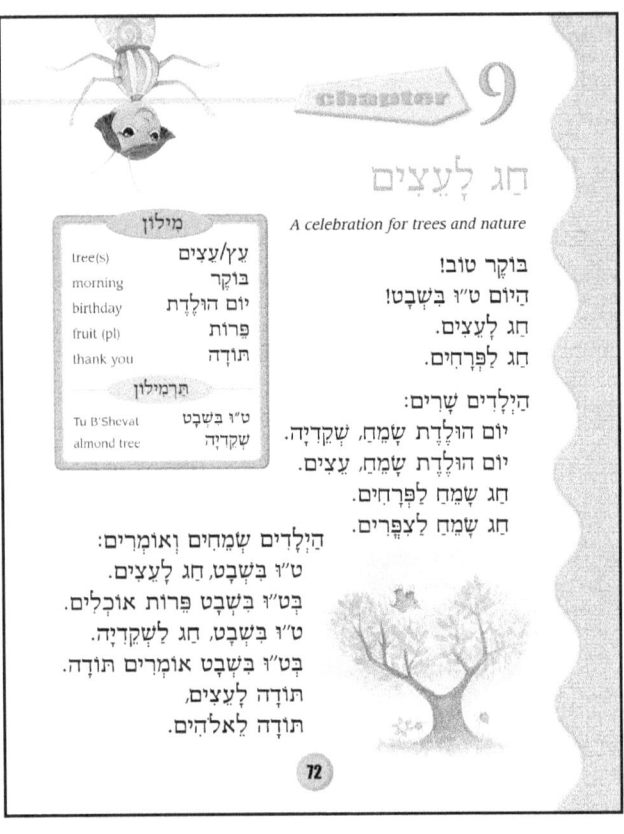

Mastering the Milon (p. 72)

• **עֵץ/עֵצִים** • Draw a tree on the board. Say: הִנֵה עֵץ.
Draw another tree, say: הִנֵה עֵצִים.
Ask: What do you think עֵץ means?

• **פֵּרוֹת** • Draw apples on one tree and bananas on another. Point to the apples and say: הָעֵץ נוֹתֵן תַפּוּחַ;
point to the bananas, say: הָעֵץ נוֹתֵן בָּנָנָה;
point to both, say: הָעֵץ נוֹתֵן פֵּרוֹת

 **Our Tradition** Say: בּוֹרֵא פְּרִי הַגָפֶן.
Ask: What do we recite this blessing over? (wine) Point out that פְּרִי is the singular form of פֵּרוֹת—fruit. Ask: What fruit is wine made from? (grapes)

• **תוֹדָה** • Extend your hand to a student holding a pencil and say: אֲנִי רוֹצֶה/רוֹצָה עִפָּרוֹן.
Receive the pencil, say, תוֹדָה!
Return the pencil, put your hand to your ear, awaiting a reply. The student should reply, תוֹדָה!
Continue this way until students understand that תוֹדָה means "thank you."

• **בּוֹקֶר** • Pretend to be waking up. Yawn and say:
בּוֹקֶר טוֹב!
Look out (or pretend to look out) the window, say:
בּוֹקֶר יָפֶה!

• **יוֹם הוּלֶדֶת** • Refer to the question asked at the end of the previous session: How do you think we say "happy birthday" in Hebrew? To the tune of "Happy Birthday," sing:
יוֹם הוּלֶדֶת שָׂמֵחַ/יוֹם הוּלֶדֶת שָׂמֵחַ...
Students should recognize יוֹם and שָׂמֵחַ—explain that הוּלֶדֶת means "birth"!

Captain Grammar Your students may wonder what the two apostrophes inside "ט״ו" stand for. Explain that in Hebrew these marks signify that letters are being used as numbers. Here, ט represents 9, and ו represents 6. Together we have the holiday's date—the 15th of Shevat!

Explain to your students that a שְׁקֵדִיָה is an almond tree.

 **Read Aloud!** Read the entire story to the class. Read slowly, with emphasis on the ים endings, to provide students with a sense of the poem's rhyme and rhythm.

Assign students to read one or two lines each. Challenge them to imagine the objects named in the poem without thinking about the English at all!

Chapter Story: חַג לָעֵצִים (p. 72)

Ready for Reading
Ask:
ט״וּ־בִּשְׁבָט יוֹם הוּלֶדֶת שֶׁל עֵצִים?
(כֵּן, ט״וּ־בִּשְׁבָט יוֹם הוּלֶדֶת שֶׁל עֵצִים.)
(Many students will know that Tu B'Shevat is the "birthday of the trees.")

Shalom Ivrit 1 • Teacher's Edition

 **The Extra Mile** Have students do a "fast read" of the poem. Ask the following questions after each paragraph, or once the entire poem has been read.

Paragraph 1:

Have your students answer these questions כֵּן אוֹ לֹא:

• ט״וּ בִּשְׁבָט חַג לִסְפָרִים? (לֹא.)
• ט״וּ בִּשְׁבָט חַג לְעַכְבָּר? (לֹא.)
• ט״וּ בִּשְׁבָט חַג לְעֵצִים? (כֵּן.)

Paragraph 2:

• מָה שָׁרִים הַיְלָדִים?
(הַיְלָדִים שָׁרִים, "יוֹם הוּלֶדֶת שָׂמֵחַ.")
• לְמִי שָׁרִים הַיְלָדִים, "חַג שָׂמֵחַ"?
(לִפְרָחִים וְגַם לַצִפֳּרִים.)

Paragraph 3:

• מָה אוֹכְלִים הַיְלָדִים בְּט״וּ-בִּשְׁבָט?
(בְּט״וּ-בִּשְׁבָט, הַיְלָדִים אוֹכְלִים פֵּרוֹת.)
• מָה אוֹמְרִים הַיְלָדִים בְּט״וּ-בִּשְׁבָט?
(בְּט״וּ-בִּשְׁבָט, הַיְלָדִים אוֹמְרִים תּוֹדָה.)

Name That Flower (p. 73)

Have students complete the exercise by finding the five Hebrew words that have the same meaning as the five numbered English words. Then have students write the letters in the shaded column in the appropriate spaces in the puzzle.

Check answers by calling on students to announce the five correct Hebrew words, then the solution to the puzzle.

Game Box Play "Scrambled!" as described on page 18.

In this version of the game, have students create as many words as they can using the 18 letters from the numbered lines on page 73. You may wish to allow students to spell any word they've learned thus far in *Shalom Ivrit*, or to concentrate only on chapters you choose.

Give students five minutes to write down as many words as they can. Unless your students are super-spellers,

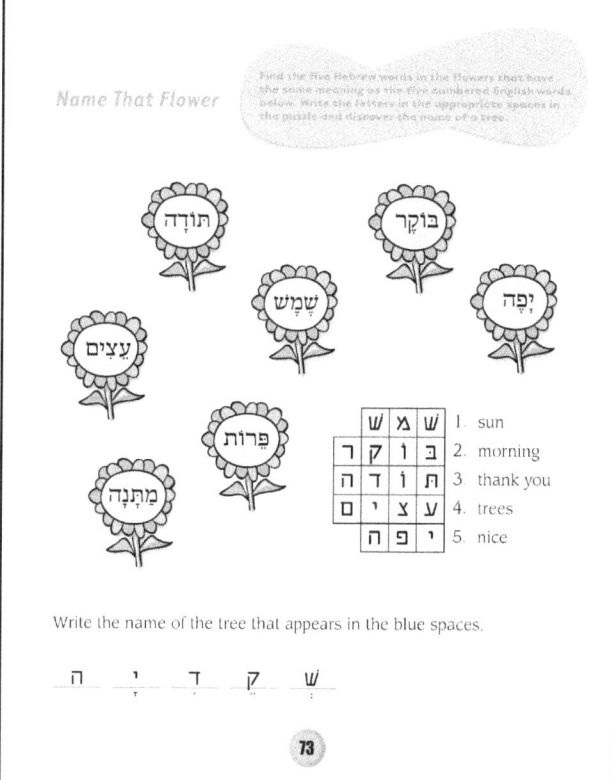

allow them to use the book. (Allow them to substitute final *mem* for "regular" *mem* at the end of a word.)

Once time is up, have students alternate reading words from their lists. Students should cross out words on their lists as they hear them. Continue until all unique words have been read.

Students receive points for unique words, based on the number of letters in the words:

2 or 3 letters: 1 point
4 letters: 2 points
5 letters: 3 points
6 letters: 4 points

The student with the most points is the winner!

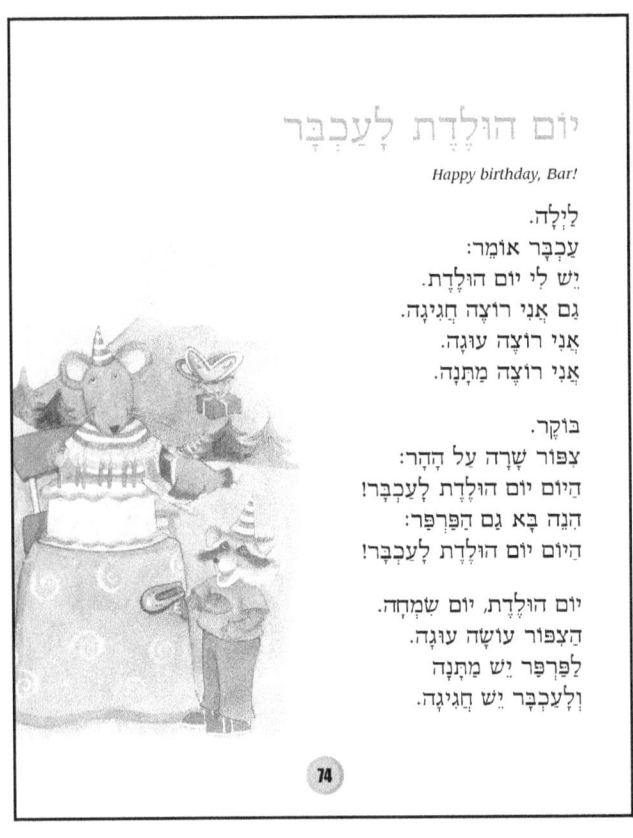

יוֹם הוּלֶדֶת לְעַכְבָּר

Happy birthday, Bar!

לַיְלָה.
עַכְבָּר אוֹמֵר:
יֵשׁ לִי יוֹם הוּלֶדֶת.
גַּם אֲנִי רוֹצֶה חֲגִיגָה.
אֲנִי רוֹצֶה עוּגָה.
אֲנִי רוֹצֶה מַתָּנָה.

בּוֹקֶר.
צִפּוֹר שָׁרָה עַל הָהָר:
הַיּוֹם יוֹם הוּלֶדֶת לְעַכְבָּר!
הִנֵּה בָּא גַם הַפַּרְפַּר:
הַיּוֹם יוֹם הוּלֶדֶת לְעַכְבָּר!

יוֹם הוּלֶדֶת, יוֹם שִׂמְחָה.
הַצִּפּוֹר עוֹשָׂה עוּגָה.
לַפַּרְפַּר יֵשׁ מַתָּנָה
וְלָעַכְבָּר יֵשׁ חֲגִיגָה.

74

Chapter Story: יוֹם הוּלֶדֶת לְעַכְבָּר

(pp. 74–75)

Ready for Reading Explain to your students that they'll see a few new words in this story, including צִפּוֹר, the singular form of צִפֳּרִים. They'll also climb onto הָהָר—the mountain, fly with a פַּרְפַּר—butterfly, and meet a new חָבֵר—friend.

Read Aloud! Divide the class into four groups. Assign each group a paragraph from the story on pages 74–75 (consider all lines on page 75 as one paragraph). Provide each group with a sheet of posterboard and markers. Have each group create an illustration based on its paragraph.

Then have groups create three new sentences based on their illustrations. For example, Group 1 might say:

1. יוֹם הוּלֶדֶת שֶׁל בָּר.
2. בָּר רוֹצֶה חֲגִיגָה.
3. בָּר רוֹצֶה עוּגָה.

Mastering the Milon (p. 75)

• **חֲגִיגָה** • Point to the picture on pages 74–75 and say:

יֵשׁ עוּגָה, יֵשׁ נֵרוֹת, יֵשׁ מַתָּנוֹת.
יֵשׁ חֲגִיגָה גְּדוֹלָה!

Ask: What do you think חֲגִיגָה means?

• **שִׂמְחָה** • Say:

שַׁבָּת יוֹם מְנוּחָה.
וְשַׁבָּת גַּם יוֹם שִׂמְחָה.
יוֹם הוּלֶדֶת יוֹם מַתָּנוֹת.
וְיוֹם הוּלֶדֶת גַּם יוֹם שִׂמְחָה!

Ask: What do you think שִׂמְחָה means?

Put It Together Have students list days of the year that are reason for שִׂמְחָה—joy or happiness. Have them also mention if it is a good day for a party! Provide an example:

יוֹם פּוּרִים יוֹם שִׂמְחָה. יֵשׁ לָנוּ חֲגִיגָה!

Other examples include:

• יוֹם הוּלֶדֶת יוֹם שִׂמְחָה. יֵשׁ לָנוּ חֲגִיגָה!
• יוֹם שַׁבָּת יוֹם שִׂמְחָה.

Captain Grammar Students may notice that the word שִׂמְחָה looks a lot like words they know: שָׂמֵחַ and שְׂמֵחָה. Explain that the words are related to one another—שָׂמֵחַ and שְׂמֵחָה mean "happy," while שִׂמְחָה means "happiness."

• **לַיְלָה** • Pretend to wake up and say:

בּוֹקֶר טוֹב!
לַיְלָה טוֹב!

Pretend to go to sleep, say:
Snore.

• **עוֹמֵד/עוֹמֶדֶת** • Sit down, then stand up tall. Say:

אֲנִי עוֹמֵד/עוֹמֶדֶת.

Gesture for a student of the opposite gender to stand, say:

_____ עוֹמֵד/עוֹמֶדֶת.

Continue until students understand that עוֹמֵד and עוֹמֶדֶת mean "stand."

Have each group present their "storyboard" to the rest of the class by:
- Reading the paragraph aloud. (Each member of the group should read at least one line.)
- Pointing to the appropriate places in the illustration as they read.
- Reading their three new sentences.

 **The Extra Mile** You may wish to ask students questions based on their "storyboards." Sample questions for each paragraph include:

Paragraph 1:
- מָה אוֹמֵר הָעַכְבָּר? (יֵשׁ לִי יוֹם הוּלֶדֶת...)
- הָעַכְבָּר רוֹצֶה חֲגִיגָה? (כֵּן, הָעַכְבָּר רוֹצֶה חֲגִיגָה.)
- הָעַכְבָּר רוֹצֶה עוּגָה? (כֵּן, הָעַכְבָּר רוֹצֶה עוּגָה.)

Paragraph 2:
- אֵיפֹה שָׁרָה הַצִּפּוֹר? (הַצִּפּוֹר שָׁרָה עַל הָהָר.)
- מָה שָׁרָה הַצִּפּוֹר? (הַצִּפּוֹר שָׁרָה, "הַיּוֹם יוֹם הוּלֶדֶת לָעַכְבָּר".)
- מָה אוֹמֵר הַפַּרְפַּר? (הַפַּרְפַּר אוֹמֵר, "הַיּוֹם יוֹם הוּלֶדֶת לָעַכְבָּר".)

Paragraph 3:
- מָה עוֹשָׂה הַצִּפּוֹר? (הַצִּפּוֹר עוֹשָׂה עוּגָה.)
- מָה יֵשׁ לַפַּרְפַּר? (יֵשׁ לַפַּרְפַּר מַתָּנָה.)
- לְמִי יֵשׁ חֲגִיגָה? (לָעַכְבָּר יֵשׁ חֲגִיגָה.)

Paragraph 4:
- אֵיפֹה עוֹמֵד בַּר הָעַכְבָּר? (בַּר הָעַכְבָּר עוֹמֵד עַל הָהָר.)
- מִי עוֹמֵד עַל הָהָר? (בַּר הָעַכְבָּר.)

 **Bring It to Life** Ask students to think of words or phrases they might use in a birthday card. Suggestions include:

חָבֵר, עוּגָה, חֲגִיגָה, יוֹם הוּלֶדֶת שָׂמֵחַ, and שִׂמְחָה.

Have students create their own birthday cards for friends or family members using markers and construction paper. Encourage them to be creative, using רַק עִבְרִית—Hebrew only!

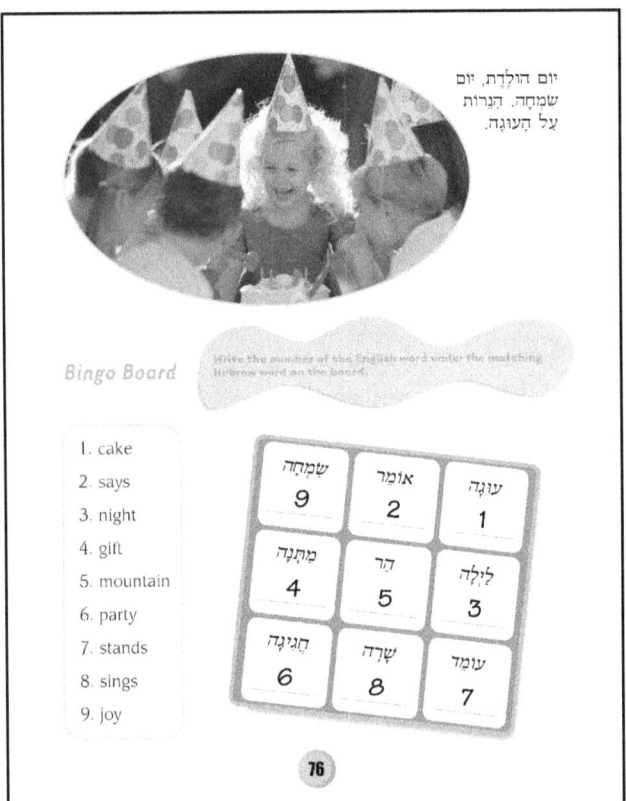

Bingo Board (p. 76)

Have students complete the exercise by writing the number of the English word beneath the matching Hebrew word. Check answers by reading through the list of English words and having students read the matching Hebrew word aloud.

Game Box Play "Tic-Tac-Toe on the Go," as described on page 17.

Arrange nine chairs in three rows of three chairs each. Prepare ten strips of paper—five white and five blue—to use as "markers."

Write the nine Hebrew words from page 76 onto nine separate index cards. Place them, face up, in random order, on each of the nine desks.

Divide the class into two teams: א and ב. Ask a member of א to choose a number between 1 and 10, and then complete the corresponding phrase from the following list. Allow students to look at the words on the desks as they choose.

1. אֲנִי עוֹמֵד/עוֹמֶדֶת עַל הָ_____. (הַר)
2. יֵשׁ מַתָּנוֹת וְעוּגָה בַּ_____. (חֲגִיגָה)
3. יֵשׁ שֶׁמֶשׁ בַּבּוֹקֶר, הַיָּרֵחַ בַּ_____. (לַיְלָה)
4. Have a boy stand next to the chalkboard, say:

   דָּוִד _____ עַל־יַד הַלּוּחַ. (עוֹמֵד)
5. FREE SPACE! Student may choose to sit at any desk.
6. פּוּרִים יוֹם _____. (שִׂמְחָה)
7. אֲנִי אוֹכֵל/אוֹכֶלֶת פִּיצָה וְ_____! (עוּגָה)
8. תּוֹדָה! הִנֵּה _____ יָפָה! (מַתָּנָה)
9. אֱלֹהִים _____: יְהִי אוֹר! (אוֹמֵר)
10. שָׂרָה _____ כָּל הַיּוֹם. (שָׁרָה)

If the student answers correctly, he or she may sit at the desk with the corresponding card. If the student answers incorrectly, then ב gets to take א's guess and the ב member can sit in the tic-tac-toe board if he or she guesses correctly. After this is completed, it is ב's turn to draw and guess.

Continue this way, alternating teams, until one team wins by occupying three desks in a row, in any direction.

Using the Photograph Have a student read the Hebrew caption to the photo on page 76 aloud. Ask: What three important ingredients make this a fun birthday party? (עוּגָה, נֵרוֹת, שִׂמְחָה)

Start a class birthday tradition. When each student's big day arrives (or is coming up), have everyone sing "Happy Birthday" in Hebrew. It's easy:
Sing "יוֹם הֻלֶּדֶת שָׂמֵחַ" four times, to the traditional "Happy Birthday" tune!

Shalom Ivrit 1 • Teacher's Edition

Mastering the Milon (p. 77)

Explain to the class that they are about to learn two new words that will help them create "real" Hebrew conversations!

• **לְךָ/לָךְ** • Give Picture Card 10 to a boy and say:

_____, אֲנִי נוֹתֵן/נוֹתֶנֶת לְךָ תַּפּוּחַ.

Give the Picture Card to a girl, say:

_____, אֲנִי נוֹתֵן/נוֹתֶנֶת לָךְ תַּפּוּחַ.

Ask: What do you think לָךְ and לְךָ mean?

 **Captain Grammar** Your students may be confused by this new use of לְךָ and לָךְ. They know יֵשׁ לְךָ/לָךְ, but this seems different. Explain to your students that לְךָ/לָךְ means "to you," and that יֵשׁ לְךָ/לָךְ means "you have," or, literally, "there is to you."

• **עִם** • Draw a חֲנוּכִּיָּה on the board and say:

הִנֵּה חֲנוּכִּיָּה.

Draw candles in the חֲנוּכִּיָּה, say:

הִנֵּה חֲנוּכִּיָּה עִם נֵרוֹת.

Point to a girl with a pencil, say:

הִנֵּה יַלְדָּה עִם עִפָּרוֹן.

Continue this way until students understand that עִם means "with."

 **Conversation Corner** Have students stand in a circle (ideally alternating boys and girls). Tell them to pretend that today is a special day—it is everyone's birthday. Give Picture Card 19 to a student and say:

1. יוֹם הוּלֶדֶת שָׂמֵחַ, _____. אֲנִי נוֹתֵן/נוֹתֶנֶת לְךָ/לָךְ עוּגָה עִם נֵרוֹת.

2. Have the student pass the card to the next student and say:

   יוֹם הוּלֶדֶת שָׂמֵחַ, _____. אֲנִי נוֹתֵן/נוֹתֶנֶת לְךָ/לָךְ עוּגָה עִם נֵרוֹת.

3. Continue this way until the card has been passed around the circle.

You may wish to time the class with a stopwatch or watch with a second hand, challenging them to complete the exercise in a time that you choose, or to repeat the exercise, getting faster and faster each time! Tell students that accuracy counts—a mistake costs two seconds.

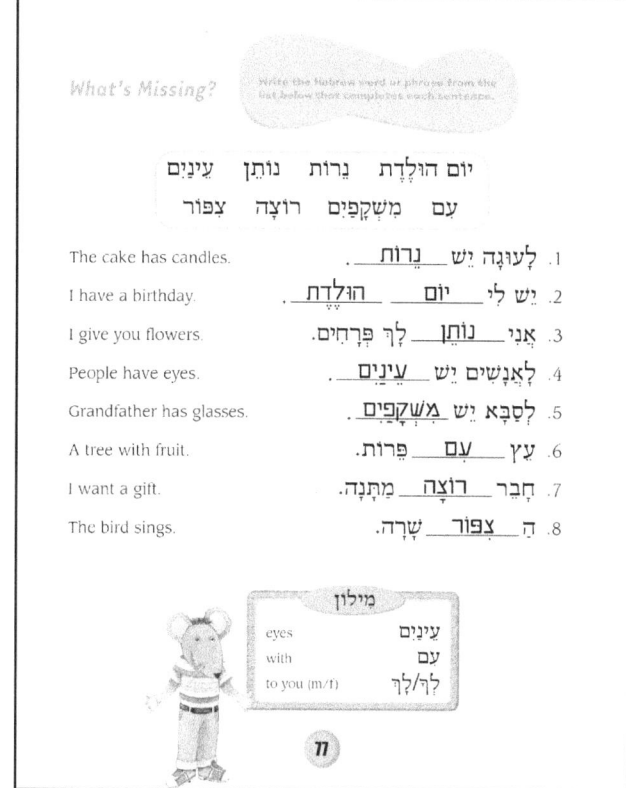

• **עֵינַיִם** • Using two fingers, point to your eyes. Say:

יֵשׁ לִי עֵינַיִם.

Point to a student's eyes, say:

יֵשׁ לְךָ/לָךְ עֵינַיִם.

Ask: What do you think עֵינַיִם are?

What's Missing? (p. 77)

Have students complete the exercise by writing the Hebrew word or phrase from the list on page 77 that completes each sentence. Check student answers by having students read each sentence aloud.

Chapter Story: לִילִי רוֹצָה מַתָּנָה
(pp. 78–79)

Ready for Reading Have a student read the Hebrew title and English sentences aloud. Ask you students: What things can help to create a perfect birthday? (*Students may answer:* חֲגִיגָה, פִּיצָה, עוּגָה, חָבֵר, מִשְׁפָּחָה, שִׂמְחָה, *etc.*)

Tell your students that this story combines lots of vocabulary—old and new. Congratulate them on coming so far in their Hebrew learning!

Read Aloud! Read the story aloud slowly, allowing students time to absorb new combinations of vocabulary (the frequent combination of יֵשׁ and לְ may be especially difficult).

Assign students to read each pair of lines. You may wish to assign all "לִילִי" lines to girls and all "סַבָּא" lines to boys, or have all "לִילִי" readers read with a high-pitched voice, and all "סַבָּא" readers read with a deep voice.

The Extra Mile Have students create their own questions to ask one another, based on the chapter story. You may wish to have each student create three questions, or divide the class into groups of three or four to create questions together.

You may wish to provide your students with some sample questions to get them started:

- מָה רוֹצָה לִילִי? (לִילִי רוֹצָה מַתָּנָה.)
- מַה יֵשׁ לַצִפּוֹר? (יֵשׁ לַצְפּוֹר נֵרוֹת.)
- יֵשׁ לַפְּרָחִים עֵינַיִם? (לֹא, אֵין לַפְּרָחִים עֵינַיִם.)

Looking Ahead

Explain to your students that the next chapter will be a treat for the artists in the class, as they will learn words that have to do with drawing and the colors we use for it.
Tell your students that they will also learn the word עוֹלָם, which may sound familiar. Ask them to think of where they've heard עוֹלָם before, and what it might mean.

לִילִי רוֹצָה מַתָּנָה

Lili wants a birthday gift.
Her grandfather gives her the best one.

לִילִי: סַבָּא, יֵשׁ לִי יוֹם הוּלֶדֶת,
אֲנִי רוֹצָה מַתָּנָה.

סַבָּא: טוֹב, אֲנִי נוֹתֵן לָךְ צִפּוֹר,
צִפּוֹר עִם נֵרוֹת.

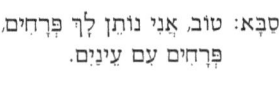

לִילִי: סַבָּא, לַצִפּוֹר אֵין נֵרוֹת.
לָעוּגָה יֵשׁ נֵרוֹת.

סַבָּא: טוֹב, אֲנִי נוֹתֵן לָךְ עוּגָה,
עוּגָה עִם דָגִים.

לִילִי: סַבָּא, לָעוּגָה אֵין דָגִים.
לָעוּגָה יֵשׁ פְּרָחִים.

סַבָּא: טוֹב, אֲנִי נוֹתֵן לָךְ פְּרָחִים,
פְּרָחִים עִם עֵינַיִם.

לִילִי: סַבָּא, לַפְּרָחִים אֵין עֵינַיִם.
לָאֲנָשִׁים יֵשׁ עֵינַיִם.

סַבָּא: טוֹב, אֲנִי נוֹתֵן לָךְ אִמָּא,
אִמָּא עִם מִשְׁקָפַיִם.

לִילִי: סַבָּא, לְאִמָּא אֵין מִשְׁקָפַיִם.
לְסַבָּא יֵשׁ מִשְׁקָפַיִם.

סַבָּא: טוֹב, אֲנִי נוֹתֵן לָךְ סַבָּא!

Checkpoint Completion (pp. 80–81)

Checkpoint 1

Have students complete the exercise by circling the word that means the same as the Hebrew.

Checkpoint 2

Have students complete the exercise by circling the word that means the same as the English.

Checkpoint 3

Instruct students to complete the exercise by drawing a line from the fish to the correct net.

Review answers by having students provide the answers for each question in all three checkpoints. Instruct students to place a checkmark next to the answers that are correct, and an X next to the answers that are incorrect. Have them place a grade at the top of each checkpoint (for example, 3/4, 4/5, or 9/10).

Review grades by checking each student's book.

Checkpoint Assessment

If possible, spend a few minutes with each student to review his or her work. Be sure to praise students for correct answers, and encourage them to find answers for incorrect ones.

For checkpoint 1, continue with the "Checkpoint Assessment" ideas on page 59. For Checkpoints 2 and 3, adjust the grading scale to students who scored: 4–5 , 3, and 2 or lower.

Keep your eyes out for words that your students consistently miss. You may wish to spend some time reviewing those words as a class.

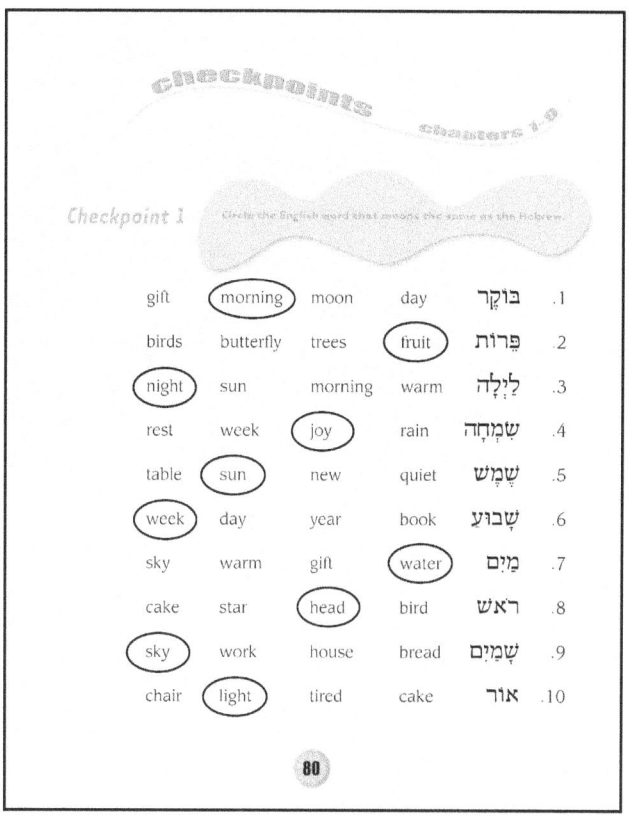

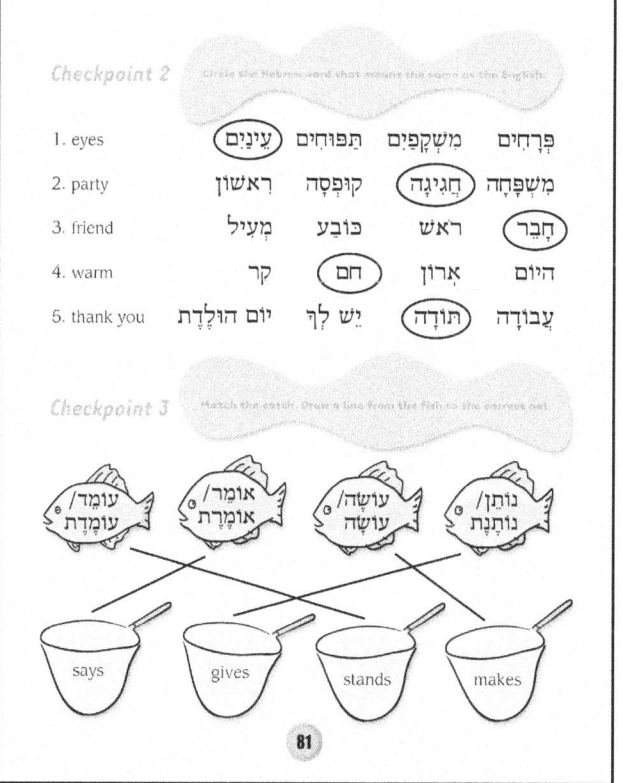

Chapter 9

Dear Parent,

During the past few weeks, our class has learned words having to do with Ḥanukkah, such as *or* (light), *neirot* (candles), and *l'vivot* (latkes); and words having to do with Tu B'Shevat, the "birthday of the trees," such as *eitzim* (trees) and *peirot* (fruit). We have also been working to build our core modern Hebrew vocabulary.

Here are some words your child has learned during the past few weeks, including ideas to incorporate these words into your daily conversations:

head	rosh	רֹאשׁ
eyes	einayim	עֵינַיִם

Refer to two important parts of the body in Hebrew.

morning	boker	בּוֹקֶר
night	lailah	לַיְלָה
today	hayom	הַיוֹם

"*Boker tov*"—good morning—is a great way to start the day, and "*lailah tov*"—good night—is a great way to end it.

birthday	*yom huledet*	יוֹם הוּלֶדֶת

Wish one another a happy birthday with "*yom huledet sameaḥ*"—happy birthday!

Thank you for helping us to learn modern Hebrew!

B'Shalom,

Lesson Objectives

Students will:

- Continue to build a base of everyday vocabulary, including colors and parts of the body.
- Learn to indicate nouns in more specific terms, with the addition of זֶה.

New Milon Words and Phrases

Core Vocabulary

world	עוֹלָם
many	הַרְבֵּה
this, this is (m)	זֶה

Art-Related Vocabulary

draws (m/f)	מְצַיֵּר/מְצַיֶּרֶת
crayon, color	צֶבַע
sheet (of paper)	דַּף

Other Useful Vocabulary

clown	לֵיצָן
garden	גַּן

What We'll need

- ❏ Text pages 82–87
- ❏ Word Cards 125–132
- ❏ Picture Card 28
- ❏ Helpful props: a notebook, a pencil, colored chalk (or dry erase markers); a variety of crayons, including the six colors shown on page 83—enough for the class to share

Where We Are

In Chapter 10, we join David and his classmates as they create their own works of art—and learn an important lesson about colors. Then we "clown around" with a new friend, Ran, as he dresses up as—you guessed it—a clown!

Let's Review

Have students create three quick drawings on index cards: a tree, a cake, and flowers.

Have the class sit in a circle on the floor. Distribute the index cards randomly. Provide directions to individual students (using the third person) that include עִם, לְךָ/לָךְ, or עוֹמֵד/עוֹמֶדֶת.

Sample directions include:

- יֶלֶד עִם עֵץ עוֹמֵד.

  (Student with "tree" card should stand.)

- שָׂרָה עוֹמֶדֶת עַל כִּסֵּא.

  (Sarah should stand on a chair.)

- דָּוִד נוֹתֵן עוּגָה לָךְ.

  (Point to a girl; David should give cake card to her.)

You may wish to make the exercise a game by having students who respond incorrectly or not at all step out of the circle.

Introducing the Lesson

Draw a sketch of the earth on the board. Say:

אֲנִי מְצַיֵּר/מְצַיֶּרֶת עוֹלָם.

Draw several tiny children on the earth, say:

אֲנִי מְצַיֵּר/מְצַיֶּרֶת יְלָדִים.

Have students come to the board and add to the drawing by following instructions you provide. Sample instructions include:

- דָּוִד מְצַיֵּר שֶׁמֶשׁ.

  (David should draw the sun.)

- שָׂרָה מְצַיֶּרֶת פְּרָחִים.

  (Sarah should draw flowers.)

- דָּנִיאֵל מְצַיֵּר עֵצִים.

  (Daniel should draw trees.)

Continue drawing more and more children, say:

יֵשׁ הַרְבֵּה, הַרְבֵּה, הַרְבֵּה יְלָדִים בָּעוֹלָם.

chapter 10

עוֹלָם יָפֶה

The children paint a colorful world.

הַיְלָדִים בַּכִּתָּה. כָּל הַיְלָדִים מְצַיְּרִים.

דָּוִד מְצַיֵּר עֵץ בְּצֶבַע יָרֹק.
רָחֵל מְצַיֶּרֶת פֶּרַח בְּצֶבַע אָדֹם.
שָׂרָה מְצַיֶּרֶת שֶׁמֶשׁ בְּצֶבַע צָהֹב.
רָן מְצַיֵּר שָׁמַיִם בְּצֶבַע כָּחֹל.

דִּינָה מְצַיֶּרֶת עֵץ בְּצֶבַע שָׁחֹר,
פְּרָחִים וְשֶׁמֶשׁ בְּצֶבַע שָׁחֹר.

הַמּוֹרָה: דִּינָה, שֶׁמֶשׁ בְּצֶבַע שָׁחֹר?
עוֹלָם בְּצֶבַע שָׁחֹר?

דִּינָה: אֵין לִי צֶבַע יָרֹק לְעֵצִים.
אֵין לִי צֶבַע אָדֹם לַפְּרָחִים.
אֵין לִי צֶבַע צָהֹב לַשֶּׁמֶשׁ.
וְאֵין לִי צֶבַע כָּחֹל לַשָּׁמַיִם.

82

---

ways to remember the names of the colors. Students may use mnemonics or other memory techniques. For example, students may say: אָדֹם is red, just like the apple אָדָם ate in the Garden of Eden.

Teach the three *tarmilon* words—all new forms of words they know. Be sure to pronounce מְצַיְּרִים slowly, so students hear all the syllables!

Have students read the English sentence in Hebrew. Explain that even though they may not know all the words, they can come very close by replacing "paint" with "draw," and "colorful" with "many colors." Allow them to refer to the *milon* and *tarmilon*. (הַיְלָדִים מְצַיְּרִים עוֹלָם בְּהַרְבֵּה צְבָעִים.)

Read Aloud! Assign six students to the parts of הַמּוֹרָה, דִּינָה, רָן, שָׂרָה, דָּוִד, and רָחֵל. Have them sit around a table with green, yellow, blue, black, white, and red crayons, and a sheet of paper for each student. Read the entire story aloud. Have them perform the story while you narrate. For example, after you read, דָּוִד מְצַיֵּר עֵץ בְּצֶבַע יָרֹק, David should find the green crayon and draw a quick sketch of a tree.

Allow ample time after each direction, as students must determine the color to use and the object to draw.

Mastering the Milon (p. 83)

• **עוֹלָם** • Remind students of the question you asked at the end of the previous lesson: Where have we heard עוֹלָם before, and what do you think it means? (*Students may recognize* עוֹלָם *from the blessing formula; many will know that* עוֹלָם *means "world."*)

• **מְצַיֵּר/מְצַיֶּרֶת** • Draw random objects on the board. Say:

אֲנִי מְצַיֵּר/מְצַיֶּרֶת עַל הַלּוּחַ.

Draw in a notebook, say:

אֲנִי מְצַיֵּר/מְצַיֶּרֶת בַּמַּחְבֶּרֶת.

Make sure that students understand that מְצַיֵּר and מְצַיֶּרֶת mean "draw" and not "write."

• **דַּף** • Display a sheet of paper. Say: דַּף גָּדוֹל.
Tear off a small piece of paper: דַּף קָטָן.
Draw on the paper, say:

אֲנִי מְצַיֵּר/מְצַיֶּרֶת עַל הַדַּף.

• **צֶבַע** • Hold up a crayon. Say: הִנֵּה הַצֶּבַע.
Hold up a different color crayon, repeat. Explain that צֶבַע means "color" as well as "crayon."

 **Put It Together** Place a sheet of paper, a notebook, a pencil, and a crayon on a table. Have students come to the table and draw using different combinations of objects. For example, instruct students:

• שָׂרָה מְצַיֶּרֶת בְּצֶבַע עַל הַדַּף.
• דָּוִד מְצַיֵּר פְּרָחִים בְּעִפָּרוֹן עַל הַמַּחְבֶּרֶת.
• רִבְקָה מְצַיֶּרֶת פֵּרוֹת בְּצֶבַע עַל הַמַּחְבֶּרֶת.

• **הַרְבֵּה** • Draw a tree on the board. Say: עֵץ
Draw five more trees, say: הַרְבֵּה עֵצִים!
Draw a child, say: יֶלֶד; draw several children, say: הַרְבֵּה יְלָדִים.
Continue this way until students understand that הַרְבֵּה means "many."

Chapter Story: עוֹלָם יָפֶה (pp. 82–83)

 **Ready for Reading** Write the names of the colors listed on page 83 on the board, using the appropriate colored chalk or markers. Read the list aloud while pointing to each color.

Have a contest to see who can come up with the most creative

 Shalom Ivrit 1 • Teacher's Edition

Assign the part of the narrator and have the class read the story a second time. (You may wish to assign different students the parts of the six characters for the second reading.) Again, have students "perform" the story.

 The Extra Mile Ask a series of "quick questions," based on the chapter story:

- אֵיפֹה הַיְלָדִים?
 (הַיְלָדִים בַּכִּתָּה.)
- מַה מְצַיֵּר דָּוִד? (דָּוִד מְצַיֵּר עֵץ בְּצֶבַע יָרוֹק.)
- מַה מְצַיֶּרֶת רָחֵל?
 (רָחֵל מְצַיֶּרֶת פֶּרַח בְּצֶבַע אָדוֹם.)
- מַה צֶבַע הַשֶּׁמֶשׁ? (הַשֶּׁמֶשׁ בְּצֶבַע צָהוֹב.)
- לְדִינָה יֵשׁ צֶבַע יָרוֹק?
 (לֹא, אֵין לְדִינָה צֶבַע יָרוֹק.)
- לְדִינָה יֵשׁ צֶבַע אָדוֹם?
 (לֹא, אֵין לְדִינָה צֶבַע אָדוֹם.)
- מַה נוֹתֵן דָּוִד לְדִינָה?
 (דָּוִד נוֹתֵן לְדִינָה צֶבַע יָרוֹק.)
- מַה נוֹתֶנֶת רָחֵל לְדִינָה?
 (רָחֵל נוֹתֶנֶת לְדִינָה צֶבַע אָדוֹם.)
- מַה נוֹתֶנֶת הַמּוֹרָה לְדִינָה?
 (הַמּוֹרָה נוֹתֶנֶת לְדִינָה דַּף לָבָן.)
- דִּינָה שְׂמֵחָה? (כֵּן, דִּינָה שְׂמֵחָה.)
- מַה אוֹמֶרֶת הַמּוֹרָה? (הַמּוֹרָה אוֹמֶרֶת, "הָעוֹלָם לֹא שָׁחוֹר וְלָבָן...")

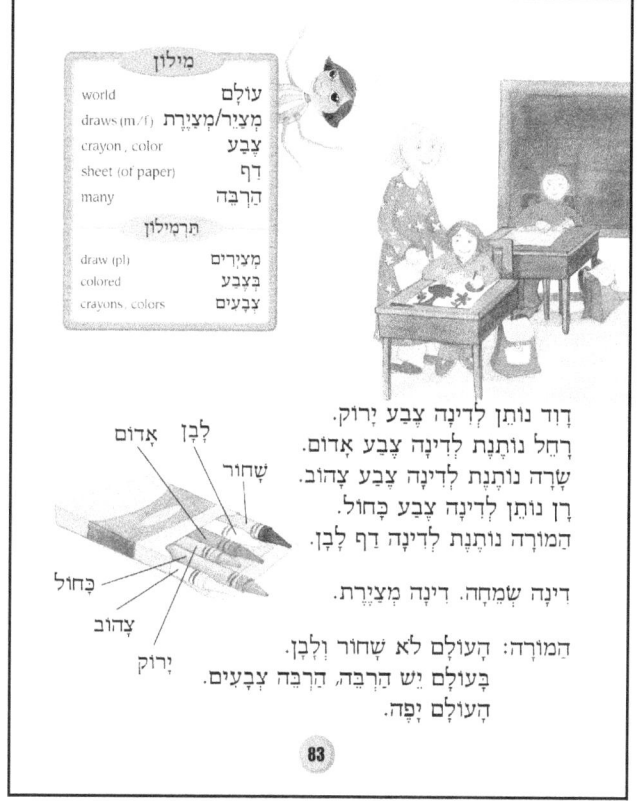

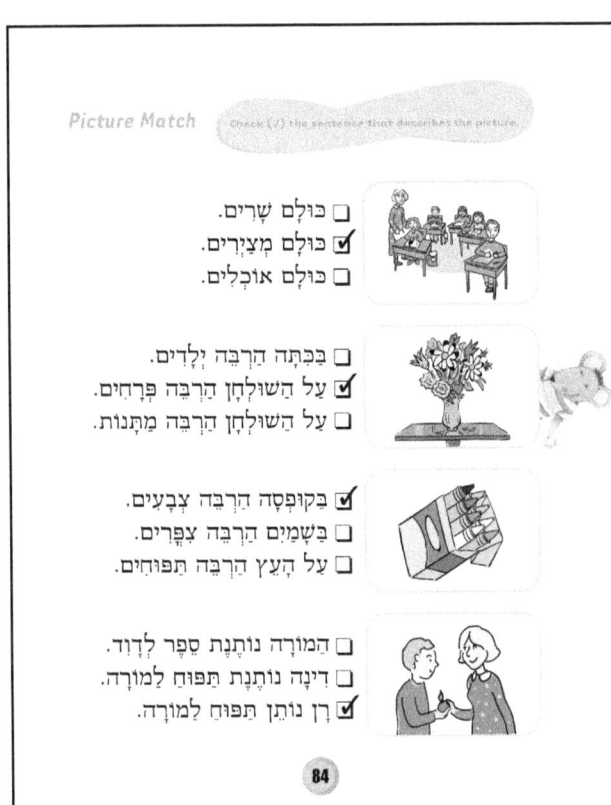

Picture Match (p. 84)

Have students complete the exercise by placing a checkmark next to the sentence that describes the picture. Check answers by having students read all three choices, then giving the correct one.

You may wish to challenge students to create new sentences based on the four illustrations on page 84. Explain to your students that the sentences may describe an actual situation in the picture, or take a more "creative" slant. For example, students may describe the top picture by saying:

- הַמוֹרָה עוֹמֶדֶת בַּכִּתָּה.
- שָׂרָה מְצַיֶּרֶת עֵצִים.
- דָּוִד מְצַיֵּר, אֲבָל דָּוִד רוֹצֶה עוּגָה.

What's the Color? (p. 85)

Have students complete the exercise by writing the color of each hat in Hebrew. Check student answers by pointing to individual hats and having students read the appropriate phrase.

**Game Box** Play "Beat the Clock," as described on page 17. Play the "individual competition" version of the game, timing each student as he or she reads lines from page 84. (Depending on the level of your students, you may wish to have them read just six or all twelve lines.) The rules of the game are:

- Read as quickly—but as clearly—as you can.
- A mistake adds two seconds to the total time.
- The teacher is the final judge!

Once the student has finished reading, he or she must pass a "color test," based on the exercise on page 85. For the test, cover the line of words across the top of the page. Point to any two hats and have students name their colors (כּוֹבַע שָׁחוֹר; כּוֹבַע אָדוֹם; *etc.*). If the student is correct, subtract three seconds from the student's total time. If the student is incorrect, add three seconds.

The student with the fewest total seconds is the winner.

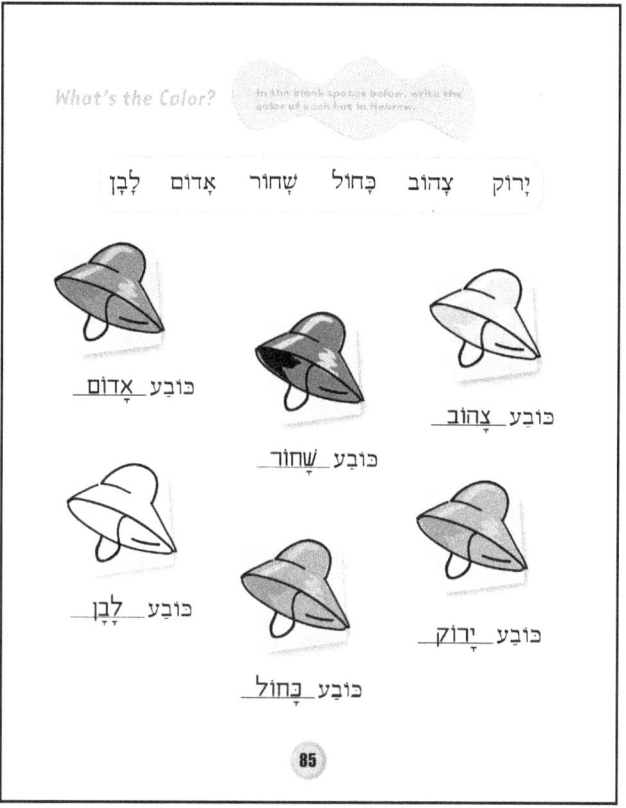

Funny Face (p. 86)

Review the parts of the clown picture with your students. Your students should be familiar with רֹאשׁ, פֶּרַח, כּוֹבַע, and עֵינַיִם. Ask them to locate these four objects in the picture.

Teach אָזְנַיִם, אַף, and פֶּה by pointing to these parts of your face and saying the words aloud.

> **Game Box**
> **Face Time!**
>
> Have students stand in a group, facing you. Tell your students that they should touch the parts of their face that you mention.
>
> Provide one direction at a time, then two and three. Speed up the frequency of your directions as the game progresses. As students are unable to respond to your instruction, they should sit down. The last student remaining standing is the winner.

Provide students with green, blue, red, and yellow crayons. Have students complete the exercise by coloring the clown's face, as per the directions provided at the top of the page.

The hat should be green, the eyes blue, the nose red, and the flower yellow. Check answers by walking around the classroom as students work.

Mastering the Milon (p. 87)

- **לֵיצָן** • Point to the picture of the clown on page 86. Say:
  הִנֵּה לֵיצָן. הַלֵּיצָן שָׂמֵחַ? (כֵּן, הַלֵּיצָן שָׂמֵחַ.)

- **גַן** • Draw a flower on the board. Say: הִנֵּה פֶּרַח.
  Draw two more flowers, say: הִנֵּה פְּרָחִים.
  Have two students come to the board and draw as many flowers as they can in one minute. Say: הִנֵּה גַן!

Our Tradition Your students may find it interesting that some words they are learning are also found in the Torah. Ask: What is the most famous גַן of all? (גַן עֵדֶן, the Garden of Eden)

- **זֶה** • Point to a boy and say: זֶה יֶלֶד.
  Pick up a pencil, say: זֶה עִפָּרוֹן.
  Pick up a book, say: זֶה סֵפֶר.
  Point to a table, say: זֶה שֻׁלְחָן.

Continue this way until students understand that זֶה means "this." Explain that זֶה means both "this" and "this is." (Note for your students: זֶה is used only for masculine words. זֹאת is used for feminine words.)

Chapter Story: רָן הַלֵּיצָן (p. 87)

Have students alternate reading lines. Challenge the class to read the story quickly and smoothly, so that the poem's rhyme and rhythm may be heard.

Have the class read the poem twice more, picking up speed each time!

The Extra Mile Ask questions based on the poem:
- רָן בַּבַּיִת? (לֹא, רָן לֹא בַּבַּיִת.)
- רָן בַּגַן? (לֹא, רָן לֹא בַּגַן.)
- מַה צֶּבַע הָרֹאשׁ? (הָרֹאשׁ לָבָן.)
- מַה צֶּבַע הָאַף? (הָאַף אָדֹם.)
- מִי הַלֵּיצָן? (רָן הַלֵּיצָן!)

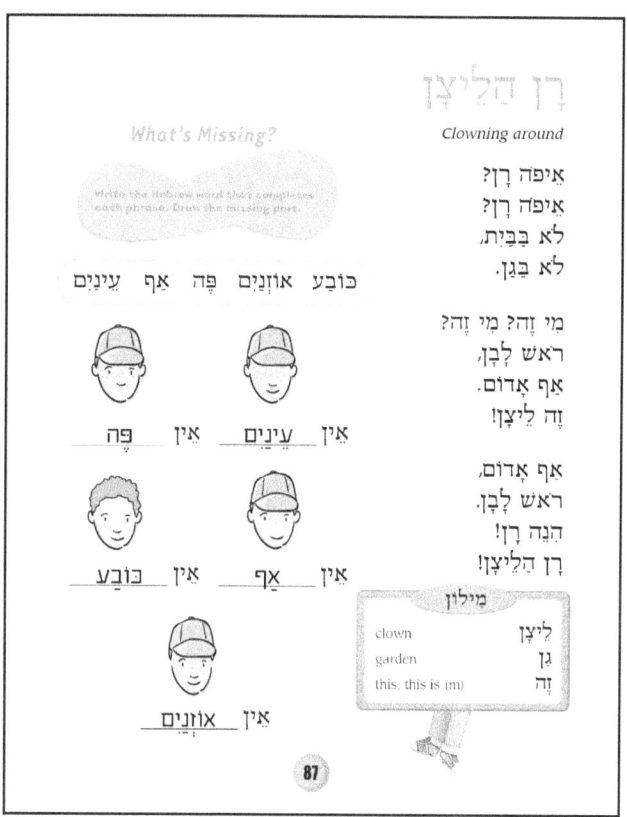

What's Missing?

Read Aloud! Have students complete the exercise by writing the word that completes each phrase, then drawing the missing part of each face. Review answers by having students say the name of the missing part, then pointing to their own faces to indicate its meaning.

 **Game Box** Play "Jeopardy!" as described on page 18. Suggested categories for this chapter are: "Colors," "Our Faces," and "New Vocabulary."

Sample questions include:

Colors:

1. Show a red crayon and ask: מַה הַצֶּבַע? (אָדוֹם)
2. Show a black crayon, ask: מַה הַצֶּבַע? (שָׁחוֹר)
3. Ask: מַה הַצֶּבַע שֶׁל הַשֶּׁמֶשׁ? (צָהוֹב)

Our Faces:

1. Say: touch your אוֹזְנַיִם. (*student should touch his or her ears*)
2. Point to your nose and ask: מַה זֶה? (אַף)
3. Ask: אֵיפֹה פֶּה, עֵינַיִם, וְאַף?
   (*student may touch his or her mouth, eyes, and nose OR say* בָּרֹאשׁ.)

New Vocab:

Have students fill in the blanks using words learned in this chapter:

1. Pretend to draw on a sheet of paper and say:
   אֲנִי ____ עַל הַדַּף. (מְצַיֵּר/מְצַיֶּרֶת)
2. Show several crayons, say:
   הִנֵּה ____ צְבָעִים! (הַרְבֵּה)
3. Say: אֱלֹהֵינוּ מֶלֶךְ הָ____. (עוֹלָם)

You may wish to include a fourth "fun" category, including general Jewish trivia.

Looking Ahead

Explain to your students that the next chapter will contain new vocabulary having to do with Purim. Have your students think about words that they would need to know to be able to tell the Purim story!

Lesson Objectives

Students will:

- Learn a new verb form—the infinitive—with the addition of לִהְיוֹת.
- Continue to strengthen general comprehension and conversational skills, with the addition of the pronouns הוּא and הִיא; verbs קוֹרְאִים and מְדַבֵּר/מְדַבֶּרֶת; and preposition אַחֲרֵי.

New Milon Words and Phrases

Core Vocabulary

read (pl)	קוֹרְאִים
to be	לִהְיוֹת
he/she	הוּא/הִיא
Jew, Jewish	יְהוּדִי
speaks (m/f)	מְדַבֵּר/מְדַבֶּרֶת
bad (m)	רַע
girls	יְלָדוֹת
after	אַחֲרֵי
if	אִם
has	יֵשׁ לְ___

Purim-Related Vocabulary

king	מֶלֶךְ
foolish (m)	טִפֵּשׁ
wise (m)	חָכָם
queen	מַלְכָּה
horse	סוּס
noise	רַעַשׁ

What We'll need

- ❏ Text pages 88–95
- ❏ Word Cards 22, 23, 48, 54, 130, and 133–148
- ❏ Picture Cards 29–31
- ❏ Helpful props: colored chalk or markers; Purim graggers (enough for each student)

Where We Are

In Chapter 11, we join David, Doron, and Dinah as they decide who in the Purim story they'd most like to be.

Then we follow David, Dinah, Doron, Dani, Malmalah, and Bar in a most unusual Purim parade.

Let's Review

Set colored chalk or markers on a table. On the board or a large sheet of paper, draw a sketch of a clown face, as it appears on page 86. Say:

זֶה לֵיצָן.

Provide students with directions to add to the picture using specific colors. For example:

- דָוִד מְצַיֵּר אַף בְּצֶבַע אָדֹם.
- שָׂרָה מְצַיֶּרֶת כּוֹבַע בְּצֶבַע צָהֹב.
- דָּנִיאֵל מְצַיֵּר פֶּרַח בְּצֶבַע יָרֹק.

Erase the drawing, or hang a new sheet of paper. Draw a landscape with a glowing sun peeking over it. Say:

הַיְלָדִים בַּכִּתָּה מְצַיְּרִים גַּן.

Call up individual students to help create a picture of a lush garden on the board.

Depending on the level of your class, you may wish to provide specific instructions, or have your students choose objects to add while describing what they are doing. For example, students might say:

- אֲנִי מְצַיֶּרֶת שֶׁמֶשׁ בְּצֶבַע צָהֹב.
- אֲנִי מְצַיֵּר פְּרָחִים בְּצֶבַע אָדֹם.
- אֲנִי מְצַיֵּר יְלָדִים בְּצֶבַע לָבָן.

Introducing the Lesson

Have your students open their books to pages 88–89.

Point to the picture of *Aḥashveirosh* and say:

אֲחַשְׁוֵרוֹשׁ מֶלֶךְ.

Point to Esther, say:

אֶסְתֵּר מַלְכָּה.

Point to Mordechai, then tap your head as if to say "smart," say:

מָרְדֳּכַי חָכָם.

Point to Haman, then shake your head, say:

הָמָן לֹא חָכָם; הָמָן רַע.

Ask the following questions based on the drawings on pages 88–89. You may wish to answer each question yourself, to help familiarize students with יֵשׁ לְ___.

הַיּוֹם פּוּרִים

Who in the Megillah would you like to be?

מוֹרָה: הַיּוֹם פּוּרִים!
הַיּוֹם קוֹרְאִים בַּמְּגִילָה.
הִנֵּה קֻפְסָה. בַּקֻּפְסָה מַסֵּכוֹת.
מִי רוֹצֶה לִהְיוֹת מֶלֶךְ?

דָּוִד: אֲנִי רוֹצֶה לִהְיוֹת מֶלֶךְ,
אֲבָל לֹא אֲחַשְׁוֵרוֹשׁ הַמֶּלֶךְ,
כִּי הוּא מֶלֶךְ טִפֵּשׁ.
אֲנִי רוֹצֶה לִהְיוֹת מֶלֶךְ חָכָם!

דּוֹרוֹן: אֲנִי רוֹצֶה לִהְיוֹת מָרְדְּכַי,
כִּי מָרְדְּכַי יְהוּדִי וְגַם אֲנִי יְהוּדִי.

דִּינָה: אֲנִי רוֹצֶה לִהְיוֹת אֶסְתֵּר,
כִּי הִיא מַלְכָּה יָפָה.

דָּנִי: אֲנִי רוֹצֶה לִהְיוֹת סוּס,
כִּי יֵשׁ גַּם סוּס בַּמְּגִילָה.

אֲחַשְׁוֵרוֹשׁ

אֶסְתֵּר

88

▼

הִיא or הוּא. For example:

הִיא רוֹצָה לִהְיוֹת מַלְכָּה.

4. Once all students have "reported," challenge individual students to remember what three of their classmates said—again using הוּא and הִיא. For example:

הִיא רוֹצָה לִהְיוֹת מוֹרָה;
הִיא רוֹצָה לִהְיוֹת מַלְכָּה;
הוּא רוֹצָה לִהְיוֹת מֶלֶךְ.

• חָכָם • Tap your head, as if to say "smart." Say:

מָרְדְּכַי חָכָם; אֲחַשְׁוֵרוֹשׁ לֹא חָכָם.

Ask: What do you think חָכָם means? (You may wish to explain that חֲכָמָה is the feminine form of חָכָם; אֶסְתֵּר חֲכָמָה.)

• טִפֵּשׁ • Say: הָמָן לֹא חָכָם. הָמָן טִפֵּשׁ!
(You may wish to explain that טִפְּשָׁה is the feminine form of טִפֵּשׁ; אֶסְתֵּר לֹא טִפְּשָׁה.)

• יְהוּדִי • Say: מָרְדְּכַי יְהוּדִי; הָמָן לֹא יְהוּדִי.

Continue this way until students understand that יְהוּדִי means "Jew" or "Jewish." (You may wish to explain that

• יֵשׁ לַאֲחַשְׁוֵרוֹשׁ כּוֹבַע?
(כֵּן, יֵשׁ לַאֲחַשְׁוֵרוֹשׁ כּוֹבַע.)
• יֵשׁ לְאֶסְתֵּר כּוֹבַע? (כֵּן, יֵשׁ לְאֶסְתֵּר כּוֹבַע.)
• יֵשׁ לְמָרְדְּכַי כּוֹבַע? (לֹא, אֵין לְמָרְדְּכַי כּוֹבַע.)

Mastering the Milon (p. 89)

• **הוּא/הִיא** • Point to individual boys and say:

הוּא בַּכִּתָּה; הוּא בַּכִּתָּה...

To girls: הִיא בַּכִּתָּה; הִיא בַּכִּתָּה...

Point to a boy and ask another student:

הוּא בַּכִּתָּה? (כֵּן, הוּא בַּכִּתָּה.)

Repeat with הִיא.

Captain Grammar You may wish to explain that even though it may sound funny to English-speakers, הִיא means "she"!

• **לִהְיוֹת** • Show Word Card 134. Ask:

לִהְיוֹת אוֹ לֹא לִהְיוֹת?

Explain that לִהְיוֹת means "to be."

• **מֶלֶךְ and מַלְכָּה** • Many students will know from their prayer study that מֶלֶךְ means "ruler." Say:

בָּרוּךְ אַתָּה יְיָ, אֱלֹהֵינוּ מֶלֶךְ הָעוֹלָם.

—Blessed are You, _____ of the world. (king) Point to the pictures on page 88, say:

אֲחַשְׁוֵרוֹשׁ מֶלֶךְ; אֶסְתֵּר מַלְכָּה.

Conversation Corner Have students practice combining לִהְיוֹת with another verb by speaking with one another:

1. Place Word Cards 22, 23, 48, 54, 130, 134, 135, and 140, on the chalkboard ledge, so that the words read: מֶלֶךְ, לִהְיוֹת, רוֹצָה/רוֹצֶה, אַתְּ, אַתָּה, לֵיצָן, אוֹ, מַלְכָּה.

2. Divide the class into pairs. Have each student ask his or her partner the question on the board. (Do you want to be a king/queen or a clown?) Remind them to be careful of gender! Answer should be:

אֲנִי רוֹצֶה לִהְיוֹת _____.

OR אֲנִי רוֹצָה לִהְיוֹת _____.

3. After each student answers the question, have the other student "report" what the partner said, using

◀

Shalom Ivrit 1 • Teacher's Edition

יְהוּדִיָה is the feminine form of יְהוּדִי;
(אֶסְתֵּר יְהוּדִיָה חֲכָמָה!)

• **רַע** • Say: מָרְדְּכַי טוֹב; הָמָן רַע.
Ask: What do you think רַע means?

• **סוּס** • Have students draw small and large horses on the board. Point to the small horse and say: סוּס קָטָן.
To the large horse: סוּס גָּדוֹל.
Ask: What do you think סוּס means?

Put It Together Have students create a fictional story based on יִצְחָק הַסּוּס—Isaac the Horse—by filling in the blanks in the paragraph below. Explain that there are many "right answers," and only two rules:
1. Students must use at least two new words from today's lesson.
2. Words must match in gender and number!

יִצְחָק הַסּוּס

יִצְחָק הַסּוּס _____ מְאֹד. הוּא הוֹלֵךְ לַמּוֹרָה וְאוֹמֵר, "_____!" הַמּוֹרָה לֹא _____. הִיא אוֹמֶרֶת לְיִצְחָק, "_____."
יִצְחָק הַסּוּס _____ מְאֹד.

• **מְדַבֵּר/מְדַבֶּרֶת** • Draw two boys' faces on the board: one with a bubble above him containing the word שָׁלוֹם, one without a bubble. Point to the first, say: הַיֶּלֶד מְדַבֵּר.
Point to the second, say: הַיֶּלֶד לֹא מְדַבֵּר.
Draw a bow on top of the faces. Point to the first drawing, ask: הַיַּלְדָּה מְדַבֶּרֶת? (כֵּן.)
To the second: הַיַּלְדָּה מְדַבֶּרֶת? (לֹא.)

Captain Grammar Your students may be confused by the similar use of מְדַבֵּר/מְדַבֶּרֶת and אוֹמֵר/אוֹמֶרֶת. Explain that אוֹמֵר/אוֹמֶרֶת is used to describe <u>what</u> someone is saying, and is often followed by a description of what is being said:

דָּוִד אוֹמֵר, "שָׁלוֹם!"

מְדַבֵּר/מְדַבֶּרֶת is used to describe the act of speaking:

שָׂרָה מְדַבֶּרֶת לְרִבְקָה.

• **רַעַשׁ** • Cover your ears, as if the classroom were loud. Say:
בְּיוֹם פּוּרִים יְלָדִים עוֹשִׂים רַעַשׁ!
Take your hands away, whisper:
שששׁ! בְּיוֹם כִּפּוּר, יְלָדִים לֹא עוֹשִׂים רַעַשׁ.
Continue this way until students understand that רַעַשׁ means "noise."

• **קוֹרְאִים** • Ask students to read the title on page 88 silently.
Say: כָּל הַיְלָדִים קוֹרְאִים.
Ask: What do you think קוֹרְאִים means? Make sure students understand that קוֹרְאִים is a plural form.

Chapter Story: הַיּוֹם פּוּרִים (pp. 88–89)

Ready for Reading Review the *tarmilon* words—many of which, such as פּוּרִים and מְגִילָה—your students will already know. They may know רַעֲשָׁן as "gragger." Explain that מַסֵּכָה means "mask," and מַסֵּכוֹת "masks."

Have a student read the Hebrew title and English question aloud. Ask students to share memories of Purim plays they've seen or been in.

מִי אֶסְתֵּר הַמַּלְכָּה?

Who's Who? Complete each sentence with the name of the correct person from the Megillah.

מָרְדְכַי הַיְהוּדִי	אֲחַשְׁוֵרוֹשׁ הַמֶּלֶךְ
אֶסְתֵּר הַמַּלְכָּה	הָמָן הָרָע

1. דָּוִד לֹא רוֹצֶה לִהְיוֹת: אֲחַשְׁוֵרוֹשׁ הַמֶּלֶךְ
2. דָּנִי לֹא רוֹצֶה לִהְיוֹת: הָמָן הָרָע
3. דִּינָה רוֹצָה לִהְיוֹת: אֶסְתֵּר הַמַּלְכָּה
4. דוֹרוֹן רוֹצֶה לִהְיוֹת: מָרְדְכַי הַיְהוּדִי

90

Read Aloud! Read the entire story aloud to the class. Read slowly to allow students time to absorb the long list of new vocabulary words. Encourage students to raise their hands and ask questions.

Assign five students to play the parts of מוֹרָה, דָּוִד, דּוֹרוֹן, דִּינָה, and דָּנִי. Have them read the entire dialog aloud. The whole class should read for יְלָדִים on page 89.

 **The Extra Mile** Have students read the story a second time (you may wish to assign new parts for students who did not read the first time). Ask the following questions after each paragraph. Encourage students to use הוּא and הִיא where appropriate.

מוֹרָה:
- מָה הַיּוֹם? (הַיּוֹם פּוּרִים.)
- אֵיפֹה מַסֵכוֹת? (מַסֵכוֹת בַּקוּפְסָה.)

דָּוִד:
- מִי רוֹצֶה לִהְיוֹת מֶלֶךְ? (דָּוִד רוֹצֶה לִהְיוֹת מֶלֶךְ.)
- הוּא רוֹצֶה לִהְיוֹת אֲחַשְׁוֵרוֹשׁ הַמֶּלֶךְ? (לֹא, הוּא לֹא רוֹצֶה...)
- מִי דָּוִד רוֹצֶה לִהְיוֹת? (דָּוִד רוֹצֶה לִהְיוֹת מֶלֶךְ חָכָם.)

דּוֹרוֹן:
- מִי דּוֹרוֹן רוֹצֶה לִהְיוֹת? (הוּא רוֹצֶה לִהְיוֹת מָרְדְכַי.)
- כִּי? (דּוֹרוֹן רוֹצֶה לִהְיוֹת מָרְדְכַי כִּי הוּא יְהוּדִי.)

דִּינָה:
- מִי דִּינָה רוֹצָה לִהְיוֹת? (דִּינָה רוֹצָה לִהְיוֹת אֶסְתֵּר.)
- כִּי? (כִּי אֶסְתֵּר מַלְכָּה יָפָה.)

דָּנִי:
- מִי דָּנִי רוֹצֶה לִהְיוֹת? (דָּנִי רוֹצֶה לִהְיוֹת סוּס.)
- כִּי? (כִּי יֵשׁ סוּס בַּמְגִילָה.)

מוֹרָה:
- מִי מוֹרָה רוֹצָה לִהְיוֹת? (מוֹרָה רוֹצָה לִהְיוֹת לֵיצָן.)
- כִּי? (כִּי לְמוֹרָה אַף אָדוֹם.)

דָּנִי:
- כִּי סוּס לֹא מְדַבֵּר, מִי דָּנִי רוֹצֶה לִהְיוֹת? כִּי? (דָּנִי רוֹצֶה לִהְיוֹת הָמָן כִּי הוּא הוֹלֵךְ עִם הַסּוּס.)

מוֹרָה (last paragraph):
- מָה הַמוֹרָה נוֹתֶנֶת לַכִּתָּה? (הַמוֹרָה נוֹתֶנֶת אָזְנֵי הָמָן לַכִּתָּה. OR הַמוֹרָה נוֹתֶנֶת רַעֲשָׁן לַכִּתָּה.)
- מָה הַיּוֹם? (הַיּוֹם פּוּרִים.)

 **Using the Photograph** Have a student read the photo caption on page 90 aloud. Ask:

מִי אֶסְתֵּר הַמַּלְכָּה?

(*the girl on the left, wearing the crown*) Ask: Whom would *you* like to dress up as next Purim?

Who's Who? (p. 90)

Have students complete each sentence with the name of the correct person from the מְגִילָה. Allow students to refer back to the chapter story on pages 88–89. Check answers by having students read each of the four complete sentences aloud.

Shalom Ivrit 1 • Teacher's Edition

Decode the Hamantash (p. 91)

Have students discover the hidden words inside the hamantash by crossing out every second letter, then writing the words in the correct spaces below. Check answers by announcing each number and calling on students to provide the word(s).

Important note: When students turn the corners in the hamantash, they should continue counting from the previous list. For example, after the first arrow (at the top of the hamantash), students should cross out the שׁ and not begin counting again.

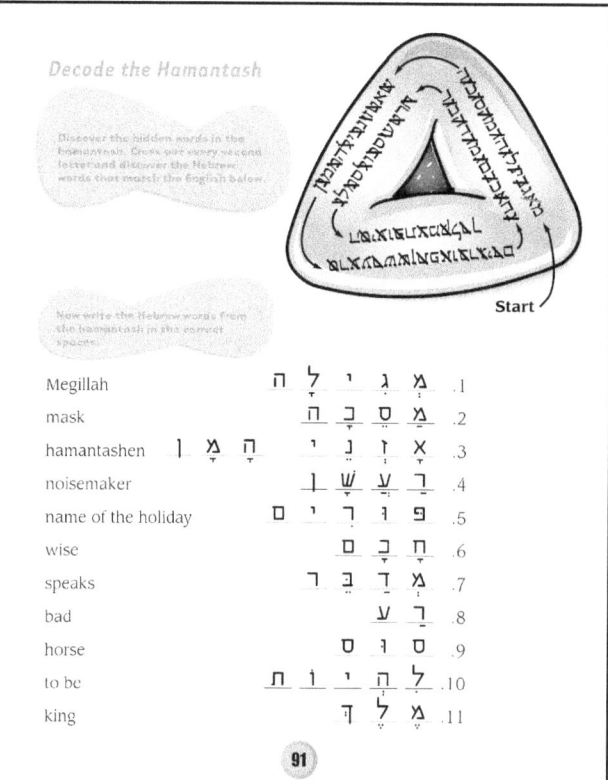

Megillah	מְגִילָה .1
mask	מַסֵכָה .2
hamantashen	אָזְנֵי הָמָן .3
noisemaker	רַעֲשָׁן .4
name of the holiday	פּוּרִים .5
wise	חָכָם .6
speaks	מְדַבֵּר .7
bad	רַע .8
horse	סוּס .9
to be	לִהְיוֹת .10
king	מֶלֶךְ .11

Game Box Play a giant game of "Concentration," as described on page 17.

Using 5" x 7" index cards, have students draw one of each of the following: מְגִילָה, מַסֵכָה, אֶסְתֵּר הַמַלְכָּה, מֶלֶךְ, סוּס, רַעֲשָׁן, אָזְנֵי הָמָן, מָרְדְכַי, and הָמָן. Also have students make creative illustrations of חָכָם, טִפֵּשׁ, קוֹרְאִים, רַעַשׁ, מְדַבֵּר/מְדַבֶּרֶת, and רַע. (Make sure the entire class has a chance to see each illustration, so they know what they'll be searching for!) Write all Hebrew words on separate index cards.

Shuffle all picture and word cards together. Lay them out in a grid on the floor or a large table. Continue as normal.

You may wish to play a special "Purim version" of the game, during which students twirl רַעֲשָׁנִים when a Haman picture or word card is found. The student who turns over a Haman card loses a turn. Students who find matching pairs of Esther or Mordechai cards receive two points for each pair.

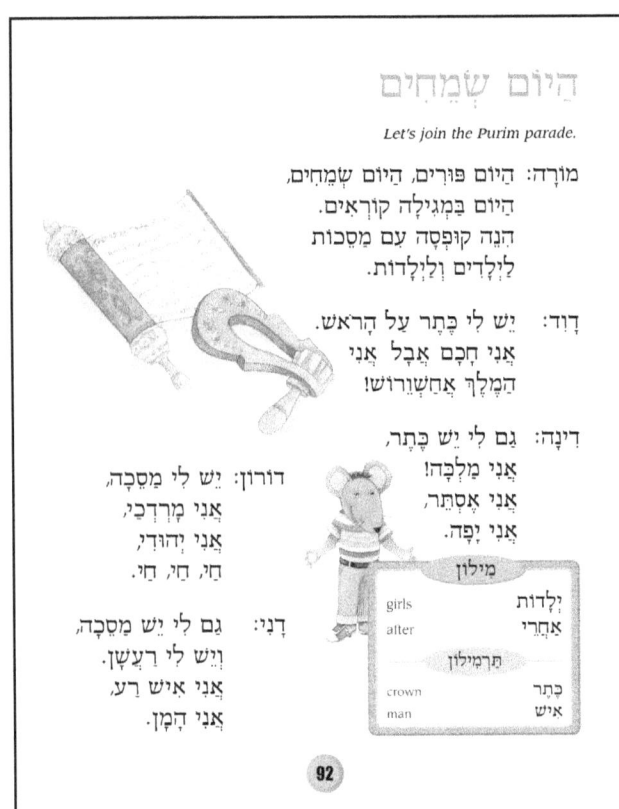

Mastering the Milon (p. 92)

• **יְלָדוֹת** • Point to each of the boys in the class and say:

_____ , _____ , _____-יְלָדִים.

Point to each of the girls, say:

_____ , _____ , _____-יְלָדוֹת.

Explain that for boys and girls together (even if there's only one boy!), we use יְלָדִים.

• **אַחֲרֵי** • Have a boy walk to the board, say:

_____ הוֹלֵךְ לַלוּחַ.

Have a girl walk to the board, say:

_____ הוֹלֶכֶת לַלוּחַ.

Say: _____ הוֹלֶכֶת לַלוּחַ אַחֲרֵי [boy's name].

Ask: What do you think אַחֲרֵי means?

Chapter Story: הַיוֹם שְׂמֵחִים
(pp. 92–93)

 **Ready for Reading** Explain that כֶּתֶר means "crown," and אִישׁ means "man." (You may also wish to have students guess what the word for "woman" is—they may deduce that it's אִשָּׁה!)

Tell students that they'll find the name of another Purim figure—Vashti, the queen who refused to dance for הַמֶּלֶךְ אֲחַשְׁוֵרוֹשׁ.

 **Read Aloud!** Assign seven students to read the parts of דּוֹרוֹן, דִּינָה, דָּוִד, מוֹרָה, נְמָלָה, and עַכְבָּר, דָּנִי. Have them read the entire story aloud. Encourage them to have fun with the reading, perhaps by using silly voices for each character.

 **The Extra Mile** At this point in the program, you may wish to challenge your students to create "The Extra Mile" questions themselves. Encourage them to ask simple questions, such as:

- הַיוֹם פּוּרִים? (כֵּן, הַיוֹם פּוּרִים.) OR
- מִי אֶסְתֵּר? (דִּינָה אֶסְתֵּר.)

If you prefer, ask the following questions once students have completed the chapter story. Or if you'd like, save them for a game of "מָצָאתִי!" (later in this chapter):

- מָה יֵשׁ בַּקּוּפְסָה? (יֵשׁ מַסֵּכוֹת בַּקּוּפְסָה.)
- לְמִי יֵשׁ כֶּתֶר עַל הָרֹאשׁ? (יֵשׁ לְדָוִד וְיֵשׁ לְדִינָה כֶּתֶר עַל הָרֹאשׁ.)
- לְמִי יֵשׁ מַסֵּכָה? (יֵשׁ לְדּוֹרוֹן וְיֵשׁ לְדִינָה מַסֵּכָה.)
- מָה הַצֶּבַע שֶׁל הַכּוֹבַע? (הַכּוֹבַע בְּצֶבַע לָבָן.)
- מִי בַּמְּגִילָה? (נְמָלָה בַּמְּגִילָה.)
- עַכְבָּר סוּס גָּדוֹל? (לֹא, עַכְבָּר סוּס קָטָן.)
- מָה אוֹכְלִים הַיְלָדִים וְהַיְלָדוֹת? (הַיְלָדִים וְהַיְלָדוֹת אוֹכְלִים אָזְנֵי הָמָן.)

מוֹרָה: וְלִי יֵשׁ כּוֹבַע,
כּוֹבַע לָבָן,
וְאַף אָדֹם,
אֲנִי לֵיצָן.

נְמָלָה: אֲנִי מִלְמְלָה,
גַּם אֲנִי בַּמְּגִילָה.
אֲנִי וַשְׁתִּי,
מַלְכָּה קְטַנְטַנָּה.

עַכְבָּר: יֵשׁ גַּם סוּס בַּמְּגִילָה.
אֲנִי סוּס קָטָן.
הַסּוּס הוֹלֵךְ
אַחֲרֵי הָמָן.

כֻּלָּם שָׂרִים, גָּדוֹל וְקָטָן,
קוֹרְאִים בַּמְּגִילָה
וְאוֹכְלִים אָזְנֵי הָמָן.

93

 **Game Box** Play "מָצָאתִי!—I Found It!" as described on page 16.

Tell students that in this version, they must do as Mordechai and Esther did—act quickly! Once they call "מָצָאתִי!," students have five seconds to follow each direction.

Sample "מָצָאתִי!" directions, in ascending order of difficulty, include:

- Find three characters in the מְגִילָה. (*Answers may include* סוּס, מָרְדְּכַי, אֶסְתֵּר, אֲחַשְׁוֵרוֹשׁ, *and* הָמָן.)
- Find the phrase that means, "I am wise." (*Page 92, line 6:* אֲנִי חָכָם.)
- מִי שָׂרִים? (*Page 93, line 13:* כֻּלָּם שָׂרִים)
- מָה אוֹמֵר דָּנִי? (*Page 92, lines 5–8*)

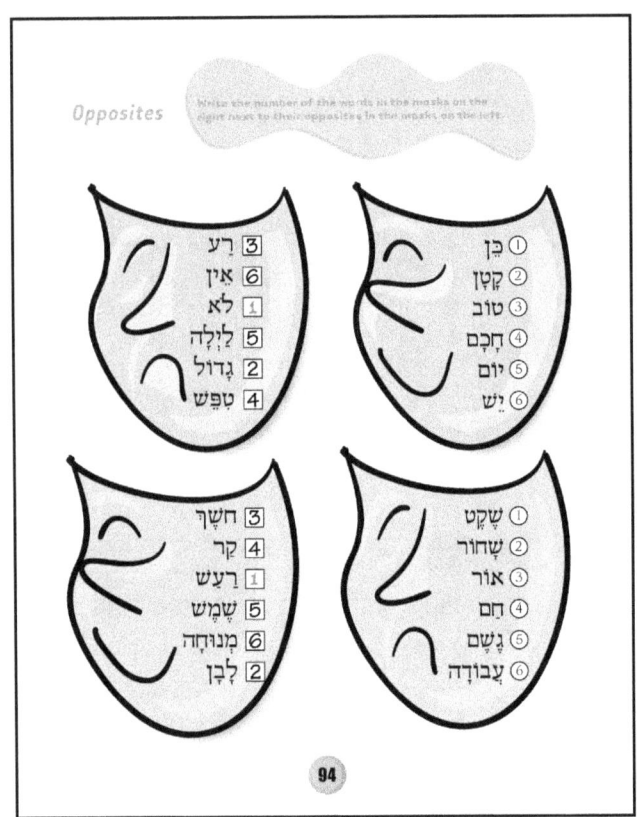

Opposites (p. 94)

Have students complete the exercise by writing the number of the words in the masks on the right next to their opposites in the masks on the left. Check answers by reading each of the words in the masks on the right side, then having students provide their opposites.

You may wish to complete the exercise as a class by having students cover the masks on the left side with books. Read each word in the masks on the right side and have students provide the opposites—without looking at the masks on the left. Students may surprise themselves by how much they know!

Game Box
Bar's Biography

Divide the class into groups of three or four. Using the pictures of Bar on page 95, have each group create four sentences that describe Bar. The sentences may be "true" (based on the pictures), or "creative."

A sample biography may be:

בָּר עַכְבָּר טוֹב. בָּר חָכָם מְאֹד. בָּר אוֹהֵב מְנוּחָה, וְהוּא לֹא אוֹהֵב עֲבוֹדָה. בָּר אוֹכֵל כָּל הַיּוֹם.

Award teams 1 point for each "mask" word they use. Award an additional 3 points for each of the following categories, based on votes from the class (the "biographers" may not vote for themselves!).

- Most interesting biography
- Most creative biography
- Best overall biography

The team with the most points is the winner!

Mastering the Milon (p. 95)

• **אִם** • Say: אִם יֵשׁ שֶׁמֶשׁ, יֵשׁ אוֹר; אִם אֲנִי עוֹבֵד/עוֹבֶדֶת, אֲנִי עָיֵף/עֲיֵפָה.

Stress the word **אִם** as you would "if."

• **יֵשׁ לְ___** • Point to individual students and say:
יֵשׁ לְ___ סֵפֶר; יֵשׁ לְ___ עִפָּרוֹן; יֵשׁ לְ___ כִּסֵּא.

Ask a student about a classmate:
יֵשׁ לְ___ מַחְבֶּרֶת? (כֵּן, יֵשׁ לְ___ מַחְבֶּרֶת.)

 **Put It Together** Review the various ways of using ___ יֵשׁ לְ:
Pick up a book and say: יֵשׁ לִי סֵפֶר.
Hand the book to a boy, say: יֵשׁ לְךָ סֵפֶר.
Ask the class: יֵשׁ לְ___ סֵפֶר?
(כֵּן, יֵשׁ לְ___ סֵפֶר.)
Hand the book to a girl, say: יֵשׁ לָךְ סֵפֶר.
To the class: יֵשׁ לְ___ סֵפֶר?
(כֵּן, יֵשׁ לְ___ סֵפֶר.)

Have the class lift their books. Say: יֵשׁ לָנוּ סְפָרִים!
You may wish to have individuals practice using each form of ___ יֵשׁ לְ.

Chapter Story (p. 95)

 **Read Aloud!** Have the class read the story in one or more of the following ways:

- Students alternate reading pairs of lines.
- All boys in the class together read the first line of each pair; the girls read the second line of each pair.
- You read the first line in each pair; the class responds by reading the second line.

If you give Bar one thing, he wants another.

אִם יֵשׁ לְבַר שֶׁקֶט,
בַּר רוֹצֶה רַעַשׁ.
אִם יֵשׁ לְבַר רַעַשׁ,
בַּר רוֹצֶה חֲגִיגָה.
אִם יֵשׁ לְבַר חֲגִיגָה,
בַּר רוֹצֶה עוּגָה.
אִם יֵשׁ לְבַר עוּגָה,
בַּר רוֹצֶה נֵרוֹת.

אִם יֵשׁ לְבַר נֵרוֹת,
בַּר רוֹצֶה מַתָּנָה.
אִם יֵשׁ לְבַר מַתָּנָה,
בַּר רוֹצֶה רַעֲשָׁן.
אִם יֵשׁ לְבַר רַעֲשָׁן,
בַּר עוֹשֶׂה רַעַשׁ.
אִם יֵשׁ לְבַר רַעַשׁ,
בַּר רוֹצֶה שֶׁקֶט!

The Extra Mile Have students, with their books, sit in a circle. Going counterclockwise, have each student read a pair of lines, replacing "Bar" with the name of the person to his or her left. Remind the class to use the correct form of רוֹצֶה/רוֹצָה!

The first three lines of the story may become:

- אִם יֵשׁ לְדָוִד שֶׁקֶט, דָּוִד רוֹצֶה רַעַשׁ.
- אִם יֵשׁ לְשָׂרָה רַעַשׁ, שָׂרָה רוֹצָה חֲגִיגָה.
- אִם יֵשׁ לְדָנִיאֵל חֲגִיגָה, דָּנִיאֵל רוֹצֶה עוּגָה.

Looking Ahead

In the next chapter, we will learn the word for "hungry," then learn all sorts of new foods to be hungry *for*—including eggs and cookies!

In preparation for the next chapter, have students think of as many Hebrew words as they can that have to do with Passover. (*Answers may include* סֵדֶר, מָרוֹר, מַצָּה, *etc.*) You may wish to start a list on the board or a large sheet of paper, then add to it as you progress through Chapter 12.

Chapter 12

Lesson Objectives

Students will:
- Develop familiarity with new verb form combinations, with the active/infinitive construction (רוֹצָה לֶאֱכוֹל).
- Develop greater command of a variety of verbs, including לוֹקֵחַ/לוֹקַחַת, קוֹרֵא/קוֹרֵאת, and חוֹשֵׁב/חוֹשֶׁבֶת.

New Milon Words and Phrases

Core Vocabulary

reads (m/f)	קוֹרֵא/קוֹרֵאת
takes (m/f)	לוֹקֵחַ/לוֹקַחַת
from	מִ—
hungry (m)	רָעֵב
to eat	לֶאֱכוֹל
thinks (m/f)	חוֹשֵׁב/חוֹשֶׁבֶת

Other Useful Vocabulary

cookie	עוּגִיָה
egg	בֵּיצָה

What We'll Need

- ❑ Text pages 96-103
- ❑ Word Cards 18, 48, 134, 136, 137, 138, 149-156
- ❑ Helpful props: markers and construction paper; cookies!

Where We Are

Chapter 12 finds us at the Passover seder. We listen in as Saba and Savta tell how Jews were slaves in Egypt, and then became free people.

Then we find a very confused Bar, who can't find a crumb of bread or cookies in the house—but who is perfectly fine with Passover cake!

Let's Review

Have students draw pictures of Haman and Mordechai on the board (using page 89 as a guide). Shuffle Word Cards 18, 48, 134, 136, 137, and 138, and place them along the chalkboard ledge, below the drawings.

Explain to students that you will provide English sentences, and they should arrange the Hebrew Word Cards in the correct order—below the correct picture!

Have students create:
Below Mordechai:
- He is wise. (הוּא חָכָם.)
- He does not want to be foolish.

(הוּא לֹא רוֹצֶה לִהְיוֹת טִפֵּשׁ.)

Beneath Haman:
- He wants to be wise. (הוּא רוֹצֶה לִהְיוֹת חָכָם.)
- He is foolish. (הוּא טִפֵּשׁ.)

Introducing the Lesson

Draw a cookie and an egg on the board. Rub your tummy as if you are hungry. Say: אֲנִי רוֹצֶה/רוֹצָה לֶאֱכוֹל.

Pointing to each drawing, ask:

אֲנִי רוֹצֶה/רוֹצָה עוּגִיָה אוֹ
אֲנִי רוֹצֶה/רוֹצָה בֵּיצָה?

Ask each student:

אַתָּה/אַתְּ רוֹצֶה/רוֹצָה לֶאֱכוֹל עוּגִיָה אוֹ בֵּיצָה?
(אֲנִי רוֹצֶה/רוֹצָה לֶאֱכוֹל עוּגִיָה OR בֵּיצָה.)

Depending on which food received the most votes, say (pointing to your head to indicate "thinking"):

אֲנִי חוֹשֵׁב/חוֹשֶׁבֶת. אֲנִי רוֹצֶה/רוֹצָה _____!

Depending on your synagogue's dietary restrictions, you may wish to distribute cookies to celebrate the beginning of a chapter that contains lots of food!

chapter 12

הַסֵּדֶר

The Passover seder is a celebration of our freedom.

כָּל הַמִּשְׁפָּחָה בַּבַּיִת.
הַשּׁוּלְחָן גָּדוֹל וְיָפֶה.
סֵדֶר פֶּסַח בַּבַּיִת.
עַל הַשּׁוּלְחָן מַצּוֹת וְיַיִן.
עַל הַשּׁוּלְחָן קְעָרָה שֶׁל פֶּסַח.

הַיְלָדִים שָׁרִים: מַה נִּשְׁתַּנָּה.
אַבָּא קוֹרֵא בַּהַגָּדָה.

סַבָּא קוֹרֵא עַל הַמֶּלֶךְ פַּרְעֹה.
הַמֶּלֶךְ פַּרְעֹה מֶלֶךְ רַע.
הַמֶּלֶךְ פַּרְעֹה לֹא אוֹהֵב יְהוּדִים.
לַיְּהוּדִים לֹא טוֹב בְּמִצְרַיִם.
הַיְּהוּדִים עֲבָדִים.

96

Chapter Story: הַסֵּדֶר (pp. 96–97)

**Ready for Reading** Without looking at the *tarmilon* on page 97, have students brainstorm a list of all Passover words they know in Hebrew. (*Most will know* סֵדֶר, הַגָּדָה, *and* מַצָּה.) Write the list on the board and keep it there throughout the lesson. Circle each word as you come across it in the chapter. Add new words, too!

Now review the *tarmilon* on page 97:

• סֵדֶר • Remind students that סֵדֶר means "order."

• פֶּסַח • Remind students that the פֶּסַח was the paschal lamb, the blood of which the Hebrew slaves used to mark their doorposts.

• מַצָּה • Ask: Why do we eat מַצָּה? (*Because in our haste to flee from Egypt, the bread did not have a chance to rise!*)

• קְעָרָה • Explain that the seder plate is called the קְעָרָה.

• מַה נִּשְׁתַּנָּה • See who in the class can remember the words and tune to מַה נִּשְׁתַּנָּה—The Four Questions.

• הַגָּדָה • Literally, "telling"—the book that contains the Passover seder.

Mastering the Milon (p. 97)

• לוֹקֵחַ/לוֹקַחַת • Walk around the classroom and collect random items (even be a little silly). Say:

אֲנִי לוֹקֵחַ/לוֹקַחַת סֵפֶר;
אֲנִי לוֹקֵחַ/לוֹקַחַת מַחְבֶּרֶת;
אֲנִי לוֹקֵחַ/לוֹקַחַת אַף שֶׁל דָּוִד...

Ask: What do you think לוֹקֵחַ and לוֹקַחַת mean?

**Captain Grammar** As you teach קוֹרֵא/קוֹרֵאת and לוֹקֵחַ/לוֹקַחַת, be careful not to use the definite article הַ___ (אֲנִי לוֹקַחַת הַסֵּפֶר), as that would require the particle אֶת, which we don't tackle quite yet!

• מִ___ • Review some English homonyms that students know (*eye, I; hi, high; etc.*). Explain that Hebrew has homonyms, too: We know that מִי means "who," but the prefix מִ—spelled without the י—means "from." Provide examples: מִכִּתָּה; מִגַּן; מִקּוּפְסָה.

**Conversation Corner** Give a book to a student and say:

אֲנִי נוֹתֵן/נוֹתֶנֶת סֵפֶר לְ___.

Extend your hand to receive the book, say:

אֲנִי לוֹקֵחַ/לוֹקַחַת סֵפֶר מִ___.

Pass the book back to student, repeat.

Have the class pass the book around the class, using the following formula (you may wish to write the following sentences on the board):

1. Student 1 passes book to Student 2, says:

אֲנִי נוֹתֵן/נוֹתֶנֶת סֵפֶר לְ___.

2. Student 2 receives book, says:

אֲנִי לוֹקֵחַ/לוֹקַחַת סֵפֶר מִ___.

• קוֹרֵא/קוֹרֵאת • Read the first line of the chapter story on page 96. Say:

אֲנִי קוֹרֵא/קוֹרֵאת.

Have a student of the opposite gender read the second line, say:

___ קוֹרֵא/קוֹרֵאת.

Continue this way until students understand that קוֹרֵא and קוֹרֵאת mean "read." You may also wish to remind them of the plural form of the word—קוֹרְאִים.

- **פַּרְעֹה** • Life was difficult for the slaves under the rule of פַּרְעֹה.

- **יְהוּדִים** • Plural of יְהוּדִי, meaning "Jews."

- **מִצְרַיִם** • Tell students that Moses freed us מִמִּצְרַיִם—"from Egypt."

- **עֲבָדִים** • Ask students to think of the word meaning "work." עֲבָדִים (עֲבוֹדָה) are workers—or slaves!

- **יוֹצְאִים** • At the Passover seder, we imagine that we יוֹצְאִים—"go out" from Egypt.

- **בְּנֵי־חוֹרִין** • Once the slaves left Egypt, they were בְּנֵי־חוֹרִין—"free people."

 **Read Aloud!** Read the entire story aloud. Encourage students to raise their hands and ask questions as you read. Congratulate them for coming so far in their studies—they are now combining more verbs, nouns, and adjectives than ever before!

Have students alternate reading lines. Do a "slow read," with students pausing before beginning each new line, to allow time to absorb all new vocabulary. Then do a "quick read"—this time with students reading different lines.

 **The Extra Mile** Tell your students that this "Extra Mile" will be slightly more difficult than usual, as they exercise their growing vocabulary:

- אֵיפֹה הַמִּשְׁפָּחָה? (הַמִּשְׁפָּחָה בַּבַּיִת.)
- הַשּׁוּלְחָן קָטָן אוֹ גָדוֹל? (הַשּׁוּלְחָן גָדוֹל.)
- מַה הַיּוֹם? (פֶּסַח הַיּוֹם.)
- אֵיפֹה יֵשׁ מַצָּה? (יֵשׁ מַצָּה עַל הַשּׁוּלְחָן.)
- אֵיפֹה הַקְּעָרָה שֶׁל פֶּסַח? (הַקְּעָרָה שֶׁל פֶּסַח עַל הַשּׁוּלְחָן.)
- מַה עוֹשִׂים הַיְלָדִים? (הַיְלָדִים שָׁרִים, "מַה נִּשְׁתַּנָּה.")
- יְהוּדִים שְׂמֵחִים בְּמִצְרַיִם? (לֹא, יְהוּדִים לֹא שְׂמֵחִים; לֹא, יְהוּדִים עֲבָדִים.)
- מַה אוֹמֵר פַּרְעֹה? (פַּרְעֹה אוֹמֵר: לֹא, לֹא!)
- מַה אוֹמֵר מֹשֶׁה? (כֵּן, כֵּן, הַיְהוּדִים יוֹצְאִים מִמִּצְרַיִם.)

Using the Photograph
Photo 1
Have a student read and translate the caption to the photo at the top of page 98. (A Passover seder is in the house. What is on the table?)

Have students list as many objects in the photograph as they can. (*Objects include:* פְּרָחִים, הַגָּדָה, מַצָּה, נֵרוֹת, יַיִן, קְעָרָה; *students may also know* מָרוֹר, חֲרוֹסֶת, *and* כַּרְפַּס.)

Refer to the brainstorming list from the beginning of the lesson. See if there are any more words to add!

Photo 2
Have a student read and translate the caption to the bottom photo. (The boy sings מַה נִּשְׁתַּנָה.)

> **Bring It to Life** If it is Passover season, you may wish to sing (or invite your synagogue's cantor to sing) מַה נִּשְׁתַּנָה with your class. Your students may be amazed to see how many words they now recognize! (מַה נִּשְׁתַּנָה, אוֹכְלִים, מִכָּל, הַזֶּה, הַלַּיְלָה, etc.)

Climb the Pyramid (p. 99)

Have students complete the exercise by writing the words from the pyramid in the correct spaces. Check answers by having students read each sentence aloud.

> **Game Box**
> **So Many Combinations!**
>
> Give each student a pencil and a sheet of paper. On the board, write line 1 from page 99:
>
> עַל הַשׁוּלְחָן ‎ ____ ‏ שֶׁל ‎ ____ ‏.
>
> Have each student write combinations of two words that would make sense in the blank spaces. See who can think of the most combinations in five minutes. Rules are:
>
> - Students may not use the same word twice.
> - Only words learned thus far in *Shalom Ivrit* are allowed.
> - Students may use their books as they create combinations, but they must write in Hebrew!
>
> Possible combinations include:
>
> פֵּרוֹת, עֵץ; פְּרָחִים, אַבָּא; לֶחֶם, עַכְבָּר...
>
> Students receive one point for each original combination. The student with the most points is the winner!

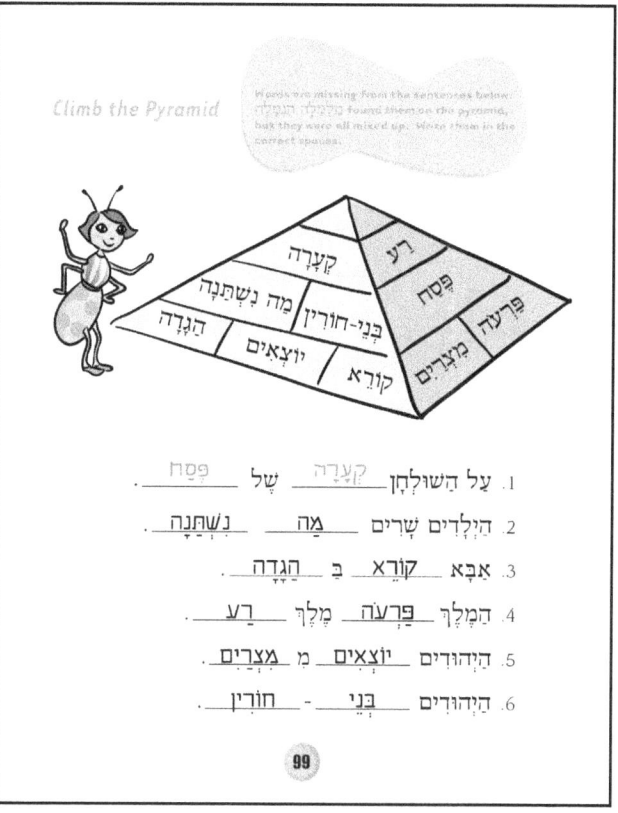

Chapter 12

Chapter Story: חַג הַפֶּסַח, חַג אָבִיב
(p. 100)

חַג הַפֶּסַח, חַג אָבִיב

Passover, a celebration of spring

מַצוֹת לַחַג, נֵרוֹת לַחַג,
יַיִן, חֲרוֹסֶת, מָרוֹר, וְדָג.
חַג הַפֶּסַח, חַג אָבִיב.
חַג הַפֶּסַח, חַג אָבִיב.

אֲנִי קוֹרֵא בַּהַגָּדָה,
אֲנִי אוֹמֵר מַה נִּשְׁתַּנָּה.
חַג הַפֶּסַח, חַג אָבִיב.
חַג הַפֶּסַח, חַג אָבִיב.

אֲנִי אוֹכֵל מַצָּה טוֹבָה,
אֲנִי גַם שָׁר חַד גַּדְיָא.
חַג הַפֶּסַח, חַג אָבִיב.
חַג הַפֶּסַח, חַג אָבִיב.

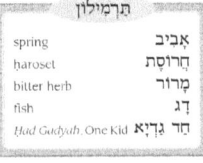

תַּרְמִילוֹן

spring	אָבִיב
haroset	חֲרוֹסֶת
bitter herb	מָרוֹר
fish	דָּג
Had Gadyah, One Kid	חַד גַּדְיָא

100

Ready for Reading Teach the *tarmilon* on page 100. Students may already know חֲרוֹסֶת—the fruity, nutty Passover mixture, and מָרוֹר—the bitter herb, from their holiday studies. They may also remember דָּג from the days of Creation all the way back in Chapter 8. Teach that אָבִיב means "spring," the season during which Passover falls, and חַד גַּדְיָא—"One Kid"—is a traditional Passover song.

Read Aloud! Divide the class into three groups. Assign each group one paragraph on page 100 to read together. Have a contest to see which group can read the most clearly and energetically. You may wish to invite the school director to listen to the reading.

The Extra Mile Have students from each group answer the following questions:

Paragraph 1:

- מַדְלִיקִים נֵרוֹת בְּחַג הַפֶּסַח?
  (כֵּן, מַדְלִיקִים נֵרוֹת בְּחַג הַפֶּסַח.)
- יֵשׁ לֶחֶם בְּחַג הַפֶּסַח?
  (לֹא, אֵין לֶחֶם בְּחַג הַפֶּסַח.)

Paragraph 2:

- מִי קוֹרֵא בַּהַגָּדָה? (הָעַכְבָּר קוֹרֵא בַּהַגָּדָה.)
- הָעַכְבָּר אוֹמֵר, "שָׁלוֹם"?
  (לֹא, הָעַכְבָּר אוֹמֵר, "מַה נִּשְׁתַּנָּה.")

Paragraph 3:

- מָה אוֹכֵל הָעַכְבָּר? (הָעַכְבָּר אוֹכֵל מַצָּה טוֹבָה.)
- הָעַכְבָּר שָׁר, "יוֹם הוּלֶדֶת שָׂמֵחַ"?
  (לֹא, הָעַכְבָּר שָׁר, "חַד גַּדְיָא.")

Shalom Ivrit 1 • Teacher's Edition

Matzah Code (p. 101)

Have students complete the exercise by writing the Hebrew word next to the English word with the same meaning. They should write one letter in each space, leaving out the vowels.

Then have students write every letter that has a number under it in the spaces at the bottom of the page to discover the new word: אֲפִיקוֹמָן.

 Bring It to Life Teach the other three seasons of the year:

חֹרֶף — winter
קַיִץ — summer
סְתָיו — autumn

Using markers and construction paper, have students draw a large circle, then divide it into quarters—representing the four seasons. Have students write the Hebrew name of each season in each quarter.

Ask students to draw objects and scenes associated with Jewish holidays that fall during each season. For example, students may draw a לוּלָב, an אֶתְרוֹג, and someone blowing a shofar in סְתָיו.

 **Game Box** Play "מָה הַמִּילָה—What's the Word?" as described on page 17.

In this version of the game, allow students to choose words from the entire book. (You may wish to allow students to fish through Word Cards 1–151 to find a really good one!)

As they now have a larger collection of words to choose from, students may wish to ask different types of questions, such as:
- Is it something you eat?
- Is it something you sing?
- Does it have to do with a holiday?

Allow each student to ask one question and offer one guess. If everyone has guessed once, allow each student a second guess. The student who guesses the word gets to choose the next one.

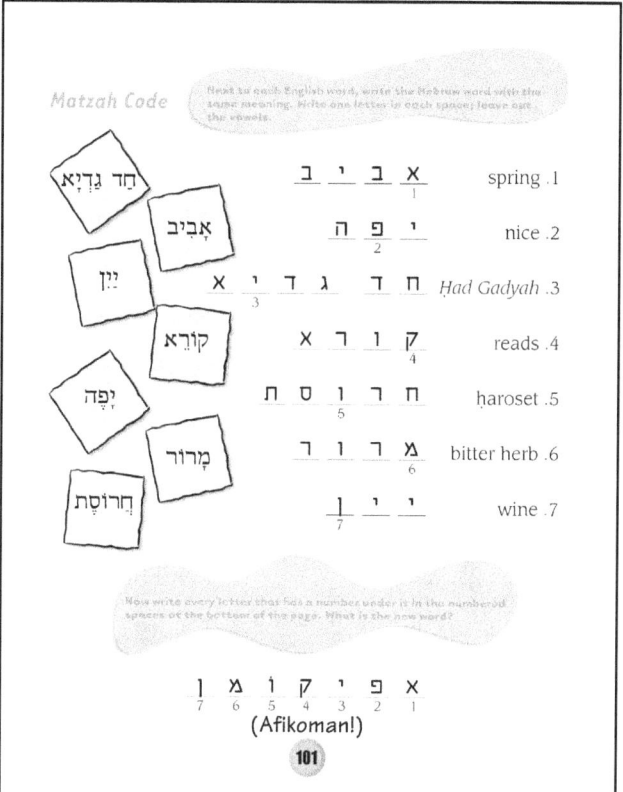

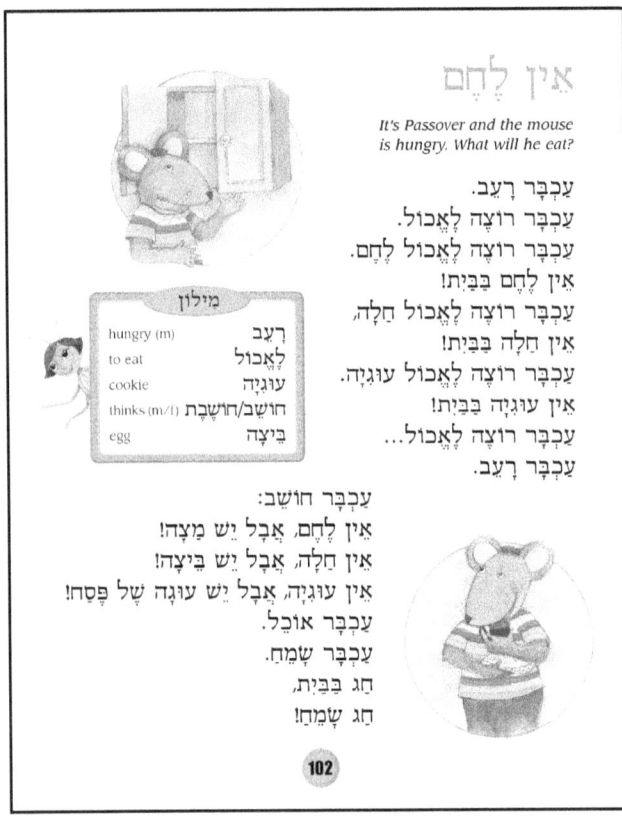

Continue until students understand that חוֹשֵׁב/חוֹשֶׁבֶת mean "thinks."

Chapter Story: אֵין לֶחֶם (p. 102)

 **Ready for Reading** Have a student read the Hebrew title and English sentences aloud. Create two lists on the board: "Passover Food" and "Non-Passover Foods." Have students include only words you've learned so far in *Shalom Ivrit*. The list may include:

Passover	Non-Passover
פֵּרוֹת	לֶחֶם
חֲרוֹסֶת	חַלָּה
דָּג	אָזְנֵי הָמָן

 **Read Aloud!** Read the entire story aloud. Then have students alternate reading lines. Challenge the class to read in a continuous, fluid rhythm. You may wish to have the class "rehearse" once through, then allow students to read "for real."

Mastering the Milon (p. 102)

• **לֶאֱכוֹל** • Display several "food" Word Cards on the chalkboard ledge. Point to each and say for example:

אֲנִי אוֹהֵב/אוֹהֶבֶת לֶאֱכוֹל עוּגָה;
אֲנִי אוֹהֵב/אוֹהֶבֶת לֶאֱכוֹל לֶחֶם;
אֲנִי אוֹהֵב/אוֹהֶבֶת לֶאֱכוֹל דָּג.

Ask a student:

מָה אַתָּה/אַתְּ רוֹצֶה/רוֹצָה לֶאֱכוֹל?
(אֲנִי רוֹצֶה/רוֹצָה לֶאֱכוֹל _____.)

• **עוּגִיָּה** • Draw a cake on the board and say: עוּגָה.
Draw a cookie on the board, say: עוּגִיָּה.
Ask a student:

אַתָּה/אַתְּ רוֹצֶה/רוֹצָה לֶאֱכוֹל עוּגִיָּה?
(כֵּן, אֲנִי רוֹצֶה/רוֹצָה לֶאֱכוֹל עוּגִיָּה.)

• **רָעֵב** • Have students look at the picture of Bar at the top of page 102. Say:

אֵין עוּגִיּוֹת, אֵין לֶחֶם, אֵין חַלָּה; בַּר רָעֵב!

Ask: What do you think רָעֵב means? (You may wish to explain that the feminine form of רָעֵב is רְעֵבָה; מַלְמָלָה רְעֵבָה)

 **Put It Together** Draw a cookie on an index card. Have students pass the card to one another, using the following dialog:

אֲנִי רָעֵב/רְעֵבָה.
אֲנִי רוֹצֶה/רוֹצָה לֶאֱכוֹל עוּגִיָּה.
אַתָּה/אַתְּ רוֹצֶה/רוֹצָה עוּגִיָּה?

(Student passes card to the next student.)

• **בֵּיצָה** • Refer to the drawing of the egg on the board. Say:

אֲנִי רוֹצֶה/רוֹצָה לֶאֱכוֹל בֵּיצָה.

Ask: What do you think בֵּיצָה means?

 **Our Tradition** On every סֵדֶר plate you'll find a בֵּיצָה—an egg—to symbolize the sacrifice that was offered at every pilgrimage holiday. Many people hard-boil the egg, then hold a burning match just under it to darken it.

• **חוֹשֵׁב/חוֹשֶׁבֶת** • Rub your chin as if you are thinking hard. Say: אֲנִי חוֹשֵׁב/חוֹשֶׁבֶת.
Point to a student, say: _____ חוֹשֵׁב/חוֹשֶׁבֶת.

The Extra Mile Have students fill in the blanks as you read each sentence:

• עַכְבָּר רוֹצָה לֶאֱכוֹל _____ וְ_____ וְ_____.
• אֲבָל אֵין _____ אוֹ _____ אוֹ _____ בַּבַּיִת.
• עַכְבָּר אוֹכֵל _____ וְ_____ וְ_____.

Ask:

• עַכְבָּר שָׂמֵחַ? (כֵּן, עַכְבָּר שָׂמֵחַ.)
• עַכְבָּר רָעֵב? (לֹא, עַכְבָּר לֹא רָעֵב.)

What's the Ending? (p. 103)

Have students complete the exercise by placing a checkmark next to the word or phrase that best completes each sentence. Check answers by having students read each complete sentence aloud.

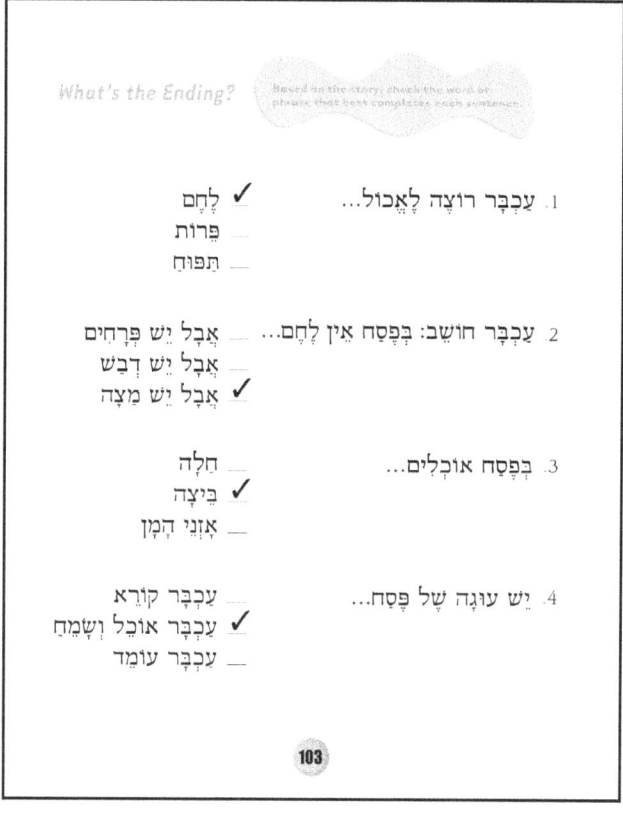

Game Box Play "Hebrew Baseball," as described on page 16. You may wish to base the questions on all the words you've learned so far, or only on words learned in this chapter.

Sample questions for this chapter include:

Single:
• Take a book from a student's desk. Say:
אֲנִי לוֹקֵחַ/לוֹקַחַת סֵפֶר _____ דָּוִד. (מִ)
• What we want to do when we are רָעֵב/רְעֵבָה. (לֶאֱכוֹל)

Double:
• The word meaning "she thinks." (חוֹשֶׁבֶת)
• Read a book and ask: מָה אֲנִי עוֹשֶׂה/עוֹשָׂה? (אַתָּה/אַתְּ קוֹרֵא/קוֹרֵאת.)

Triple:
• יְלָדִים שָׁרִים _____ וְ_____ בְּפֶסַח. (מַה נִּשְׁתַּנָּה and חַד גַּדְיָא)
• חֲרֹסֶת וְגַם מָרוֹר וְגַם בֵּיצָה עַל הַ_____. (קְעָרָה)

Home Run:
• יְהוּדִים _____ מִמִּצְרַיִם. (יוֹצְאִים)
• יְהוּדִים לֹא עֲבָדִים, יְהוּדִים _____. (בְּנֵי־חוֹרִין)

Introduce a new way to steal a base: Pick a word (for an object) from this chapter. Provide three clues about the object. (For example: לֶחֶם, פֶּסַח, and סֵדֶר might be clues for מַצָּה.) Students have ten seconds to guess the correct word or they're out!

Looking Ahead

In the next chapter, we will take a journey to Israel and learn the words for "flag," "nation," and "land."

We will also learn how to say "to me"—a contraction of two words your students already know. Have them think of the words for "to" and "me" ("I") and see if they can guess—without looking!—how to say "to me."

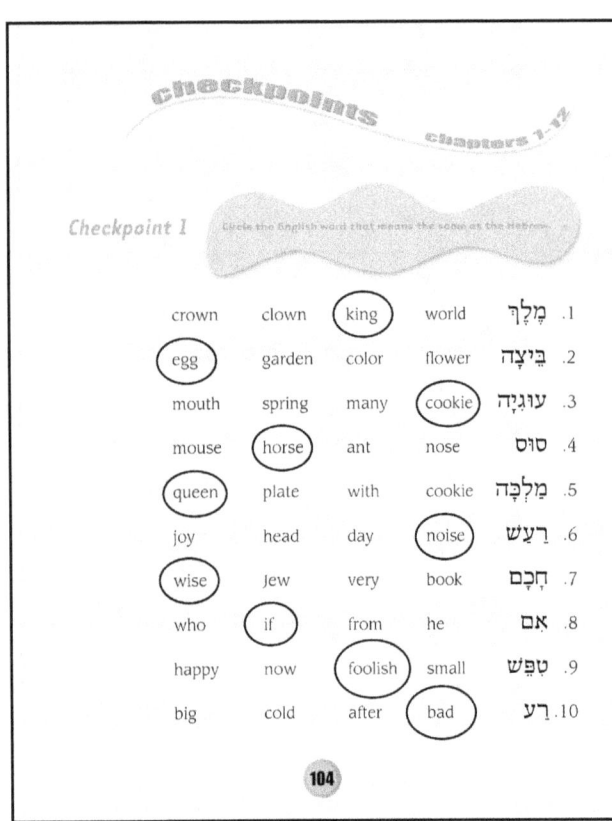

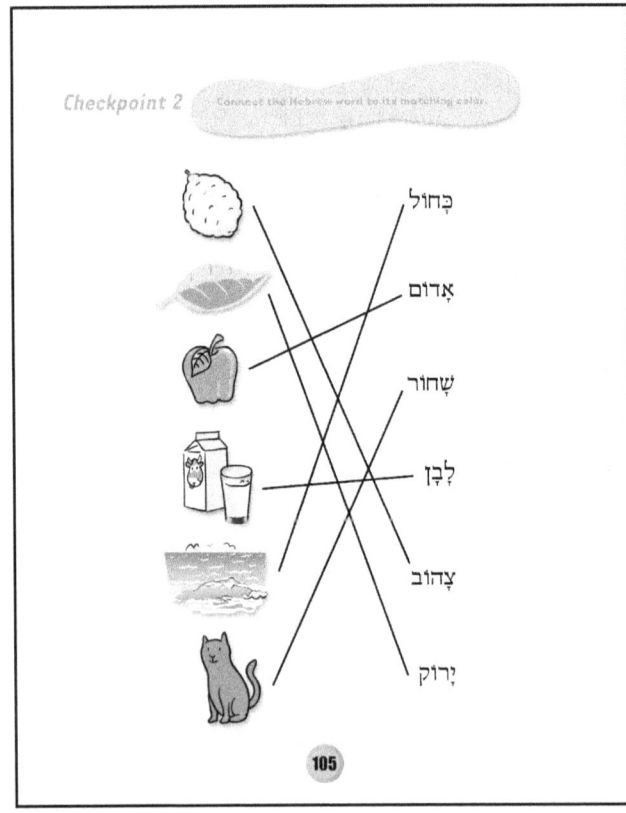

Checkpoint Completion

(pp. 104–107)

Checkpoint 1

Have students complete the exercise by circling the English word that means the same as the Hebrew.

Checkpoint 2

Have students complete the exercise by connecting the Hebrew word to its matching color.

Continue on the next page.

Checkpoint 3

Have students complete the exercise by circling the Hebrew word that means the same as the English.

Checkpoint 4

Have students complete the exercise by writing the Hebrew word for each picture, then writing one letter in each blank space, leaving out the vowels.

Review answers by having students provide the English for each of the ten Hebrew words in Checkpoint 1, and the six Hebrew words in Checkpoint 2. Then have students provide the Hebrew for each of the ten Engish words in Checkpoint 3, and the seven pictures in Checkpoint 4. Instruct students to place a checkmark next to the answers that are correct, and an X next to the answers that are incorrect. Have them place a grade at the top of each page (for example, 4/6 or 9/10).

Review grades by checking each student's book.

Checkpoint Assessment

If possible, spend a few minutes with each student to review his or her work. Be sure to praise students for correct answers, and encourage them to find answers for incorrect ones.

For checkpoints 1 and 3, continue with the "Checkpoint Assessment" ideas on page 59. For Checkpoint 2, adjust the grading scale to students who scored: 5–6, 4, and 3 or lower. For Checkpoint 4, adjust the grading scale to students who scored: 6–7, 4–5, and 3 or lower.

Keep your eyes out for words that your students consistently miss. You may wish to spend some time reviewing those words as a class.

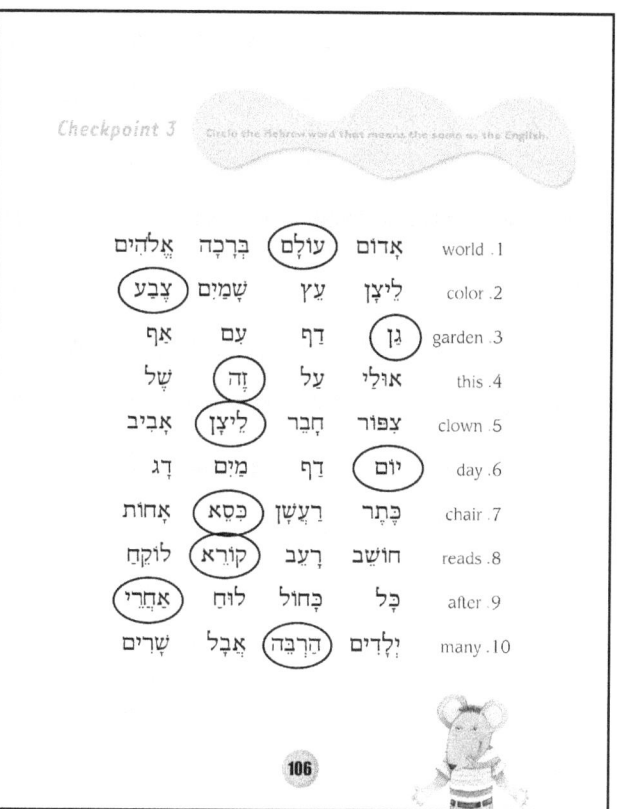

145

Chapter 12

Dear Parent,

During the past few weeks, our class has learned words and phrases having to do with Purim, such as *ra'ash* (noise), *melech* and *malkah* (king and queen), and *oznei haman* (hamentashen); and words having to do with Passover, such as *mitzrayim* (Egypt), *avadim* (slaves), and *b'nei ḥorin* (free people). We have also been working to build our core Hebrew vocabulary.

Here are some words your child has learned during the few weeks, including ideas to incorporate these words into your daily conversations:

garden	*gan*	גַּן

Why not plant a *gan* in honor of Tu B'Shevat?

to eat	*le'echol*	לֶאֱכוֹל

Everyone loves to hear that it's time *le'echol*!

cookie	*ugiyah*	עוּגִיָּה
egg	*beitzah*	בֵּיצָה

No one gets an *ugiyah* without using its Hebrew name!

Thank you for helping us to learn modern Hebrew!

B'Shalom,

Lesson Objectives

Students will:

- Further develop expertise in combining vocabulary, verb forms, and concepts learned throughout *Shalom Ivrit*.
- Learn a new construction of the prefix ‎לְ‎___, with the addition of ‎לִי‎.

New Milon Words and Phrases

Core Vocabulary

why	לָמָה
to me	לִי

Israel-Related Vocabulary

flag	דֶּגֶל
nation, people	עַם
land	אֶרֶץ

What We'll Need

- ❏ Text pages 108–113
- ❏ Word Cards 157–161
- ❏ Picture Card 32
- ❏ Helpful props: markers and posterboard; a map of Israel

Where We Are

In Chapter 13, we celebrate Yom Ha'atzma'ut—Israel's birthday—with David, Lili, and an Israeli flag cake!

We also join Bar and Malmalah as they each offer a song about the Jewish homeland—"*Eretz Yisrael*."

Let's Review

Have students draw cookies on index cards or strips of paper (one for each student). Place them in a box.

Write the following three sentences on the board:

1. אֲנִי _____ [hungry].
2. אֲנִי רוֹצֶה/רוֹצָה _____ [to eat].
3. אֲנִי _____ [take] _____ [a cookie] _____ [from a box].

Extend the box to each student and have him or her take a "cookie" while completing the sentences. A student might answer: אֲנִי רְעֵבָה; אֲנִי רוֹצָה לֶאֱכוֹל; אֲנִי לוֹקַחַת עוּגִיָּה מְקוּפְסָה.

Remind your students to use the correct forms of רָעֵב/רְעֵבָה and לוֹקֵחַ/לוֹקַחַת!

If possible, prepare Israeli flag cookies for the class to enjoy. Have students complete the exercise above with the *real* cookies, then enjoy the snack together as you begin the lesson on אֶרֶץ יִשְׂרָאֵל.

Introducing the Lesson

Explain to students that in this chapter they will learn their fourth "question word." (Remind them that they already know מִי, מָה, and אֵיפֹה.)

Ask students:

אַתָּה/אַתְּ רוֹצֶה/רוֹצָה לֶאֱכוֹל?
(כֵּן, אֲנִי רוֹצֶה/רוֹצָה לֶאֱכוֹל. OR
לֹא, אֲנִי לֹא רוֹצֶה/רוֹצָה לֶאֱכוֹל.)

Follow up with:

לָמָה אַתָּה/אַתְּ לֹא רוֹצֶה/רוֹצָה לֶאֱכוֹל?
(Be sure to stress לָמָה as you would "why?")

(כִּי אֲנִי רָעֵב/רְעֵבָה. OR
כִּי אֲנִי לֹא רָעֵב/רְעֵבָה.)

Have a student read the Hebrew title and English sentence aloud. Ask the class to read the sentence again to themselves, this time restating the sentence in Hebrew. (Tell them to change "wants to draw" to "draws.") Encourage students to try their best!

(לִילִי מְצַיֶּרֶת דֶּגֶל שֶׁל יִשְׂרָאֵל, אֲבָל אֵין לְלִילִי צֶבַע כָּחוֹל.)

Mastering the Milon (p. 109)

• **לִי** • Give a book to a student. Say:

אֲנִי נוֹתֵן/נוֹתֶנֶת סֵפֶר לְ_____.

Have the student return the book to you, say:
_____ נוֹתֵן לִי סֵפֶר. (לִי).
(point to yourself as you say
Ask: What do you think לִי means?

 **Captain Grammar** In English we say, "David gives the book *to me*," while in Hebrew we say, "David gives *to me* the book." Provide a series of examples to help your students become familiar with the "switch":

• אַתָּה קוֹרֵא לִי סֵפֶר.
• אַתְּ אוֹמֶרֶת לִי, "שָׁלוֹם".
• אַתָּה אוֹמֵר לִי, "מַה נִּשְׁתַּנָּה".

• **לָמָּה** • Ask your students a series of random questions. (אַתָּה קוֹרֵא סְפָרִים?; אַתְּ אוֹהֶבֶת עוּגָה?; etc.) As you receive answers, ask: לָמָּה? OR לָמָּה לֹא? Continue this way until students understand that לָמָּה means "why?"

• **דֶּגֶל** • Display Picture Card 32. Say: דֶּגֶל שֶׁל יִשְׂרָאֵל.
Ask: What do you think דֶּגֶל means?

Chapter Story: דֶּגֶל כָּחוֹל וְלָבָן
(pp. 108–109)

 **Ready for Reading** Teach the two *tarmilon* words. Most students will know that יִשְׂרָאֵל means "Israel" and that יוֹם הָעַצְמָאוּת is Israel's Independence Day.

You may wish to tell your students that יוֹם הָעַצְמָאוּת is one of the newest Jewish holidays; we've only been celebrating it since 1948, when Israel was born!

 **Our Tradition** Israel is the name of our Jewish state, but it is also used to refer to כְּלַל יִשְׂרָאֵל—the world Jewish community.

Shalom Ivrit 1 • Teacher's Edition

 **Read Aloud!** Tell the class that they will now compete in a new Olympic sport: cross-country Hebrew reading. In this sport, speed does not count—but pronunciation and enthusiasm do!

Divide the class into "countries" of three student each. Have each group decide who will play the parts of אִמָּא, לִילִי, and דָּוִד. Give the groups 10 minutes to rehearse the dialog. (For fun, you may wish to allow the groups a few minutes to create their own דֶּגֶל, to post on the board as they read. If you do, have each group list the colors on the flag of their "country.")

Have each group, in turn, perform the entire dialog. Again, praise your students on how much they've learned! Then have the class vote on whose "performance" was the best, based on the two criteria of pronunciation and enthusiasm ("countries" may not vote for themselves).

You may wish to hold a "medal ceremony," during which the winning "country" stands before the class (perhaps holding up their דֶּגֶל!).

 Bring It to Life Teach your students—or invite your synagogue's cantor to teach—*Hatikvah*, Israel's national anthem. (Many *siddurim* include the words to *Hatikvah*.)

 **The Extra Mile** Direct the following questions to the entire class:

- לָמָה אִמָּא עוֹשָׂה עוּגָה הַיּוֹם? (הַיּוֹם יוֹם הוּלֶדֶת. OR הַיּוֹם יוֹם הָעַצְמָאוּת לְיִשְׂרָאֵל.)
- מָה מְצַיֵּר דָּוִד? (דָּוִד מְצַיֵּר דֶּגֶל כָּחוֹל וְלָבָן.)
- מָה צֶבַע הַשָּׁמַיִם? (צֶבַע הַשָּׁמַיִם כָּחוֹל.)
- מָה צֶבַע הַשָּׁלוֹם? (צֶבַע הַשָּׁלוֹם לָבָן.)
- אֵיפֹה רוֹצָה אִמָּא שָׁלוֹם? (אִמָּא רוֹצָה שָׁלוֹם בַּבַּיִת, בָּעוֹלָם, וְגַם בְּיִשְׂרָאֵל.)

Chapter 13

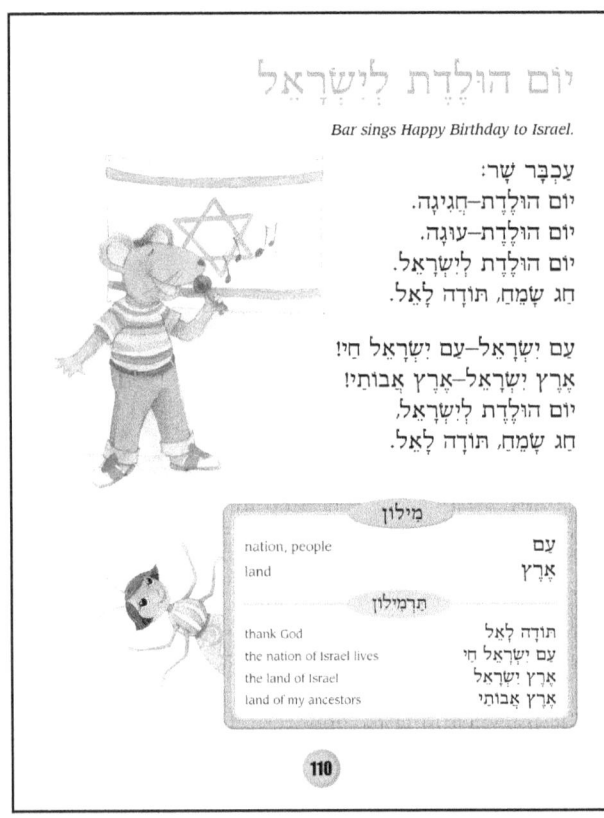

Mastering the Milon (p. 110)

• **עַם** • Sing:

עַם יִשְׂרָאֵל חַי/עַם יִשְׂרָאֵל חַי/עַם יִשְׂרָאֵל חַי.

Remind your students that יִשְׂרָאֵל means "Israel," and חַי means "lives." Ask: What do you think עַם means? Explain that עַם means "nation," or "people," usually the Jewish people!

• **אֶרֶץ** • Display a map of Israel. Say: הִנֵה אֶרֶץ יִשְׂרָאֵל. Many students will know that אֶרֶץ means "land."

Chapter Story: יוֹם הוּלֶדֶת לְיִשְׂרָאֵל (p. 110)

 **Ready for Reading** Teach the four common expressions found in the *tarmilon* on page 110:

• **תּוֹדָה לָאֵל** • Ask students for examples in their lives when they might say, תּוֹדָה לָאֵל—Thank God!

• **עַם יִשְׂרָאֵל חַי** • As the song says—the nation of Israel lives!

• **אֶרֶץ יִשְׂרָאֵל** • Ask students to name three cities found in אֶרֶץ יִשְׂרָאֵל (*Tel Aviv, Jerusalem, Haifa, Eilat, Be'er Sheva, etc.*)

• **אֶרֶץ אֲבוֹתַי** • Explain that אֶרֶץ אֲבוֹתַי means "land of my ancestors." Ask students to name some of our biblical ancestors (*Abraham, Sarah, Isaac, Rebecca, etc.*)

 **Read Aloud!** Have students alternate reading lines, first a "slow read," allowing them to become familiar with the poem's rhythm and new vocabulary, then a "quick read," allowing them to read smoothly and playfully—perhaps in their squeaky "Bar" voices.

For fun, have the entire class sing the melody of עַם יִשְׂרָאֵל חַי as they read the sixth line!

 **Bring It to Life** Have three or four volunteers lead groups of four or five students in creating their own melody for Bar's song. Have each group sing its melody to the class!

 **The Extra Mile** Ask students:

• מָה שָׁר הָעַכְבָּר?
(הָעַכְבָּר שָׁר יוֹם הוּלֶדֶת לְיִשְׂרָאֵל.)

• לָמָה שָׁר הָעַכְבָּר?
(הָעַכְבָּר שָׁר כִּי הַיוֹם יוֹם הוּלֶדֶת לְיִשְׂרָאֵל.)

• יוֹם הָעַצְמָאוּת חַג שָׂמֵחַ?
(כֵּן, יוֹם הָעַצְמָאוּת חַג שָׂמֵחַ.)

Bring It to Life Using markers or water colors and posterboard, have students create their own יוֹם הָעַצְמָאוּת decorations. Encourage them to include images and colors of the Israeli flag and Hebrew expressions from the chapter, including אֶרֶץ יִשְׂרָאֵל and עַם יִשְׂרָאֵל חַי.

Then display the Israel decorations in the classroom, the school hallways, or during a Yom Ha'atzma'ut celebration. (If the decorations will be on public display, you may wish to have your students include English translations as well.)

Shalom Ivrit 1 • Teacher's Edition

True or False? (p. 111)

Have students complete the exercise by reading each of the sentences on page 111 and deciding—based on "דֶגֶל כָּחוֹל וְלָבָן" on pages 108–109—whether they are true or false. Then have them circle the letter in the correct column—כֵּן or לֹא.

Once they have finished, have students copy each circled letter in the matching blank space at the bottom of the page to find the name of the holiday—יוֹם הָעַצְמָאוּת!

For the three "לֹא" sentences, have students provide versions of the sentences that would make them "כֵּן." Remind your students to be careful of verb forms! Answers are:

- Sentence 2: לִילִי מְצַיֶּרֶת דֶגֶל.
- Sentence 5: יוֹם הָעַצְמָאוּת לֹא חַג לָעֵצִים. OR יוֹם הָעַצְמָאוּת יוֹם הוּלֶדֶת לְיִשְׂרָאֵל.
- Sentence 7: אִמָּא רוֹצָה שָׁלוֹם בַּבַּיִת.

Game Box Play "Hebrew Match-Up," as described on page 18.

Prepare by assigning students to write each of the sentences on page 111—with question marks at the end of each—on slips of colored paper. Instruct your students to write neatly and clearly. Meanwhile, prepare the answers to the questions on slips of white paper. Answers are:

1. כֵּן, דָוִד מְצַיֵּר דֶגֶל כָּחוֹל וְלָבָן.
2. לֹא, אִמָּא לֹא מְצַיֶּרֶת דֶגֶל.
3. כֵּן, אִמָּא עוֹשָׂה עוּגָה.
4. כֵּן, לִילִי מְצַיֶּרֶת דֶגֶל יָרוֹק וְלָבָן.
5. לֹא, יוֹם הָעַצְמָאוּת לֹא חַג הָעֵצִים.
6. כֵּן, כָּחוֹל צֶבַע הַשָּׁמַיִם.
7. לֹא, אִמָּא רוֹצָה שָׁלוֹם בַּבַּיִת.
8. כֵּן, יוֹם הָעַצְמָאוּת יוֹם הוּלֶדֶת לְיִשְׂרָאֵל.
9. כֵּן, אִמָּא רוֹצָה שָׁלוֹם בָּעוֹלָם.
10. כֵּן, לָבָן צֶבַע הַשָּׁלוֹם.

Have students place the colored slips of paper into a "question box," and the white slips of paper into an "answer box." Divide the class into א and ב. Have א draw slips of paper from the "question box," while ב draws from the "answer box." The two teams should stand in lines, facing one another.

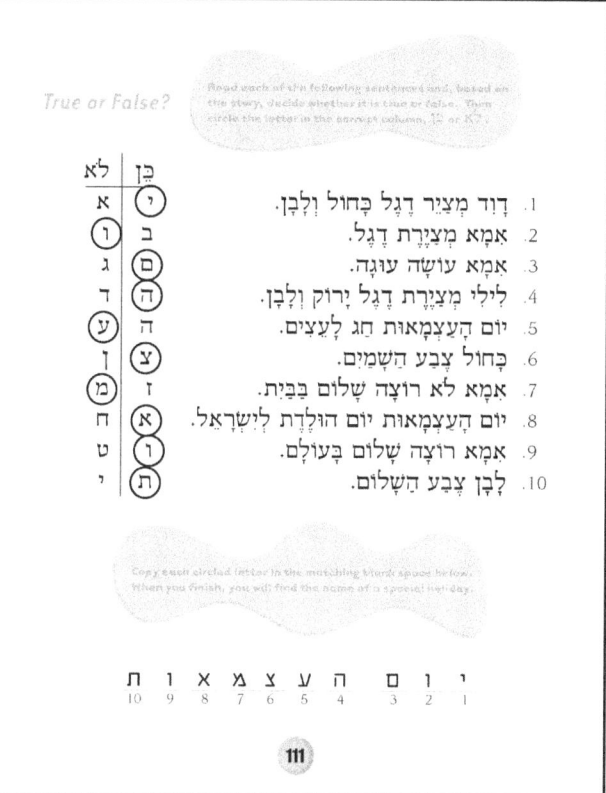

The first student in the א line should ask his or her question. The player on ב holding the correct answer then has ten seconds to step forward and read it aloud. If the student on ב is correct, ב receives a point. If not, א receives the point.

After all questions have been read, have the teams replace their slips of paper into their boxes and switch. ב now chooses from the "question box," א from the "answer box."

The team with the most points at the end of both rounds is the winner.

Chapter 13

Chapter Story: יֵשׁ לָנוּ דֶגֶל (p. 112)

Read Aloud! We've heard Bar's song to Israel, now it's time for Malmalah's. As you did for "יוֹם הוּלֶדֶת לְיִשְׂרָאֵל" on page 110, have students read the story twice, alternating lines: a "slow read," then a "quick read"—this time with feeling!

The Extra Mile Ask the following questions:

- יֵשׁ לָנוּ דֶגֶל גָדוֹל? (לֹא, יֵשׁ לָנוּ דֶגֶל קָטָן.)
- יֵשׁ לָנוּ דֶגֶל יָרוֹק? (לֹא, יֵשׁ לָנוּ דֶגֶל כָּחוֹל וְלָבָן.)
- יֵשׁ לָנוּ אֶרֶץ גְדוֹלָה? (לֹא, יֵשׁ לָנוּ אֶרֶץ קְטַנָה.)

Our Tradition What does Malmalah mean by "אֶרֶץ קְטַנָה"? Is Israel really that small? Explain to your students that in fact Israel is one of the smallest countries in the world—but it is gigantic in the hearts of the Jewish people!

Map of Israel (p. 113)

Have students complete the exercise by connecting the English and Hebrew names of each city. Then have students write the Hebrew names of the cities on the map in the blank spaces at the bottom of the page. Check answers by having students read each number and the city that corresponds to it.

Bring It to Life Invite an Israeli teenager to speak to your students about life in Israel. Have the class prepare a series of questions to ask. Sample questions include: What are the different cities in Israel like? How is life for kids different in Israel than it is here? How is it the same?

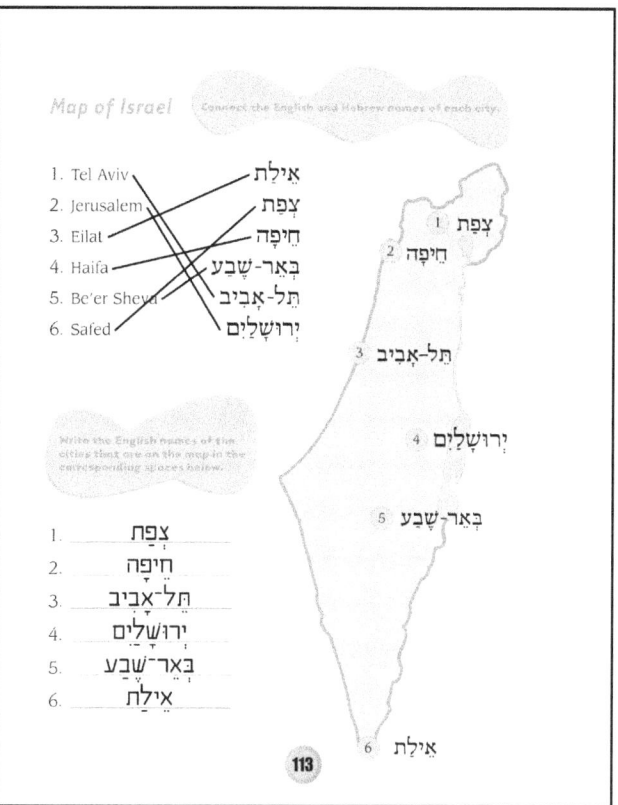

Looking Ahead

Explain that in the next chapter, we will take a tour through all of *Shalom Ivrit*, including all the holidays we've learned.

We will also learn an important word that sums up much of what we've learned this year: the word for "year." Ask your students to think about all the holidays you've studied together. Instruct students—or groups of students—to prepare to present words having to do with holidays that you assign.

Lesson Objectives

Students will:
- Create new combinations of nouns and verbs learned in previous chapters.
- Review vocabulary learned throughout *Shalom Ivrit*.

New Milon Words and Phrases

Core Vocabulary

year   שָׁנָה

What We'll need

☐ Text pages 114–121
☐ Word Cards 22, 23, 44, 84, and 162
☐ Helpful props: markers or crayons and construction paper

Where We Are

In Chapter 14, we take a tour through all the holidays we've learned throughout *Shalom Ivrit*, with a special stop at the one holiday that comes every week.

Then we are reminded that—not surprisingly—Bar is happiest when he is eating!

Let's Review

Ask each of your students to hand you one object in the classroom. (You may wish to collect the items in a box, or make it silly by collecting everything in your hands and arms). As students hand you objects, say:

נוֹתֵן/נוֹתֶנֶת לִי סֵפֶר; _____
נוֹתֵן/נוֹתֶנֶת לִי מַחְבֶּרֶת... _____

Then return the objects to your students. Have them "narrate" the exchange using נוֹתֵן/נוֹתֶנֶת and לִי. For example:

מוֹרָה נוֹתֶנֶת לִי עִפָּרוֹן;
מוֹרָה נוֹתֶנֶת לִי כּוֹבַע...

Introducing the Lesson

Explain that in this lesson the class will review all the holidays they've learned throughout *Shalom Ivrit*.

Introduce this lesson with a quick review of all the previous ones:

- Assign groups of two or three students to each of the previous chapters (1–13). Depending on the size of your class, you may need to assign more than one chapter per group.
- You may wish to distribute Word Cards to the appropriate groups (see chart on pages 19–20).
- Have students prepare to read selections from their assigned chapters (suggested list below), then "teach" four words by showing their Word Cards and asking the class for the English (the words need not correspond to the reading selections).

Appropriate selections include:

Chapters:

1. All of מִי בַּבַּיִת?, page 5.
2. The first 8 lines of אֵיפֹה הַדְבַשׁ?, page 10.
3. The first 10 lines of גֶּשֶׁם, page 25.
4. The first 7 lines of מִשְׁפָּחָה, page 28.
5. The first 9 lines of דּוֹרוֹן בַּכִּתָּה, page 38.
6. All of יוֹם שַׁבָּת, יוֹם מְנוּחָה, page 50.
7. Lines 5–12 of חֲנוּכָּה, page 57.
8. The first two lines of each day of Creation, pages 66–69.
9. Lines 10–16 of חַג לָעֵצִים, page 72.
10. The first 7 lines of עוֹלָם יָפֶה, page 82.
11. Lines 13–20 of הַיּוֹם פּוּרִים, pages 88–89.
12. Lines 13–21 of הַסֵּדֶר, page 97.
13. The first 13 lines of דֶּגֶל כָּחוֹל וְלָבָן, pages 108–109.

Congratulate your students on how much they've learned so far (almost 250 words!), and for successfully reaching the book's final chapter!

Mastering the Milon (p. 114)

- שָׁנָה • Say:
  בְּרֹאשׁ הַשָּׁנָה, אֲנִי אוֹמֶרֶת, "שָׁנָה טוֹבָה!"
  Ask: What do you think שָׁנָה means? Most students will know that שָׁנָה means "year."

> **Our Tradition** Explain to your students that the Jewish year is different from the secular—or "regular"—year. Ask: When does the Jewish year begin? (רֹאשׁ הַשָּׁנָה). Ask: According to Jewish tradition, when does the Hebrew calendar begin to count years? (*When God created the world!*)

Chapter Story: כָּל שָׁנָה (pp. 114–115)

Ready for Reading Teach the *tarmilon* words on page 114: הוֹלְכִים, מְבָרְכִים, and דְּגָלִים are plural forms of words your students already know. Most students will recognize שָׁבוּעוֹת, the holiday during which we celebrate מַתַּן תּוֹרָה—the giving of the Torah.

Ask your students to list other holidays during which we honor and read the Torah. (*On Simḥat Torah we begin the Torah reading again; on Rosh Hashanah and Yom Kippur we dress the Torah in white; etc.*)

Read Aloud! Have students alternate reading pairs of lines aloud. You may wish to have the entire class read "כָּל שָׁנָה" together in each stanza.

Using the Photograph Have a student read and translate the photo caption on page 115 aloud. (*Day of Shabbat, day of blessing. Shabbat shalom.*) Have students list objects in the photo. (חַלָּה, נֵרוֹת, יַלְדָּה, יֶלֶד, אִמָּא, etc.)

Ask the class to think of another holiday that would include חַלּוֹת, and a holiday that would not. (*Rosh Hashanah would; Passover would not*)

Shalom Ivrit 1 • Teacher's Edition

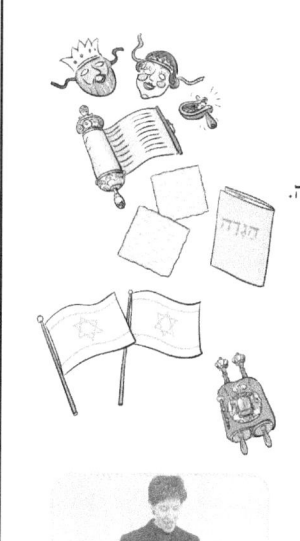

בְּחַג פּוּרִים, כָּל שָׁנָה,
שְׂמֵחִים וְקוֹרְאִים בַּמְּגִילָה.

בְּחַג הַפֶּסַח, כָּל שָׁנָה,
אוֹכְלִים מַצָּה וְקוֹרְאִים בַּהַגָּדָה.

בְּיוֹם הָעַצְמָאוּת, כָּל שָׁנָה,
לְאֶרֶץ יִשְׂרָאֵל יֵשׁ חֲגִיגָה.

בְּחַג הַשָּׁבוּעוֹת, כָּל שָׁנָה,
חַג שָׂמֵחַ, מַתַּן תּוֹרָה.

אֲבָל כָּל שָׁבוּעַ בַּשָּׁנָה
יֵשׁ לָנוּ חַג שֶׁל מְנוּחָה.
יוֹם שֶׁל נֵרוֹת, יַיִן, וְחַלָּה,
יוֹם שַׁבָּת, יוֹם שֶׁל בְּרָכָה.

יוֹם שַׁבָּת, יוֹם שֶׁל בְּרָכָה.
שַׁבָּת שָׁלוֹם.

115

▼ וְגַם...
Say:
(Answers may include:
בֵּיצָה, חֲרוֹסֶת, מָרוֹר...)
• בְּחַג הַפֶּסַח קוֹרְאִים בַּ_____. (הַגָּדָה)

Stanza 8:
• בְּיוֹם הָעַצְמָאוּת, אוֹמְרִים,
"יוֹם הוּלֶדֶת שָׂמֵחַ" לְ_____. (יִשְׂרָאֵל)
• הַ_____ שֶׁל יִשְׂרָאֵל כָּחוֹל וְלָבָן. (דֶּגֶל)

Stanza 9:
• חַג הַשָּׁבוּעוֹת חַג שָׂמֵחַ?
(כֵּן, חַג הַשָּׁבוּעוֹת חַג שָׂמֵחַ.)
• אֱלֹהִים נוֹתֵן לְיִשְׂרָאֵל _____. (תּוֹרָה) OR
חַג הַשָּׁבוּעוֹת, חַג מַתַּן _____. (תּוֹרָה)

Stanza 10:
• כָּל שָׁבוּעַ שְׂמֵחִים בְּיוֹם _____. (שַׁבָּת)
• שַׁבָּת יוֹם שֶׁל _____.
(Answers may include:
בְּרָכוֹת, חַלָּה, יַיִן, נֵרוֹת, מְנוּחָה)

 **The Extra Mile** Ask students these review questions after each stanza:

Stanza 1:
• מָה אַתָּה/אַתְּ אוֹכֵל/אוֹכֶלֶת
בְּרֹאשׁ הַשָּׁנָה?
(Answers may include:
אֲנִי אוֹכֵל/אוֹכֶלֶת תַּפּוּחַ, דְּבַשׁ, חַלָּה...)
• מָה אוֹמְרִים בְּרֹאשׁ הַשָּׁנָה?
(אוֹמְרִים, "שָׁנָה טוֹבָה!")

Stanza 2:
• עַל מָה מְבָרְכִים בְּסֻכּוֹת?
(מְבָרְכִים עַל לוּלָב וְאֶתְרוֹג.)
• מָה יֵשׁ בַּסֻּכָּה בְּסֻכּוֹת?
(Answers may include:
שֻׁלְחָן, יְלָדִים, פֵּרוֹת, פְּרָחִים...)

Stanza 3:
• בְּשִׂמְחַת תּוֹרָה קוֹרְאִים בְּמָה?
(קוֹרְאִים בַּתּוֹרָה בְּשִׂמְחַת תּוֹרָה.)
• יֵשׁ שֶׁקֶט אוֹ רַעַשׁ בְּשִׂמְחַת תּוֹרָה?
(יֵשׁ רַעַשׁ.)

Stanza 4:
• מָה מַדְלִיקִים בַּחֲנֻכָּה?
(מַדְלִיקִים נֵרוֹת בַּחֲנֻכָּה.)
• מָה אוֹכְלִים בַּחֲנֻכָּה?
(אוֹכְלִים לְבִיבוֹת בַּחֲנֻכָּה.)

Stanza 5:
• לָמָּה שָׁרִים בְּט"וּ בִּשְׁבָט?
(שָׁרִים לָעֵצִים בְּט"וּ בִּשְׁבָט.)
• ט"וּ בִּשְׁבָט אוֹמְרִים לָעֵצִים,
"יוֹם _____ שָׂמֵחַ!" (הוּלֶדֶת)

Stanza 6:
• בְּחַג פּוּרִים קוֹרְאִים בְּמָה?
(קוֹרְאִים מְגִילָה בְּחַג פּוּרִים.)
• מִי מַלְכָּה יָפָה בַּמְּגִילָה?
(אֶסְתֵּר מַלְכָּה יָפָה בַּמְּגִילָה.)

Stanza 7:
• מָה אוֹכְלִים בְּחַג הַפֶּסַח?
(אוֹכְלִים מַצָּה בְּחַג הַפֶּסַח.) ▶

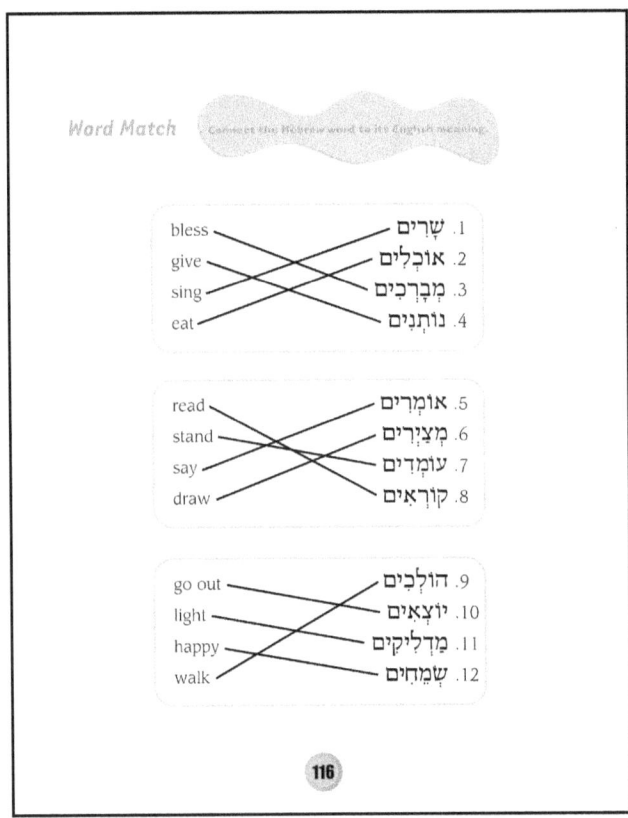

Word Match (p. 116)

Have students complete the exercise by connecting each Hebrew word to its English meaning. Check answers by reading each English word and having students provide the Hebrew.

Have a contest to see who can read the most Hebrew words on page 116 without getting tongue-tied! If a student is able to read the entire list without stumbling, have him or her begin again!

Captain Grammar Remind your students that to make a word plural when only girls are present, we add וֹת (as in יְלָדוֹת).

See if your students can change all the Hebrew words on page 116 into their feminine plural forms. Answers are: שָׁרוֹת; אוֹכְלוֹת; מְבָרְכוֹת; נוֹתְנוֹת; אוֹמְרוֹת; מְצַיְּרוֹת; עוֹמְדוֹת; קוֹרְאוֹת; הוֹלְכוֹת; יוֹצְאוֹת; מַדְלִיקוֹת; שְׂמֵחוֹת.

Game Box Play "מָצָאתִי!—I Found It!," as described on page 16.

In this version of the game, have students read the word or phrase in question, then the entire line that the word or phrase appears on. All pronunciation must be correct in order to receive a point. Or else the rest of the class has an opportunity to call "מָצָאתִי!"

Sample questions for "מָצָאתִי!" (in ascending order of difficulty) include:

- Find the word נֵרוֹת. (p. 114, line 8)
- Find the phrase מַתַּן תּוֹרָה. (p. 115, line 8)
- Find the word that means "Israel." (יִשְׂרָאֵל; p. 115, line 6)
- Find the phrase that means "every week." (כָּל שָׁבוּעַ; p. 115, line 9)
- בְּסוּכּוֹת, מְבָרְכִים עַל לוּלָב וְ_____. (אֶתְרוֹג; p. 114, line 4)
- בְּשִׂמְחַת תּוֹרָה, הוֹלְכִים עִם _____. (דְּגָלִים; p. 114, line 6)
- בְּחַג הַפֶּסַח, קוֹרְאִים בְּמָה? (הַגָּדָה; page 115, line 4)
- אֵיפֹה יֵשׁ נֵרוֹת בַּחֲנוּכָּה? (בַּחֲנוּכִּיָּה; p. 114, line 8)
- שַׁבָּת חַג שֶׁל מְנוּחָה אוֹ עֲבוֹדָה? (שֶׁל מְנוּחָה; p. 115, line 10)

Shalom Ivrit 1 • Teacher's Edition

He, She, or They? (p. 117)

Complete the exercise by having students circle the correct form of the verb for each sentence below, then write it in the blank space. Check answers by having students read each complete sentence.

Game Box
Listen Up!

Divide the class into teams of boys and girls. Have one girl and one boy come to the front of the class. Announce a verb (in any form you choose) from page 117, and have the appropriate student or students pantomime the word. For example, if you say אוֹכְלִים, both the girl and the boy should pretend to eat. If you say אוֹכֵל, only the boy should pretend; אוֹכֶלֶת, only the girl.

If both the boy and the girl respond correctly (inaction may be a correct response), both teams receive a point. If a student responds incorrectly, his or her team does not receive a point.

The team with the most points after ten verb forms (rounds) is the winner.

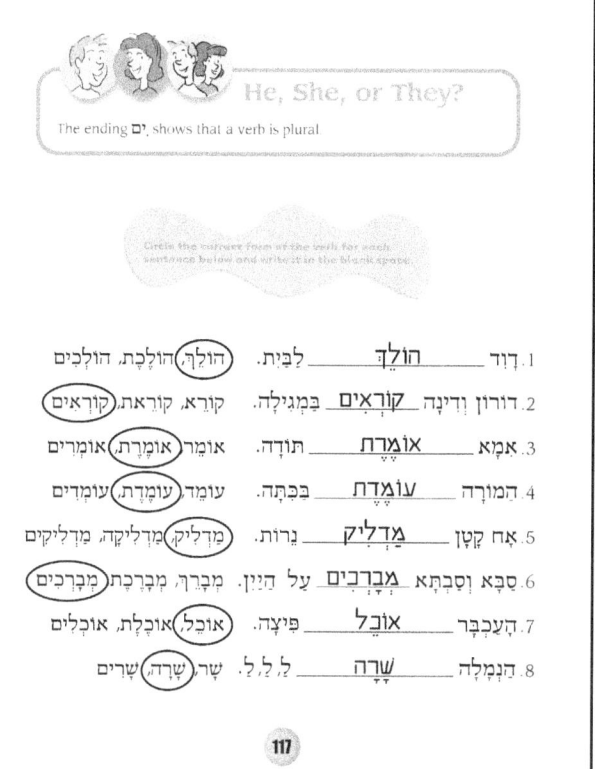

Chapter Story: עַכְבָּר שָׂמֵחַ (p. 118)

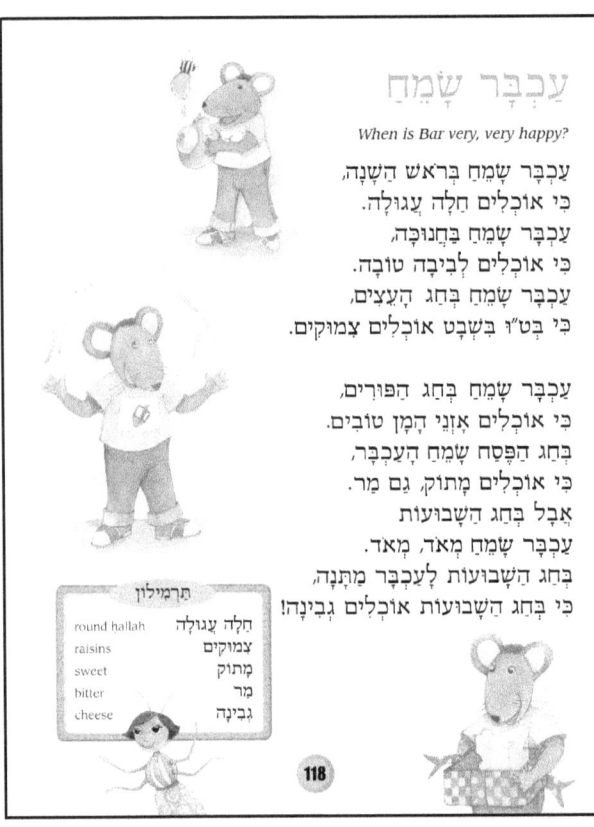

 **Ready for Reading** Teach the list of *tarmilon* words on page 118:

- **חַלָה עֲגוּלָה** • חַלָה—a round חַלָה • We eat חַלָה עֲגוּלָה on Rosh Hashanah, to symbolize the cycle of the year.

- **צְמוּקִים** • Some people prefer their חַלָה with צְמוּקִים—raisins! Take a vote in your classroom to see who prefers plain חַלָה or חַלָה עִם צְמוּקִים!

- **מָתוֹק** • Have students list foods that are מָתוֹק—sweet. Ice cream, candy, and chocolate included!

- **מַר** • See which of your students can demonstrate מַר—bitter—with the best facial expression.

- **גְבִינָה** • See who can be the first to guess the meaning of גְבִינָה from this list: American, Swiss, provolone, mozzarella.

Have a student read the Hebrew title and English question aloud. Ask your students: When are you very, very happy? Allow each student to answer. Then ask: When do you think Bar is very, very happy? (*Students may know by now that it's when he's eating!*)

 **Read Aloud!** Read the entire story aloud. Read slowly to allow students to absorb the new vocabulary. Then have students alternate reading lines. It may be fun to have girls read the first line, boys the second, then alternate this way.

 **Conversation Corner** Divide the class into pairs. Review the chapter story by having students ask one another what they would like to eat on various holidays.

Write the following question on the chalkboard:

מָה אַתָּה/אַתְּ אוֹכֵל/אוֹכֶלֶת בְּ_____?

Have students ask their partners the question on the board twice, each filling in the blank with a holiday on which we eat special foods. Have students "report" what their partner likes to eat to the class.

Sample answers include:

- דָוִד אוֹכֵל תַּפּוּחַ בְּרֹאשׁ הַשָׁנָה.
- שָׂרָה אוֹכֶלֶת לְבִיבוֹת בַּחֲנוּכָּה.
- רִבְקָה רוֹצָה לֶאֱכוֹל אָזְנֵי הָמָן בְּחַג פּוּרִים.

Shalom Ivrit 1 • Teacher's Edition

Name That Holiday (p. 119)

Have students complete the exercise by writing the name of the holiday under the matching food. Check answers by pointing to each picture and having students provide the answer.

Bring It to Life Have students write three-sentence stories about Bar ha'achbar, based on the illustrations on pages 118–119. Allow students to use their books. The stories should contain words from at least five different *Shalom Ivrit* chapters.

A sample story may be:

בָּר גָּר בַּבַּיִת. בָּר הָעַכְבָּר אוֹהֵב לֶאֱכוֹל.
הוּא אוֹהֵב מַצָּה, גְּבִינָה, וְחַלָּה.

You may wish to have students illustrate their stories using markers or crayons, then present their stories to the class.

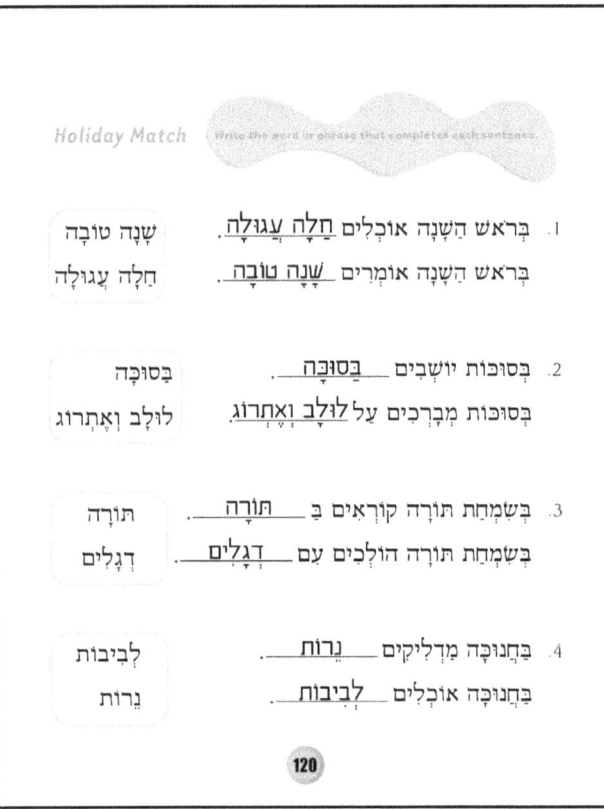

Holiday Match (pp. 120–121)

Have students complete the exercise by writing the word or phrase that completes each sentence. Check answers by having students read each sentence aloud.

Or, assign students to read each pair of sentences aloud. Challenge the rest of the class to complete each sentence without looking in the book!

Game Box Play a gigantic version of "Concentration," as described on page 17.

In this version of the game, have students create 50 (yes, 50!) pairs of picture cards and Hebrew word cards on 5" x 7" index cards (you may wish to determine a list of appropriate words, or allow the class to choose). Shuffle all cards and lay them out in rows and columns on a large table or on the floor.

For a super way to end the book, have students create picture cards and Hebrew word cards on 8½ x 11 sheets of paper (construction paper will work best), and lay them out on the floor of the social hall or another large room in your synagogue.

You may wish to invite younger classes to come watch, and to cheer your students on!

Looking Ahead

Congratulate your students on a job well done in *Shalom Ivrit 1*. Teach one final phrase: כָּל הַכָּבוֹד—well done!

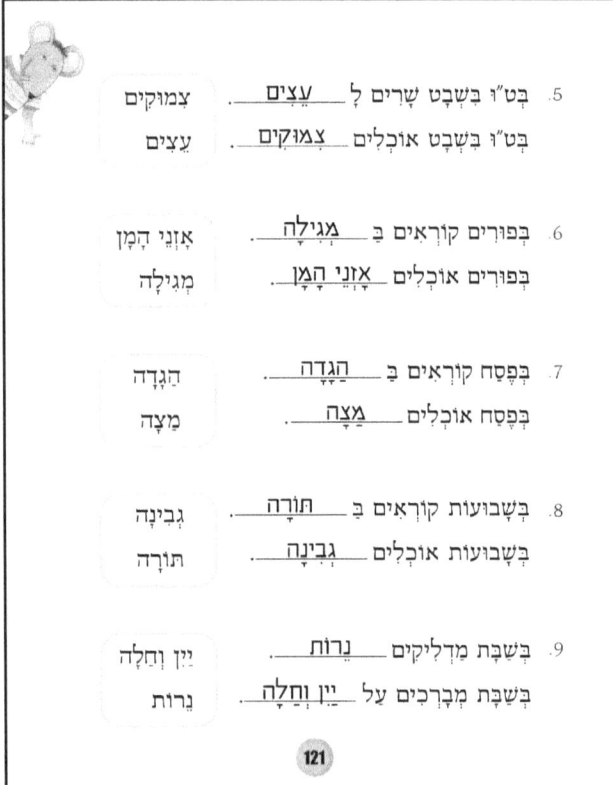

Checkpoint Completion

(pp. 122–123)

Checkpoint 1

Have students complete the exercise by circling the Hebrew word that means the same as the English.

Checkpoint 2

Have students complete the exercise by writing the Hebrew word that completes each sentence.

Review answers by having students provide the answers for each question in both checkpoints. Instruct students to place a checkmark next to the answers that are correct, and an X next to the answers that are incorrect. Have them place a grade at the top of each page (for example, 7/10 or 9/10).

Review grades by checking each student's book.

Checkpoint Assessment

If possible, spend a few minutes with each student to review his or her work. Be sure to praise students for correct answers, and encourage them to find answers for incorrect ones.

Continue with the "Checkpoint Assessment" ideas on page 59.

Keep your eyes out for words that your students consistently miss. You may wish to spend some time reviewing those words as a class.

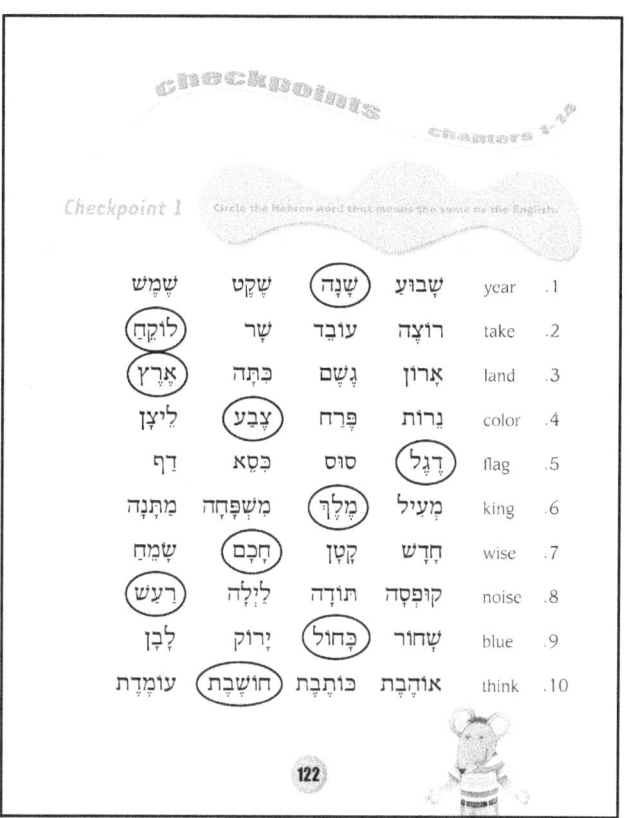

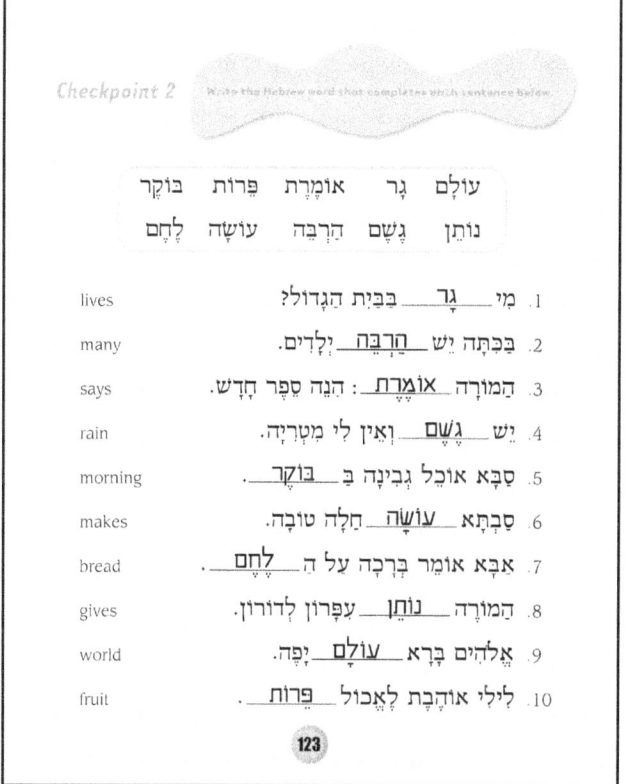

English Translations of Chapter Stories, Poems, and Songs

Chapter 1

page 4:

Hello

I am Doron, I am a boy.
Hello Doron.

I am Dinah, I am a girl.
Hello Dinah.

I am Bar, I am a mouse.
Hello Bar.

page 5:

Who Is In The House?

Here is a house.
Who is in the house?

Mother is in the house.
Father is in the house.

Hello Mother.
Hello Father.

A mouse is in the house!
A mouse is in the house?
Yes, a mouse is in the house.

I am Bar.
I am a mouse.
I live in the house.

Chapter 2

page 10:

Where Is The Honey?

Rosh HaShanah (The New Year).
The family is in the house.

Father: Are there candles?
Mother: Yes, here are candles.

Doron: Is there ḥallah?
Dinah: Yes, here is ḥallah.

Mother: Is there wine?
Father: Yes, here is wine.

Dinah: Is there an apple?
Doron: Yes, here is an apple.

Father: Is there honey?
Dinah: No!

Doron: No!

Family: Where is the honey?

page 11:

Mother: Here is honey!
          The honey is good.

Doron: Happy New Year Mother.
Dinah: Happy New Year Father.

Mother: Happy New Year Dinah and Doron.
Father: Happy New Year family.

page 14:

The Sound of the Shofar

Tu, tu, tu,
The sound of the shofar.

Happy New Year,
Happy New Year.

Happy New Year to Father,
Happy New Year to Mother.

Happy New Year,
Happy New Year.
To a boy and a girl.

page 16:

The Mouse in the Shofar

In the house lives
Bar the mouse.
It is good in the house
for the mouse.

Tu tu tu
here is a shofar.
Who is in the shofar?
Bar the mouse!

Bar the mouse
lives in the shofar!

Chapter 3

page 18:

In the Sukkah

Mother: Father, are you in the sukkah?
Father: No, I am in the house.

Mother: Doron, are you in the sukkah?
Doron: No, I am not in the sukkah.

Mother: Dinah, are you in the sukkah?
Dinah: No, I am not in the sukkah.

Mother: The family is not in the sukkah…
Who is in the sukkah?

page 19:

Grandfather: I am in the sukkah.
Here is a lulav.
Grandmother: Also I am in the sukkah.
Here is an etrog.
Mouse: Also I am in the sukkah!
Happy holiday!

page 20:

A Mouse in the Sukkah

Rain. Cold.
Who is in the sukkah?

Is the family in the sukkah? No.
Are the children in the sukkah? No.

Who is in the sukkah?
The mouse is in the sukkah!

page 21:

Bar the mouse
lives in the sukkah.
Lives in the sukkah?
It is cold in the sukkah!

Isn't the mouse cold?

Bar the mouse
lives in the box.
It is not cold in the box.
It is good for the mouse.

page 24:

Torah—A Good Gift

Happy holiday, happy holiday,
the holiday of Simḥat Torah.

Happy holiday, happy holiday,
the holiday of Simḥat Torah.

Torah, Torah,
a good gift.

Torah, Torah,
a good gift.

page 25:

Rain

Doron: Goodbye Mother,
I am going.
Mother: Doron, are you going?
There is rain…it is cold!
Doron: Yes, I am going.
Goodbye Mother.

Mother: Here is a coat.
Doron: Good, goodbye Mother.

Mother: Here is a hat.
Doron: Good, goodbye Mother.

Mother: Here is an umbrella.
Doron: Mother…goodbye.
Mother: Goodbye Doron.

Doron has a coat,
Doron has a hat,
Doron has an umbrella.
Doron is not cold.
Doron goes.

Chapter 4

page 28:

Family

I am David.
I have a family.
Brother is Dani
and Sister is Lili.

The brother Dani—big.
The sister Lili—small.
I—not big and not small.

page 29:

David: Dani, am I big?
Dani: No, you are small!

David: Lili, am I small?
Lili: No, you are big!

David: Mother, am I big?
Am I small?
What am I?

page 32:

Lili No, No

Everyone is next to the table.
Everyone is eating.

English Translations

Mother:	Lili, do you want bread?
Lili:	No, no.
David:	Lili, do you want ḥallah?
Lili:	No, no.
Dani:	Lili, do you want an apple?
Lili:	No, no.
Mother:	David, maybe Lili wants cake?
David:	No, no.

page 33:

Everyone is eating cake.
Everyone is happy.
Lili is not happy, Lili is crying.

Lili:	I want cake. I want cake.
Dani:	Lili no, no. Lili doesn't want…
Lili:	I want, I want, yes, yes, yes!
David:	Lili no, no or Lili yes, yes?

page 35:

I Am Very Small

I am an ant
I am Malmalah.

I am not big
I am very small.

Is there bread in the house?
The bread is small.

Is there cake in the house?
The cake is small.

Is there ḥallah in the house?
The ḥallah is big!

Yes, yes, yes, I want!
I want a big ḥallah.

Chapter 5

page 36:

In the Class

David comes to the class.
The children are in the class. It is quiet in the class.

David:	Is the teacher in the class?
Children:	No, the teacher is not in the class.
David:	Who is the teacher?
Sarah:	A new teacher.
David:	A good teacher?
Sarah:	Yes, a very good teacher.

page 37:

The teacher comes to the class.

Teacher:	Hello children.
Children:	Hello teacher.

The teacher writes on the chalkboard:
    A good class.

Sarah:	The class is good because the teacher is good.
Teacher:	The teacher is good because the children are good!

page 38:

Doron Is In The Class

Teacher:	Hello Doron.
Doron:	Hello Teacher.
Teacher:	Here is a chair, here is a desk. Do you have a notebook?
Doron:	I have a notebook but I do not have a pencil.
Teacher:	Do you have a book?
Doron:	I have a book but I do not have eyeglasses.
Teacher:	Where are the (your) eyeglasses, Doron? Where is the pencil?
Doron:	Maybe in the house? Maybe in the closet?

page 42:

An Ant In the Class

Here is the teacher
coming to the class.

Teacher:	Who is in the class? David, Sarah?
Ant:	I am in the class! I am Malmalah. I am in the class. Malmalah the ant.

page 43:

There are books in the class,
notebooks in the class,
but there are no apples
and also there are no cakes.

Maybe there is honey?
Maybe there are ḥallahs?
Maybe in the desk, in the closets?

Here is ḥallah!
The ant is happy.
Malmalah sings:
La, la, la, la, la.

Chapter 6

page 44:

Shabbat Shalom (Sabbath Peace)

Father is in the house.
Also Mother is in the house.
Doron is in the house.
Also Dinah is in the house.
It is good in the house.

Candles are on the table.
Ḥallahs are on the table.
Wine is on the table.
Flowers are on the table.
It is nice in the house.

Shabbat is in the house,
peace is in the house,
peace is in the family.
Shabbat Shalom (Sabbath Peace)

page 46:

Who Is In the House on Shabbat?

Who is in the house?
The children are in the house.
The family is in the house.
Also a mouse is in the house!

Mouse:	Yes, I am in the house!
	I love ḥallah.
	I love wine.
	I love flowers.
	I love Shabbat!
The mouse sings:	I am Bar the mouse.
	I live in the house.
	In the house it is not cold.
	On Shabbat I sing!
	I sing a blessing.
	I eat ḥallah.

page 50:

Shabbat Day, A Day of Rest

Malmalah the ant
is not tired.
Malmalah the ant
loves work.

Every day Malmalah works,
every day Malmalah spins.
But on Shabbat there is no work,
because Shabbat is a day of rest.

Chapter 7

page 56:

Ḥanukkah

The holiday of Ḥanukkah is coming!
Ḥanukkah is a nice holiday.
Ḥanukkah is a happy holiday.
Ḥanukkah is the holiday of light.

page 57:

The family is in the house.
Today is the first day of Ḥanukkah.

Dani:	I light the first candle!
Lili:	No, no!
	I light the first candle!
David:	I also want to light a candle.
Dani:	I am the first (eldest) brother,
	I light the first candle.
Mother:	David, here is a Ḥanukkah menorah.
	Lili, here is a Ḥanukkah menorah.
	Dani, here is a Ḥanukkah menorah.
	Everyone is happy.
	Dani, David and Lili
	light the first candle.
	Everyone sings blessings
	for Ḥanukkah.

page 60:

The Holiday of Light

In the Ḥanukkah menorah are candles—light.
In the Ḥanukkah menorah is a helper candle—light.
Children sing—light.
We eat latkes—light.
To light a candle—light.
Of Ḥanukkah —light.

A great miracle—light.
Happened there—light.
It is warm in the house,
it is good in the house,
we have light.

page 62:
The Mouse in the Dreidel
Mother sings blessings,
the children light candles,
Father makes latkes,
Grandmother gives gifts.
And a mouse…

Where is Bar?
Where is the mouse?
The mouse is in the dreidel!
The dreidel spins…

page 63:
The mouse spins…
The children say: "nun" —a miracle!
The mouse spins…
The children say: "gimel" —great!
The mouse spins…
The children say: "hay" —happened!
The mouse spins…
The children say: "shin" —there!

The mouse says: "shin" —quiet!
The dreidel spins,
the house spins,
the table spins,
the (my) head spins,
I am tired!

Chapter 8

page 64:
Dinah is Happy
All week Dinah does not go to the class.

Sunday	Dinah is happy because there is no class.
Monday	Dinah says: Today there is rain.
	Dinah does not go to the class.
Tuesday	Dinah says: Today is cold!
	Dinah does not go to the class.
Wednesday	Dinah says: Today is warm.
	Dinah does not go to the class.
Thursday	Dinah says: I don't have (my) eyeglasses.
	Dinah does not go to the class.
Friday	Dinah says: I am tired.
	Dinah does not go to the class.

page 65:

Shabbat	Dinah says: Today I am going to the class.
	Goodbye Father. Goodbye Mother.

Father says: Dinah, today is Shabbat.
          Today there is no class.
          Today is a day of rest.
Dinah is in the house, Dinah is happy because there is no class.

page 66:
What Did God Create?
On the first day God created
darkness and light.
On the first day, on the first day,
darkness and light.

On the second day God created
sky (on) over the water.
On the second day, on the second day,
sky (on) over the water.

page 67:
On the third day God created
flowers and trees.
On the third day, on the third day,
flowers and trees.

On the fourth day God created
sun, moon, and stars.
On the fourth day, on the fourth day,
sun, moon, and stars.

page 68:
On the fifth day God created
fish and birds.
On the fifth day, on the fifth day,
fish and birds.

On the sixth day God created
animals and people.
On the sixth day, on the sixth day,
animals and people.

page 69:
Shabbat day, Shabbat day,

a day of rest.
Shabbat day, Shabbat day,
a day of rest.
Shabbat Shalom! (Sabbath Peace!)

Chapter 9

page 72:

A Holiday for the Trees

Good morning!
Today is Tu B'Shevat!
A holiday for the trees.
A holiday for the flowers.

The children sing: Happy Birthday, almond tree.
  Happy Birthday, trees.
  Happy holiday to the flowers.
  Happy holiday to the birds.

The children are happy and say:
  Tu B'Shevat, a holiday for the trees.
  On Tu B'Shevat we eat fruit.
  Tu B'Shevat, a holiday for the almond tree.
  On Tu B'Shevat we say thank you.
  Thank you to the trees,
  Thank you to God

page 74:

The Mouse's Birthday

Night.
Mouse says:
I have a birthday.
I also want a party.
I want cake.
I want a gift.

Morning.
A bird sings on the mountain:
Today is the mouse's birthday!
Here the butterfly is also coming:
Today is the mouse's birthday!

Happy Birthday, happy day.
The bird makes a cake.
The butterfly has a gift
and the mouse has a party.

page 75:

Bar the mouse
stands on the mountain.
Bar the mouse
stands and sings:

I have a day, a happy day.
I have a holiday, a party.
Thank you bird,
says Bar.
Thank you butterfly,
thank you friend.

page 78:

Lili Wants a Gift

Lili: Grandfather, I have a birthday,
  I want a gift.

Grandfather: Good, I am giving you a bird,
  a bird with candles.

Lili: Grandfather, a bird does not have candles.
  A cake has candles.

Grandfather: Good, I am giving you a cake,
  a cake with fish.

Lili: Grandfather, a cake does not have fish.
  A cake has flowers.

page 79:

Grandfather: Good, I am giving you flowers,
  flowers with eyes.

Lili: Grandfather, flowers do not have eyes.
  People have eyes.

Grandfather: Good, I am giving you Mother,
  Mother with eyeglasses.

Lili: Grandfather, Mother does not have eyeglasses.
  Grandfather has eyeglasses

Grandfather: Good, I am giving you Grandfather!

Chapter 10

page 82:

A Pretty World

The children are in the class. All the children are drawing.

David draws a tree colored green.
Rachel draws a flower colored red.
Sarah draws a sun colored yellow.
Ron draws a sky colored blue.

Dinah draws a tree colored black,
flowers and a sun colored black.

Teacher: Dinah, a sun colored black?
  A world colored black?

English Translations

Dinah: I don't have a green crayon for the trees.
I don't have a red crayon for the flowers.
I don't have a yellow crayon for the sun.
And I don't have a blue crayon for the sky.

page 83:

David gives Dinah a green crayon.
Rachel gives Dinah a red crayon.
Sarah gives Dinah a yellow crayon.
Ron gives Dinah a blue crayon.
The teacher gives Dinah a white sheet of paper.

Dinah is happy. Dinah draws.

Teacher: The world is not black and white.
In the world there are many, many colors.
The world is pretty.

page 87:

Ron the Clown

Where is Ron?
Where is Ron?
Not in the house,
not in the garden.

Who is this? Who is this?
A white head,
a red nose.
This is a clown!

A red nose,
a white head,
Here is Ron!
Ron the clown!

Chapter 11

page 88

Today is Purim

Teacher: Today is Purim!
Today we read in the Megillah.
Here is a box. Masks are in the box.
Who wants to be king?

David: I want to be king,
but not King Aḥashverosh,
because he is a stupid king.
I want to be a smart king!

Doron: I want to be Mordecai,
because Mordecai is a Jew and also I am a Jew.

Dinah: I want to be Esther,
because she is a pretty queen.

Dani: I want to be a horse,
because there is also a horse in the Megillah.

page 89:

Teacher: A horse does not speak!
But Dani does speak.

Dani: Good, I want to be Haman,
because he walks with the horse.

Teacher: I want to be a clown,
because I have a red nose.

Children: Ha, ha, ha, the teacher has a red nose!

Teacher: Here is a noisemaker for everyone,
today we make noise.
Here are hamantashen,
today everyone is happy.
Today is Purim!

page 92:

Today We Are Happy

Teacher: Today is Purim, today we are happy,
today we read in the Megillah.
Here is a box with masks
for the boys and for the girls.

David: I have a crown on the (my) head,
I am wise but I am
King Aḥashverosh!

Dinah: I also have a crown,
I am a queen!
I am Esther,
I am pretty.

Doron: I have a mask,
I am Mordechai,
I am a Jew,
Live, live, live.

Dani: I also have a mask,
and I have a noisemaker.
I am a bad man,
I am Haman.

page 93:

Teacher: And I have a hat,
a white hat,
and a red nose,
I am a clown.

Ant: I am Malmalah,
I am also in the Megillah.
I am Vashti,
a very small queen.
Mouse: There is also a horse in the Megillah.
I am a small horse.
The horse walks
after Haman.

Everyone sings, big and small.
We read in the Megillah
and eat hamantashen.

page 95:

If Bar has quiet,
Bar wants noise.
If Bar has noise,
Bar wants a party.
If Bar has a party,
Bar wants cake.
If Bar has cake,
Bar wants candles.

If Bar has candles,
Bar wants a gift.
If Bar has a gift,
Bar wants a noisemaker.
If Bar has a noisemaker,
Bar makes noise.
If Bar has noise,
Bar wants quiet!

Chapter 12

page 96:

The Seder
All the family is in the house.
The table is big and pretty.
The Passover Seder is in the house.
Matzahs and wine are on the table.
The Passover Plate is on the table.

The children sing: *Mah Nishtanah* (The Four Questions).
Father reads in the Haggadah.

Grandfather reads about Pharaoh the king.
Pharaoh the king is a bad king.
Pharaoh the king does not like Jews.
It was not good for Jews in Egypt.
The Jews are slaves.

page 97:

Grandmother says:
It is bad for the Jews in Egypt.
Moses takes the Jews from Egypt.
Pharaoh says: No, no!
But Moses says:
Yes, yes, the Jews are going out from Egypt.
Moses and the Jews go out from Egypt.
The Jews are not slaves.
The Jews are free people.

page 100:

The Holiday of Passover—A Holiday of Spring
Matzahs for the holiday, candles for the holiday,
wine, ḥaroset, bitter herbs, and fish.
The holiday of Passover, a holiday of spring.
The holiday of Passover, a holiday of spring.

I read in the Haggadah,
I say *Mah Nishtanah*.
The holiday of Passover, a holiday of spring.
The holiday of Passover, a holiday of spring.

I eat good matzah,
I also sing *Ḥad Gadya* (One Kid).
The holiday of Passover, a holiday of spring.
The holiday of Passover, a holiday of spring.

page 102:

There Is No Bread
Mouse is hungry.
Mouse wants to eat.
Mouse wants to eat bread.
There is no bread in the house!
Mouse wants to eat ḥallah,
there is no ḥallah in the house!
Mouse wants to eat a cookie.
There isn't a cookie in the house!
Mouse wants to eat …
Mouse is hungry.

Mouse thinks:
There is no bread, but there is matzah!
There is no ḥallah, but there is an egg!
There isn't a cookie, but there is Passover cake!
Mouse eats.
Mouse is happy.
A holiday in the house,
Happy Holiday!

Chapter 13

page 108:

A Blue and White Flag

Lili: Mother, why are you making a cake today?

Mother: Today is Israel's birthday!
Today is Independence Day.
I am making a cake colored blue and white.

page 109:

David: I am drawing a blue and white flag.
Blue—the color of the sky.
White—the color of peace.

Lili: I am also drawing a flag.

David: Lili, the flag of Israel is blue and white,
not green and white.
Today is not the holiday for the trees…

Lili: But Dani is not giving me a
a blue crayon.

Mother: Lili, here is a blue crayon.
I want peace.
Peace in the house,
peace in the world,
and peace in Israel.

page 110:

A Birthday for Israel

Mouse sings:
A birthday—party.
A birthday—cake.
A birthday for Israel.
Happy holiday, Thank God.

The nation of Israel—the nation of Israel lives!
The land of Israel—the land of my ancestors!
A birthday for Israel,
happy holiday, thank God.

page 112:

We Have a Flag

The ant sings:
We have a small flag,
we have a white flag,
we have a blue flag,
the flag of Israel.

We have a small land,
we have a pretty land,
we have a good land,
the land of Israel.

Chapter 14

page 114:

Every Year

On Rosh HaShanah (the New Year), every year,
we say Happy New Year.

On the holiday of Sukkot, every year,
we recite blessings over a lulav and an etrog in the sukkah.
On Simhat Torah, every year,
we walk with flags and read in the Torah.

On Hanukkah, every year,
we light candles in the Hanukkah menorah.

On Tu B'Shevat, every year,
we sing thanks to the trees.

page 115:

On the holiday of Purim, every year,
we are happy and read in the Megillah.

On the holiday of Passover, every year,
we eat matzah and read in the haggadah.

On Independence Day, every year,
there is a party for the land of Israel.

On the holiday of Shavuot, every year,
happy holiday, the giving of the Torah.

But every week in the year
we have a holiday of rest.
A day of candles, wine, and hallah,
Shabbat day, a day of blessing.

page 118:

Mouse is Happy

Mouse is happy on Rosh Hashanah (the New Year),
because we eat round hallah.
Mouse is happy on Hanukkah,
because we eat a good latke.
Mouse is happy on the holiday of the trees,
because on Tu B'Shevat we eat raisins.

Mouse is happy on the holiday of Purim,
because we eat good hamantashen.
On the holiday of Passover the mouse is happy,
because we eat sweet, and also bitter.
But on the holiday of Shavuot
Mouse is very, very happy.
On the holiday of Shavuot the mouse has a gift,
because on the holiday of Shavuot we eat cheese!